List of contributors:

Ronnie Wilbur

ASL Linguistics Research Laboratory, Interdepartmental Program in Linguistics and Department of Audiology and Speech Sciences, Purdue University, West Lafayette, Indiana, USA

Maria del Pilar Fernández

Center for the Study of Catalan Sign Language, Department of Developmental and Educational Psychology, Faculty of Psychology, University of Barcelona, Spain

Josep Maria Segimon

Center for the Study of Catalan Sign Language, Department of Developmental and Educational Psychology, Faculty of Psychology, University of Barcelona, Spain

Ninoslava Šarac

Zagreb, Croatia, Purdue, USA

Tamara Alibašić

Zadar, Croatia, Purdue, USA

Stane Košir

School of Education, University of Ljubljana, Slovenia

Milon Potmesil

The Institute for the Deaf, Beroun, Czech Republic

Linda Lupton

Saint John's Health System, Anderson, Indiana, USA

Richard A. van Royen

Seminarium voor Orthopedagogiek, University of Professional Education, Utrecht, the Netherlands

Paddy Ladd

Center for Deaf Studies, University of Bristol, United Kingdom

Angel Naumovski

Deaf Theatre, Visual Arts and Culture "DLAN", Zagreb, Croatia

Alena Macurova

Faculty of Arts and Philosophy, Charles University, Prague, Czech Republic

Ila Parasnis

National Technical Institute for the Deaf, Rochester Institute of Technology, Rochester, New York, USA

Susan Gregory

School of Education, University of Birmingham, United Kingdom

Roger Carver

Deaf Children's Society, Burnaby, Canada

Lisbeth Henning   School for the Deaf, Lund, Sweden

Signild Salander   School for the Deaf, Lund, Sweden

Klaus B. Günther   Institute of Special Education, University of Hamburg, Germany

Ilka Schäfke   Institute of Special Education, University of Hamburg, Germany

Peter Oracha Adoyo   Institute of Special Education, University of Hamburg, Germany

Nicole Kuplenik   School for Deaf and Hard of Hearing Children, Ljubljana, Slovenia

Vesna Ivasović   School for the Deaf "Slava Raškaj", Zagreb, Croatia

Tvrtko Maras   Zagreb, Croatia

Lidija Andrijević   School for the Deaf "Slava Raškaj", Zagreb, Croatia

Tereza Szavai   School for the Deaf "Slava Raškaj", Zagreb, Croatia

Sandra Bradarić-Jončić   Department of Hearing Impairments, Faculty of Education and Rehabilitation Sciences, University of Zagreb, Croatia

Sanja Tarczay   Croatian Association of Deaf-Blind Persons "Dodir", Zagreb, Croatia

Noel T. Traynor   Deaf Studies, Department of Education and Social Science, University of Central Lancashire, Preston, United Kingdom

Johannes Fellinger   Out-patient Clinic for the Deaf and Hard of Hearing, Hospital of St. John of God, Linz, Austria

D. Holzinger   Out-patient Clinic for the Deaf and Hard of Hearing, Hospital of St. John of God, Linz, Austria

R. Schoberberger   University of Vienna, Austria

G. Lenz   Department of Psychiatry, Allgemeines Krankenhaus, Vienna, Austria

Sign Language, Deaf Culture & Bilingual Education

Sandra Bradarić-Jončić & Vesna Ivasović (Eds.)

Published by Faculty of Education .... University of Zagreb,
Kušlanova 59a, 10000 Zagreb, Croatia

Editors:
Sandra Bradarić - Jončić & Vesna Ivasović

Cover design:
Dario Sošić

English language advisor:
Tatjana Majić

Printed by:
Kratis, Zagreb

CIP - Katalogizacija u publikaciji
Nacionalna i sveučilišna knjižnica - Zagreb

UDK   376.33:81'221.24>(082)
           81'221.24(082)
           316.723-056.263(082)

Sign Language, Deaf Culture & Bilingual
Education / Sandra Bradarić-Jončić & Vesna
Ivasović (eds.) ; <contributors Ronnie
Wilbur ... et al.>. - Zagreb : Faculty of
Education and Rehabilitation Sciences, 2004.

Bibliografija iza većine radova.

ISBN 953-6418-23-1

1. Bradarić-Jončić, Sandra
I. Gluhe osobe -- Znakovni jezik
II. Gluhe osobe -- Kvaliteta življenja
III. Djeca oštećena sluha -- Dvojezična komunikacija

440923047

Contents:

Preface

The aim of this book of selected papers related to sign language, and bilingual education Deaf culture is to contribute to a change in the status of Croatian Sign Language (HZJ), in the understanding of the identity of the deaf and, particularly, in the role and place of Croatian Sign Language in the education of the deaf in Croatia, as well as in other countries where such changes are needed.

Theoretical considerations and researches of contributors from twelve countries will be presented, some of which are very distinguished experts from the area of sign language linguistics, psychology and sociology of deafness, and deaf education. Many of these papers have been presented at the Symposium "Sign Language and Deaf Culture", organized in Zagreb in 2001 by the Department of Hearing Impairments of Faculty of Education and Rehabilitation Sciences, the Faculty of Philosophy of the Society of Jesus and the Croatian Association of Deaf-blind Persons "Dodir". Over 200 participants from more than 20 countries of the world participated in this Symposium, with the total of 79 presentations. It was successfully organized thanks to the intensive cooperation between deaf and hearing people. Of particular importance is the fact that a big number of deaf experts and university professors actively participated in the Symposium.

By this Symposium we intended, among other things, to show to a wider public that the deaf community really has interesting and valuable things to say about its art and language. Therefore, we included in the concept of the Symposium an exhibition of deaf painters, as well as two theater performances using sign language. Deaf painting and exhibitions have existed in Croatia for a long time, but the deaf theater did not exist, and one of the aims of the Symposium was to establish it. On the occasion of the Symposium, a play in sign language, "The Planet of Silence", was performed for the first time by the newly established theater of the deaf "Dlan" in the Zagreb Drama Theater. We also wanted to show the expressivity and actual presence of sign language theaters in Europe and the world by inviting the Common Ground Sign Dance Theatre from Liverpool, whose actors performed their play "Territories" in an eminent theater in Zagreb.

In Croatia we still feel a strong need for offering deaf children different educational options, beside the exclusively oral educational approach. Deaf children and their parents must have the possibility of choosing between different educational options: 1) special schools with oral approach; 2) special schools with bilingual-bicultural approach; and 3) inclusive education in regular schools using oral and bilingual approach.

We hope that this book will bring about a change in the attitudes toward the communication and education of the deaf as one of the assumptions of implementing bi-bi education for deaf children in Croatia. However, it is not enough just to change the attitudes. We are faced with the more complex task of creating other, more challenging prerequisites. The basic prerequisite is the existence of curricula of the sign language as the second language for present and future professionals, as well as hearing parents of deaf children. An important part of every curriculum of the second language is grammar. The Department of Hearing Impairments has recently begun researches aimed at describing HZJ grammar, the results of which will be implemented thereafter in teaching and learning HZJ as a second language.

In Strasbourg in April 2003 Croatia accepted the European Council's recommendation to protect and promote national sign languages. We hope this book will contribute to the realization of this recommendation, to a further development of deaf education, as well as to an affirmation and empowerment of the deaf community in Croatia and other countries.

We wish to thank all the contributors who made the publishing of this book possible.

Editors

AFTER 40 YEARS OF SIGN LANGUAGE RESEARCH, WHAT DO WE KNOW?

Ronnie Wilbur

Purdue University, West Lafayette, Indiana, USA

Abstract

Research on sign languages is gaining momentum around the world. It is useful to review what is already known in general because this frees researchers to concentrate on the details that are specific to each sign language and prevents wasted efforts. For example, we know that there are naturally-evolved sign languages, that these differ from pedagogical signing systems that aim to present the dominant spoken language in signs, and that these also differ from naturally-developing sign languages (e.g. in Nicaragua) and "home signs". There is no universal, international sign language, although there is a European "International Sign (IS)". Naturally-evolved sign languages are not dependent on the structure of the dominant spoken language even though they may be presented that way in classes; this does not mean that the spoken and signed languages cannot be similar. Our research shows more similarity between German and Austrian Sign Languages and spoken German than there is between American Sign Language and English. Because sign languages evolve on their own, with sociolinguistic influence from the dominant spoken language through the educational system, we expect to see both similarities and differences. Researchers should not have to prove that their specific sign language is a language (unless it is clearly a developing one) and they should not have to prove that it is different from the spoken language. Naturally--evolved sign languages are produced with multiple articulators: two hands, head, body, upper face (including eyebrows, eye gaze, eye lids for blinks), nose, mouth/cheeks, chin, and tongue. The productions of these articulators is "layered" so that several articulations can occur at once and the messages do not interfere with each other but rather contribute to the overall meaning. Researchers should be able to concentrate on the specific messages being sent by each articulator. Naturally-evolved sign languages do not interfere with the acquisition of the dominant spoken language. Research shows that individuals who learn a sign language from birth (deaf children of deaf parents) outperform their later-learning peers (deaf children of hearing parents) on most measures of language, speech, reading, writing, social development, and academic performance (e.g. math). There is no significant difference in the overall outcome for speech when early sign learners are compared to oral learners. Researchers should not have to prove that learning sign language is critical to deaf children's overall successful achievement. They should be able to concentrate instead on the structural differences between the sign language and the spoken language to create appropriate materials to teach the second language (spoken) to children who already know a first language (signed).

Key words: *sign language, deaf, bilingual education, literacy, linguistic skills, deaf education*

1. Introduction and terminology

The objective of this paper is to provide research support for the use of natural sign languages in the early education of deaf children, especially when the aim is to develop sophisticated language and literacy skills. To achieve this objective, it is necessary that the reader understand a number of conceptual and terminological distinctions. After those distinctions have been articulated, the remainder of the paper will address the benefits of early sign language acquisition available to all deaf children. A review of the literature indicates that early learning of sign language does not cause deaf students' problems learning English, does not interfere with cognitive development and memory, and does not limit speech potential. Furthermore, it does benefit language learning and overall socioeducational performance, and can be used to improve reading and writing by providing a necessary language base.

1.1 'Language' and 'speech' and its relevance to bilingual development

The term 'language' is not synonymous with the word 'speech', as speech is only one way of transmitting language between users of that language. This distinction is demonstrated by talking parrots, which can 'speak' (produce speech-like sounds) but which do not 'know a language'. Other means of transmitting language include the use of different styles of print and script, and encoded alphabets such as Braille and fingerspelling. In fact, language transmission does not have to be by alphabetical methods at all, as Chinese characters demonstrate. Furthermore, languages do not necessarily have an associated print system: many existing writing systems were invented not by the speakers of the language but by outsiders to the cultural community, such as missionaries (in order to translate the Bible), linguists (to be able to investigate the language), and others (conquerors solidifying dominance over the conquered).

With respect to the role of sign language in the education of deaf children, it is important to recognize that researchers have known for over 20 years that there is no evidence to support the belief that early use of sign language interferes with the development of speech abilities. A study of children using Swedish Sign (Ahlstrom, 1972) reported that "speech was not adversely affected by knowledge of signs" (Power, 1974). A study comparing non-ASL users (deaf children with hearing parents) with early intensive oral training to ASL users (deaf children with deaf parents) with no intensive speech training showed no differences in oral skills, but the ASL users were superior in reading and general achievement (Vernon and Koh 1970). Other studies comparing ASL users to non-ASL users showed the ASL users to be superior on some or all of the English skills and general measures of ability. Three of these studies reported no difference between the two groups on measures of speech production, but the fourth reports that the deaf children of hearing parents were better. When they are compared on measures of speechreading ability, three studies report no differences between the two groups and a fourth reports that the ASL users are better (Meadow, 1966; Quigley and Frisina, 1961; Stevenson, 1964; Stuckless and Birch, 1966; for a description of these, see Bonvillian, Charrow, and Nelson, 1973; Moores, 1971, 1974). Finally, it should be noted that a study to determine the effect of early oral preschool training shows no difference in oral skills (speech and speechreading) between two groups of deaf children of hearing parents (Moores 1971). What is striking about these studies is the lack of any direct evidence that the use of signing is detrimental to the development of speech skills. If such an interference relationship existed, one would expect to see it reported in study after study. Its absence is thus noteworthy.

It is important to understand further that the challenge facing deaf children is not really the acquisition of fluent speech skills, although those can be extremely useful in interactions with the hearing world, but the acquisition of the language skills that underlie successful use of speech, signing, reading, and writing. That is, it is critical to develop the underlying concepts (knowledge) and the linguistic mechanisms necessary to map those concepts onto meaningful forms of expression, regardless of the form that the output will take (spoken, written, signed, fingerspelled). There is very strong evidence that deaf children can be taught to articulate speech at a decent level of intelligibility and can be taught to make perceptual distinctions in speech sounds, especially when properly aided. These skills, however, are peripheral motor skills, not central cognitive and linguistic skills. Thus, it is possible to learn to produce speech without understanding what one is saying. Parrots do it. A linguist trained in phonetic transcription (the International Phonetic Alphabet) can read aloud any spoken language written in it and still have no idea what the passage means. To be fully understood, the input (sound, print, sign) must be received by the brain centers that are involved in cognitive and linguistic skills, where the processing that is required to parse syntax, identify lexical items and morphological markers, and construct an understanding of the semantics of the message takes place. Speech reception and production at the level of a parrot is not sufficient for a lifetime of human cognitive and linguistic potential.

1.2 'Naturally evolved languages' and 'artificially created systems'

Another distinction that needs to be made is that between 'naturally evolved languages' and 'artificially manipulated language-like systems'. Natural languages are learned by babies from birth without formal pedagogical intervention (teaching and consistent correction). Two examples of natural languages are English (hearing babies with hearing parents) and American Sign Language (deaf babies with deaf parents). In contrast, artificial systems require a variety of formal procedures, such as training adult users to provide specific input in a specific way, and as such are not learned by babies in the home environment without intervention. An example of an artificially manipulated system is signed English (SE), of which there are many variations because different educators choose different pedagogical principles to follow (Wilbur 1987, 2000a).

1.3 'Bilingual', 'bimodal', and 'typical bilingual situation'

Here, the term 'bilingual' is used to refer to naturally evolved languages, both spoken and signed. Much of the available research concentrates on American Sign

Language (ASL) and English, hence they will be used in this discussion as exemplars representing the larger set of natural languages. It is important to note that artificial signing systems such as SE do not qualify as natural languages and hence cannot be included in the notion 'standard bilingual situation'. The potential role of such signing systems as classroom educational tools is discussed later in this paper. Critically, speaking and signing at the same time, as one can do with signed English, is not bilingual, but 'bimodal', that is, using two modes – speaking and signing – to convey a single message. The large literature on the ways that these two modes can interact to carry information is reviewed in Wilbur & Petersen (1998).

The global benefit of learning a natural sign language as a first language (L1) is that it creates a 'typical bilingual situation'. This term refers first to situations in which young children (0 to 5 years of age) are exposed to, and interact with, at least one language in the course of daily home and family conversations. It also requires that there be no language disorders or other anomalies that prevent the children from acquiring at least one language fluently and fully (e.g., no specific language impairment (SLI)). In typical bilingual situations, the 'bilingual' part (L2) may come from a variety of sources, including family, community, school, and so on. Because at least one language is being acquired naturally, teachers and learners can take advantage of the first language to assist children in acquiring the second language and in the transfer of general knowledge. Thus, the term 'bilingual' does not require that the child learn two languages at the same time, but rather that the second language is learned either simultaneously with, or sequentially dependent on, knowledge of the first language. This wording reflects the fact that 'balance' and 'dominance' between the two languages in these early stages is not important to the eventual outcome. Instead, at least one language must be learned naturally and the acquisition of the other, whether natural or taught or both, must utilize architecture established during the acquisition of the first language. Relevant to the present discussion, the first language can be either (spoken) English for hearing children or ASL for deaf children, but not signed English (because it is not a natural language and lacks critical aspects of the linguistic architecture that children must learn, for example, the natural prosodic structure of language). Another language can then be built on top, or co-extensive with, the first language and for deaf children, this would be English (or any other appropriate spoken language from the surrounding community).

These definitions clarify the problem with early learning of SE as opposed to ASL. SE is not a natural language and its early acquisition does not include many of the universal characteristics of natural languages, such as modality-appropriate intonation patterns (Wilbur & Petersen 1998). Thus it does not provide the necessary initial language learning experience and therefore does not provide the basis for the acquisition of a second language. Wilbur and Petersen (1998) document the distortion of speech and the absence of systematic facial expressions in 'fluent' adult users of signed English. Wilbur (2000b) discusses naturally evolved intonational systems such as those in ASL and English, and provides an explanation for the absence of natural systems in artificially created signing and speaking systems like signed English.

These observations and conclusions are further confirmed by a recent study comparing the outcomes of two groups of Dutch deaf children. Hoiting and Slobin (2002) analyze data from deaf children aged 1;3 to 3;0 years collected over a 12 year period, during which time the educational policy was changed from 'Sign Supported Dutch' (SSD, parallel to signed English) to Sign Language of the Netherlands (SLN, a sign language unrelated to ASL). They report significant advantages of the SLN input compared to the SSD input, such as more varied structures, wider choice of lexical items, and more modeling of appropriate uses of language (requests, demands, plans). As for the children's output, those children receiving SLN input produced longer and more complex output than the SSD children. Thus, signing while speaking does not provide the natural linguistic requirements for true bilingual development. All the advantages are with the natural sign languages.

2. What is the problem that deaf children have learning English and what causes it?

The overall difficulty that deaf children have learning English has been very well documented (Quigley and Kretschmer 1982; Quigley and Paul 1984; Wilbur 1979, 1987). As a general observation, by age 18, deaf students do not have the linguistic competence of 10-year-old hearing children in many syntactic structures of English, and studies report that less than 12 percent of deaf students at age 16 can read at a fourth-grade reading level or higher as measured on the Metropolitan Reading Achievement Test (see Wilbur 2000a). These classic papers demonstrate clearly that whether or not deaf children are able to speak, there is still a larger overriding problem of syntax that renders the children unable to understand what they read (or speak, when reading out loud).

In contrast, by the time hearing children begin to learn to read, they have already developed conversational fluency in their native language, including sophisticated syntactic skills, and can be taught to transfer this knowledge to reading and to the acquisition of other languages, in the way that has been described under 'typical bilingual situation' above. Deaf children who have lost their hearing at an early age do not have this knowledge; thus, they do not come to the task with the same skills in sentence formation, vocabulary, and world knowledge as hearing children.

The powerful role that early learning of sign language plays in linguistic and educational achievement is reflected in the fact that deaf children whose deaf parents use sign language at home with them are exceptional in their accomplishments. This success is a result of the fact that they have a fully-established language base prior to learning to read. These children are more similar to (hearing) children who must learn to read and write in a second language (typical bilingual). For this group, early ASL use provides a significant advantage, not interference.

Early studies overwhelmingly reported better overall achievement for ASL users, although there are differences on some measures, and, in some cases, no differences at all (Moores 1974). Stevenson (1964) reported higher educational achievement for the deaf students of deaf parents in 90% of the comparisons, with 38% going on to college, compared to only 9% of the students with hearing parents. Stuckless and Birch (1966) reported superior reading, speechreading, and written language for the ASL users, with no differences noted in speech or psychosocial development. Meadow (1966) reported higher self-image and academic achievement (arithmetic, reading, and overall) for this group. Teachers' ratings of the students were in favor of this group on maturity, responsibility, independence, sociability, appropriate sex role, popularity, appropriate responses to situations, fingerspelling ability, written language, signing ability, absence of communicative frustration, and willingness to communicate with strangers. No difference was noted in speech or speechreading. Vernon and Koh (1970) likewise reported that the ASL users were superior in reading, vocabulary, and written language. No differences were found in speech, speechreading, or psychosocial adjustment. Quigley and Frisina (1961) reported higher vocabulary levels for the ASL users, no differences in speechreading or educational achievement, and better speech for the deaf students of hearing parents. Furthermore, Vernon and Koh (1970) compared the academic achievement of ASL users to deaf students of hearing parents with early intensive oral training. The ASL users were ahead in all areas and had superior reading skills. No differences were found in speech or speechreading. These early studies established to the satisfaction of more than a generation of researchers that knowledge of ASL is invaluable in the education of deaf children.

More recent research (Strong & Prinz 1997; Prinz 2002; Hoffmeister 2000; Padden & Ramsey 2000; Singleton, Supalla, Litchfield & Schley 1998) have confirmed many of these findings. Significantly, there is, as indicated by the older research, a strong correlation between ASL fluency and English literacy. Furthermore, there is an improvement in English literacy as ASL skills improve, indicating that the early benefit of having deaf parents fades as children acquire ASL in contact with other fluent users. This finding is significant because some have tried to suggest that the educational advantage shown by deaf children of deaf parents was not due to knowledge of sign language but rather to social development issues such as greater parental acceptance of deaf parents of a deaf children than that of hearing parents, who might be distressed at the presence of a deaf child in their family. We now know that it is the ASL skills that are important, and that as deaf children, even with hearing parents, become more fluent in ASL, they become better readers of English.

My own experience confirms this finding. The successful deaf individuals in my professional field either have deaf parents or they have hearing parents who began signing with them, however awkwardly, when they were diagnosed as deaf as children. While parents may worry about never becoming good enough signers, in fact poor parental signing skills are easily overcome by providing deaf children with interactional opportunities with ASL-fluent members of the Deaf community (deaf clubs, deaf schools, deaf athletics). The best general discussion of these conclusions is contained in Johnson, Liddell, and Erting (1989; readily available from Gallaudet University), in which they outline a model program for the education of deaf children with ASL as a central focus and family support provided by Deaf community interaction (among other sources). Crucially, they set a clear goal for deaf education: access to age-appropriate curriculum (also called 'on-grade-level'). For example, are third grade deaf children able to demonstrate competency in the standard third grade curriculum in math, history, science, and whatever else is typical for third grade? Johnson et al. argue that anything less is unacceptable.

Finally, studies of the acquisition of English by deaf learners reveal that their acquisition strategies, such as interpreting sentences based on surface rather than deep word order, are like other young learners. However, unlike other young learners, deaf children tend to persist in their erroneous strategies long after they should have been replaced with more sophisticated strategies. Research indicates that this persistence results from a) inadequate language skills, compounded by limited input due to the hearing loss, b) inadequate teaching methods, including teaching selected structures in isolation, due to concerns over communication modality and lack of appreciation of the complexities of language acquisition, and c) teacher focus on sentence structure over other aspects of language use (inferencing, paragraph structure, conversational and story structure as transmission of sequenced information). These problems are discussed at length in Wilbur (1987, 2000a, 2001).

3. How can a bilingual situation help with respect to language and literacy development?

Consider the benefits that all deaf children would receive from early exposure to ASL. One would be the fully developed language base that deaf children of deaf parents are already getting. A fully developed language base provides normal cognitive development within the critical language acquisition period (Newport and Meier 1985; Petitto 1993; Lillo-Martin 1994). Teacher-child and parent-child communication is vastly improved and there is no longer a limited input problem. Instead, ASL-signing deaf children become another bilingual minority learning English (Charrow & Wilbur, 1975).

It is already known that deaf children learn English as though it were a foreign language. Charrow and Fletcher (1974) gave the Test of English as a Foreign Language (TOEFL) to deaf high-school students of college-entrance age. Although the deaf subjects did not perform as well as foreign college entrants, in general their results more closely resemble foreign students than native speakers of English. From the perspective of treating deaf children like other second language learners, one should expect on-grade-level performance. Some of that performance may be demonstrated in the first, rather than the second, language. Hakuta (1986) has shown that there is no problem with transfer of curricula material learned in one language to eventual use in the other language, thus this is not a concern.

3. 1 Advantages of having a fully developed first language

From a linguistic perspective, knowledge of ASL as a first language is beneficial because it taps normal capacities at the appropriate stage of development. As Lillo-Martin (1993, 1994) discusses, when children have a first language (ASL or other language), their linguistic competence is constrained by Universal Grammar, that is, the normal language acquisition process takes place within the confines of what all natural languages have in common (see also Petitto 1993; Newport and Meier 1985; Pinker 1993). As a result of this first language acquisition process, there is less need for concern about teaching particular syntactic structures in the second language (see also discussion of knowledge transfer in Hakuta 1986). Given knowledge of a first language, learners of a second language have some idea of what to expect, making the acquisition of the second language simpler.

VanPatten (1995, 1996) has argued that for successful language acquisition, learners need access to input which is communicatively and/or meaningfully oriented and comprehensible in nature. He notes that there are three corollaries to this observation: 1) the learner must interact with the input to maximize language acquisition, 2) the input must not only be comprehensible, it must be comprehended with ease, and 3) the degree and quality of language acquisition is partially determined by degree and quality of input received. Deaf children of deaf parents are clearly provided with quality input that is easily understood and they are able to interact with their parents and other signer. Thus, they have the basis for successful acquisition of English, and this is reflected in their academic and professional accomplishments.

3.2 Improved literacy

Learning to read requires an already developed language base. As deaf children are traditionally taught, they are asked to learn English language structure, speech, and reading at the same time. The problem with this is that students cannot understand what they are being told until they have mastered English well enough to understand the teacher's instructions. This vicious cycle is broken when the children come to school with a fully established ASL language base — then a normal situation is encountered for teaching English as a second language (ESL). Properly trained teachers of the deaf should have substantial expertise in ESL methods, and speech-language pathologists and audiologists working to develop speech and listening skills should have conversational fluency in ASL in order to be able to work with the children.

Consider reading readiness, that is, what children are expected to be able to do with language before learning to read. They should have a well-developed vocabulary, otherwise they will not recognize a written word even if they sound it out. They should be able to handle sentences of some complexity. One reason for this is that even though books for beginning readers limit the number of words per sentence, actual syntactic structure is not properly regulated (Quigley, Wilbur, Power, Montanelli, and Steinkamp, 1976; Wilbur and Nolen 1986b). Finally, they should be able to draw on their conversational skills and their knowledge of story structure to draw inferences and conclusions so that they can "read between the lines". Deaf children with competency in a natural sign language should be expected to meet reading readiness milestones as well. Even though they might not be able to recognize words that they sound out, they should be able to do the equivalent with fingerspelling (Padden and Hanson 2000). Certainly, they should be able to understand those concepts when signed, and this is precisely where knowledge of ASL makes a difference. Stuckless (1981) noted that whereas deaf children exposed only to a graphic form of English are working with a clear and complete code (written English), they still need to have an established language base in order to derive meaning from it. Similarly, Hirsh-Pasek and Treiman (1982) note that deaf children rarely possess a strong language base that is compatible with the alphabetic writing system and that sounding out or spelling aloud in the absence of extensive articulatory or fingerspelled vocabularies is unprofitable. They suggest that teachers working with signing deaf children can increase the child's fingerspelled lexicon, but that explicit instruction in using fingerspelling as a coding strategy related to print may be necessary because children may not discover it without assistance. Thus, the process of learning to deal with printed material is separate from the task of learning a language in the first place. As long as the two goals continue to be confused, progress towards both will continue to be hindered.

One of the most significant advantages of working with deaf children who already have a well-developed first language base is that many opportunities for learning can be found outside of the traditional classroom situation. For example, a trip to the zoo becomes more than just an opportunity to learn the names of animals; with extensive communication provided through the sign language, teacher and students can have a discussion about which animals are more interesting to write stories about and why. Children can make up short stories and tell them in ASL, enjoying the experience without the frustration of English structure, spelling, and writing. When the children do finally write stories, the task is different, but typical for bilingual children: translating into another language. For children who do not know ASL, writing the story is not just a translation task and requires attention to factors other than just the structure of English (for example, the notion of a story grammar has to be developed, whereas children who can use ASL will have already learned many things about normal story grammar structure, such as creating the setting, introducing participants, etc.)

4. Understanding ASL as a natural language

ASL is a naturally evolved complex language that varies significantly from English. Like many other languages (e.g., Russian, Spanish), it has a flexible word order, preferring that sentence elements reflect discourse roles (topic, focus) rather than the grammatical relations (subject, object) that English prefers (Wilbur 1997). Another difference between ASL and English is that ASL has what is called fixed phrasal stress, that is, it does not allow stress to shift to different words in a sentence in order to focus on different items (Wilbur 1997). Instead, ASL takes advantage of its more flexible word order to ensure that the desired focus will receive stress only in sentence-final position. Languages that allow phrasal stress shift, like English and Russian, are referred to as [+plastic], whereas languages like ASL and Catalan are [-plastic], where [plastic] is a typological feature that reflects how a language brings stress prominence and information focus together (Vallduví 1991).

An illustration of the differences between the two types may be helpful here. English allows the following sentences, each one with a different stressed item (in **bold**) but with the same word order:

1a. Carolina saw Julija put the book on the **TABLE**   (not the SHELF)
1b. Carolina saw Julija put the **BOOK** on the table.   (not the MANUSCRIPT)
1c. Carolina saw **JULIJA** put the book on the table.   (not Adriana)
1d. **CAROLINA** saw Julija put the book on the table.   (it was not Martina)

Stress movement cannot be done in languages with fixed phrasal stress. Instead, in ASL the word order must be changed so that the item to be stressed is put in the reserved place for focused items; in ASL and many other languages, this position is at the end of a sentence (Wilbur 1994b, 1995b, 1996). ASL has a very common structure that translates into English in two ways, either as in (1a-d) or as the wh-cleft as in (2); signs are glossed in small capitals, the extent of required brow raise (br) is marked with a line:

                                                              br
2a. CAROLINA SEE JULIJA PUT BOOK WHERE, TABLE
    'The place where Carolina saw Julija put the book was the table.'

                                                              br
2b. CAROLINA SEE JULIJA PUT-ON-TABLE WHAT, BOOK
    'What Carolina saw Julija put on the table was the book.'

                                                           br
2c. CAROLINA SEE BOOK PUT-ON-TABLE WHO, JULIJA
    'The person who Carolina saw put the book on the table was Julija.'

                                                    br
2d. SEE JULIJA BOOK PUT-ON-TABLE WHO, CAROLINA
    'It was Carolina who saw Julija put the book on the table.'

The ASL structure can be expanded to create further structures that are considered exceptionally complex in English:

                                            br
2e. CAROLINA SEE JULIJA DO++, BOOK PUT-ON-TABLE
    'What Carolina saw Julija do was put the book on the table.'
                                      br
2f. CAROLINA DO++, SEE JULIJA BOOK PUT-ON-TABLE
    'What Carolina did was see Julija put the book on the table.'

                                                     br
2g. CAROLINA SEE JULIJA DO++ WITH BOOK, PUT-ON-TABLE
    'What Carolina saw Julija do with the book was put it on the table.'

The basic form of this construction in ASL is 'old information + wh-word, new information', with the old information clause marked by a brow raise (Wilbur 1996). Brow raises and other nonmanual markers are integral components of the ASL grammatical system (Baker and Padden, 1978; Battison, 1974; Frishberg, 1978; Siple, 1978; Wilbur, 1991, 1994b, 1995a, 1999b; Wilbur and Patschke 1999). These differences in prosodic structure are primary contributors to significant differences in syntactic structure between ASL and English (Wilbur 1999a, 1999c). The prosodic, intonational, and syntactic structures evolved together to provide natural language capability in the signed modality (Allen, Wilbur, and Schick 1991; Wilbur and Allen 1991; Wilbur 1997, 2000b).

The nonmanual markers comprise a number of independent channels: head; body position; eyebrow and forehead; eyeblink and eye gaze; nose; and mouth, tongue, and cheek (Wilbur 1994a). Nonmanual cues provide morphemic information on lexical items, or indicate the ends of phrases (boundary markers) or their extent (domain markers, such as the brow raise in the examples above). The nonmanual signals made on the face can be roughly divided into two groups, lower and upper. The lower portion of the face is used to provide adverbial and adjectival information. The mouth, tongue, and cheeks provide meaningful markers that associate with specific lexical items or phrases (Liddell 1978, 1980; Wilbur 2000b) and the nose can be used for discourse marking purposes (Wood 1996).

The nonmanuals supplied by the upper part of the face and the head (eyebrows, head nods, tilts, and shakes, eyegaze; Wilbur 2000b) occur with higher syntactic constituents (clauses, sentences), even if such constituents contain only a single sign (e.g., a topicalized noun). Liddell (1978, 1980) noted the larger scope of upper face/head nonmanuals when he discussed the nonmanual marking 'q' for yes/no questions, as in (3):

3. MAN FISH[I:continuous]   'Is the man fishing with relaxation and enjoyment?'

This single example illustrates inflectional modification on the predicate sign itself (continuous), lower mouth adverbial modification of the predicate ('mm'), and upper face, head, and body marking for the entire question ('q', lean forward, head forward, brows raised), all on only two sequential lexical items. Information corresponding to English intonation is provided throughout the ASL clause from beginning to end by the upper face and head, and differs in production from what hearing people might also do with their face and head (Veinberg and Wilbur 1990).

In Wilbur (2000b), I discuss various nonmanuals and how and why they may be layered, where by 'layered' I mean simultaneously produced without interfering with the perception and production of the signs themselves or with other co-occurring nonmanuals. It is the presence of this layering in ASL, and its absence in signed English, that makes the prosodic difference between natural language and artificial system, respectively. Similarly, spatial arrangement in ASL can convey syntactic, semantic, and morphological information. If a verb is inflected for its arguments by showing starting and ending locations, then the nouns or pronouns do not need to be separately signed. Aspectual information carried in English by adverbs and prepositions phrases can be conveyed in ASL by modifying the verb's temporal and rhythmic characteristics. Information is layered, and thus ASL does not need separate signs for many of the concepts that English has separate words for. In this respect, the fact that ASL is a naturally evolved language in the visual/manual modality can be fully appreciated — more information is conveyed simultaneously than in comparable English renditions. Development of abilities to read and write the equivalents in English can take advantage of what the children already know.

5. Why signing the spoken language, for example, signed English, does not provide the same benefits

There are many situations in the daily lives of deaf children, especially those who have hearing parents, where communication in a form of signed English between adult and child is acceptable and adequate for information transfer. Those situations arise when, and only when, the child has acquired a sufficient knowledge of English for the signed English to be meaningfully interpreted. It is clear from the research and the success of deaf children of deaf parents who use ASL that one can reasonably expect to reach this point sooner and more efficiently with ASL as the first, early established language. When English syntax is the focus of educational attention, signed English usage may have an appropriate place as an effective educational tool. (For a review of the history of the debate surrounding signed English as an educational tool back to 1834, see Lane 1992.) This does not mean that signed English should be used with very young deaf children, as it is quite clear that there are many stages of language acquisition that must come before one can be concerned with syntactic structures, such as lexical development, lexical categorization such as transitive vs. intransitive verbs, concepts of aspect and time, morphological marking, among many others (see Radford 1990; Atkinson 1992; Lust, Suñer, and Whitman 1994; Lust, Hermon, and Kornfilt 1994). There are also many cognitive and socioemotional things that children must develop during the early years in addition to language (see relevant discussions in Bloom 1993; Fletcher and Garman 1986; Slobin 1985).

With respect to the disadvantages of early use of signed English, it is clear that natural languages have certain linguistic characteristics in common, including those features that linguists refer to as Universal Grammar. I have argued that 'layering' is one such characteristic (Wilbur 2000b). The question could be raised why signed English, as a code for English, which is a natural language, should be problematic.

Two criterial features for defining a natural language are that 1) it has a community of users and 2) it can be learned by babies from birth. It must be a perfect fit with the perception and production characteristics of the human user, and over time, natural languages evolve to fit the modality in which they are produced and perceived. Obviously, spoken languages are designed to be communicative with ease by people who speak and hear. Similarly, signed languages are evolved to provide communication with ease by people who sign and see. It is only when spoken languages and signed languages are compared for what they have in common, despite their modality differences, that these linguistic design features become obvious.

What signing the spoken language lacks is adaptation to the signing modality, which would allow it to take advantage of simultaneity rather than sequentiality. For example, signed English has not developed an intonational and rhythmic system that is designed to be seen by the eyes and produced by the hands and face. This evolution does not take place because of the goal is to mimic the lexicon, morphology and syntax of English. Thus, when it is learned by deaf children, it is learned with the over-riding constraint that it must follow English word order. This means that the syntactic structure cannot be adapted for modality purposes. So flexible word order cannot develop. However this fact by itself is not a problem as there is no linguistic reason why a signed language could not have the word order of English, if by 'syntax' we mean merely the basic word order.

A bigger problem is that SE is supposed to follow English morphology, which morphology cannot be modified for modality purposes. There is substantial overlap between the lexical vocabulary of ASL and SE (Wilbur, 1987). But these signs do not provide an exact match with English because certain information in ASL is not carried by separate signs, but by morphological modifications in the form of spatial or temporal adjustments to the sign movement (Klima and Bellugi 1979). English morphology involves affixes which are added to the stems (plural, past tense, progressive, comparative, superlative, possessive) and freestanding grammatical words (future, prepositions, infinitival 'to', and determiners). Because ASL uses other grammatical methods such as spatial arrangement in place of several types of prepositional phrases, signs for many function words and morphemes (e.g., at, to, the, -ing) that are not needed in ASL were invented for SE. These are translated into SE as separate signs, each requiring independent articulation in sequence; the result is that SE sentences have substantially more signs per sentence than ASL. Therefore, SE takes at least 50% longer to produce the same set of propositions than the two natural languages, spoken English and ASL, which are roughly comparable (Bellugi and Fischer, 1972).

The constraint that SE should follow English morphology encourages sequentiality and prevents layering mechanisms from arising. Given the requirement that SE should match English, any child inventions for SE (such as those reported by Supalla, 1991; Gee and Mounty, 1991) involving the types of manual or nonmanual mechanisms seen in ASL will be under pressure to normalize to the proper English sequence of signs. For example, Supalla (1991) reports that despite pure signed English input containing no spatially modified verbs or pronouns (and no known contamination by ASL signers), 10 year-old deaf students produced signing in which 80% of the verbs and 86% of the pronouns were spatially modified. The total absence of these devices in the teacher's signing suggests that these innovative spatial modifications will be treated as unacceptable errors by the teacher until they are completely eliminated from the students' signing and are replaced by the proper signed English forms. Under these circumstances, grammaticization of nonmanuals or manual sign modifications for functions like verb agreement cannot evolve. Furthermore, when adults (usually hearing) learn to sign English, they are already fluent in English and find it convenient to follow English principles, making innovations by this older population less likely. In essence, then, the dominance of English sequentiality of words and morphemes in this communication situation suppresses layering adaptations of signed English.

Wilbur and Petersen (1998) studied two groups of fluent SE users, one which also knows ASL (adult children of deaf parents) and one which does not (teachers, parents, audiologists, speech-language pathologists). In this study, the signers who know ASL were relatively diligent in using ASL nonmanual markers to convey information while producing SE (with or without speech), that is, they extended layering from ASL to SE. The signers who do not know ASL used minimal and occasionally incorrect nonmanual marking while signing SE. For example, some of their SE productions of yes/no questions had correct ASL brow raise on them whereas other productions were inappropriately marked with brow lowering. Fully 81% of the yes/no questions produced by these signers were not correctly marked by ASL standards. Other nonmanuals (blinks, negative headshakes) clearly differed between the two groups even though both groups were supposed to be producing the same SE content. The signers who knew ASL were able to transfer nonmanuals to SE because SE has no specified nonmanuals of its own. As a group, the signers who did not know ASL but who are nonetheless fluent users of SE were not homogeneous in their use of nonmanuals because no such system has developed for SE. If this is true for the general population of SE signers who do not know ASL, then it is clear that children are not presented with a consistent adult model of SE in the settings in which it is used.

Finally, the observation that there are systematic cues for intonation in signed languages provides insight into the universal structure of natural languages (Wilbur 1991, 1997, 2000b). One may infer that intonational information is a necessary component of the human linguistic and cognitive systems, and that at the prosodic level, the central processing mechanisms of the brain is indifferent to the modality in which such information is received by the peripheral mechanisms (ear or eye), so long as the information is present and appropriate to the linguistic content and communicative situation. There are clear differences between naturally evolved languages prosodically suited to their modality by appropriate layering (ASL and English) and artificial systems like signed English which take structure from one modality (spoken English) and attempt to convey it in another modality (signed English) without regard to modifications that might be appropriate for the production modality.

The solution that I am arguing for here is one where ASL is used as the initial language of communication and instruction for deaf children and where English is treated as a second language. That second language has a signed form (SE), a spoken form, and a written form. I have identified problems with signed English and indicated why I do not think it should be the first method of communication and language instruction. However, I want to make it clear that I think there is a role for signed English, and that this role is separate from signing and speaking at the same time. Signed English can be used to assist deaf children as they struggle to understand the differences between ASL and English. It can be used to concentrate on English syntax and morphology and on its written form (reading and writing).

Speaking and signing at the same time is another matter altogether. First, it should be clear from the above description of ASL that it is impossible to sign ASL and speak English at the same time. There are cognitive, linguistic, and motoric reasons for the presence of English-based signing and the absence of ASL-based signing when speaking English.

Second, questions have arisen about the quality of speech that serves as input to deaf children in SC situations. The Wilbur and Petersen (1998) study reported that in the production of simultaneous communication, speech duration increased as compared to producing speech alone. As part of the original design of the Wilbur and Petersen study, the speech with and without accompanying signs was also recorded on audiotapes so that the speech could be presented to 'blind' duration-measurers who would not know if the speakers were signing or not. It proved impossible to carry out this portion of the experimental design, as even naive listeners were instantly able to identify from the speech when there was signing at the same time. Slower, elongated speech such as that produced in simultaneous communication sounds less natural than speech produced alone. The source of these speech production modifications was not signer fluency (see similar findings in Whitehead et al. 1995; Schiavetti et al 1996). Rather, the observed modality interaction is likely the result of the prosodic structural mismatches between spoken and signed English. Theoretically, simultaneous speaking and signing contains the same number of words in each modality as they both code English. However, the number of syllables in the two modalities and the rhythmic pattern are extremely unlikely to match (Wilbur 1990c, 1993; Wilbur and Petersen 1997). There are numerous mismatches in the number of forms produced because SE frequently requires a separate sign for spoken English suffixes (e.g., -s); hence a single syllable word in spoken English (e.g. 'cats') may be two separate signs in SE (e.g., CAT + Plural). Every sign is given full metrical timing (e.g., full sign duration) regardless of whether its corresponding English translation is a lexical item or suffixal morpheme (Wilbur and Nolen 1986a). Hence, the single spoken syllable for 'cats' is matched by two full sign productions. Furthermore, spoken English has many words that have two or more syllables, but SE, which gets its basic vocabulary from ASL, contains mostly monosyllabic signs (Coulter, 1982; Wilbur, 1990). For example, the English word meaning 'eliminate' has 4 spoken syllables but only 1 signed syllable. Thus, in simultaneous signing and speaking, the number of syllables being produced is usually different in the two modalities.

6. Summary

The research that has been reviewed here provides strong support for the use of ASL as a means of communication before the deaf child enters school to develop cognition, socialization, and an age-appropriate knowledge base, as well as providing a basis for learning English and English literacy. Its use should continue into the classroom. Consider the ways in which knowledge of ASL can be helpful in improving acquisition of English and literacy proficiency with deaf children.

Conversational use of ASL models important features of ASL discourse, and discourse in general (Wilbur and Petitto 1983). As we have seen, ASL requires more obvious attention to what is the focus of the sentence in order to construct sentences in accordance with the requirement that the focus should be at the end of the sentence. This structural requirement in turn requires the signer to separate old and new information, placing the discourse old information prior to the new. Deaf students' difficulty with determiner usage ('a/the'), pronoun usage, and the stiltedness of their paragraphs, is precisely that they do not understand when and how to push old information to the background and how to bring new information to the foreground. The mechanisms for accomplishing these tasks in ASL are clear and consistent, so that children who know ASL come to the task of learning the English counterpart constructions with a strong base of understanding of the differences in meaning that need to be encoded in English syntax. That is, they would already know how to separate old from new information and have a sense of how conversational flow affects individual sentence structure. The task then becomes one of presenting these children with a situation in the form of 'if this is what you mean in ASL, here's how you express it in English.' When phrased this way, the task is not confounded by the necessity to also teach the notions of old and new; in short, we now have a typical bilingual learning environment.

Prosodic structure (intonation, stress placement) provides cues to the listener as to where sentences end and new ones begin, as well as providing cues as to whether the speaker intends to continue, plans to yield the floor, expects a response from the addressee, and other conversational controlling functions. These functions are only partially represented in the written form of English, through the use of punctuation and novelty uses of capitals, italics, bold, and graphic symbols ('!@$%#'). In ASL, sentence boundaries, signer intentions, and conversational controllers are all provided by cues other than the signs themselves. Various nonmanual cues provide overt information about phrasing and syntactic constituency. The difference between a string of words and a real sentence is the 'sentence glue' that binds the words into phrases and the phrases into sentences. In ASL, eyeblinks, head nods, and when the brows are raised or lowered all signal the ends of clauses and sentences. The height of the hands signals whether the signer intends to continue, yield, or interrupt someone else (Wilbur and Petitto 1983). Focus, contrast, emphasis, and other more subtle functions, such as uncertainty, specificity, and inclusion/exclusion, are carried by the face, head, and body (Wilbur and Patschke 1998). Deaf children who learn ASL first are prepared with full conversational fluency before they begin the task of learning to use English fluently. Full conversational fluency includes the signer's responsibility to ensure that the addressee can follow the topic, who is doing what to whom, and how much certainty the signer places in the truth of the assertions. These are all things that are coded in normal English usage, but are not part of the standard English lessons that are provided for deaf students. Again, the task of acquiring English is already simplified when learners have a first language that has prepared them with notions of conversational structure.

Along the same lines, ASL provides clear cues to which noun phrase is the subject/agent and which is the object/undergoer. For many verbs, formation is adjusted so that the verb production starts at a location representing the subject and moves to a location representing the object (see Meir 1998 for a complete linguistic discussion). In addition, eyegaze and head tilt are also used as subject and object markers (Bahan 1996). Information about subject and object in English is carried strictly by word order, subject before the verb and object after. Students with knowledge of ASL will find this aspect of English syntax fairly easy to acquire. More importantly, they will then be prepared to deal with exceptional constructions, such as the passive where the agent is not the subject, because it can be explained to them how the two structures (active and passive) differ with respect to the placement of the agent. The use of nonmanuals and spatial modifications of sign formations is one of the reasons why ASL does not need separate signs for many of the concepts that (spoken/signed) English has separate words for. In this respect, the fact that ASL is a naturally evolved language in the visual/manual modality can be fully appreciated — more information is conveyed simultaneously than in comparable English renditions.

As we have seen in the section on the development of speech skills in deaf learners, early acquisition of ASL does not affect the development of speech production or speechreading skills. Deaf children who have deaf parents who use ASL as the primary means of communication perform at a level comparable to orally trained deaf children from hearing households with respect to speech skills. Deaf children of deaf parents, like other deaf children, routinely receive speech skill training in school. ASL does not compete or interfere with this training; clearly it can produce speech results as effective as oral-only training in children who may not be specially 'gifted' for oral performance. In addition, deaf children who know ASL have the further advantages of superior performance on measures of cognitive, linguistic, and social skills.

Finally, there is the fact that sign languages have no written form. This is also not a major concern; consider the functions that writing serves: long-distance (not face-to-face) communication and preservation of documents for future use. For signed languages, these functions are easily served by videotape. The history, stories, biographies, theatrical performances, poetry, and other linguistic expressions of American Deaf culture in ASL are preserved in videorecordings (and earlier, on film) dating back to the beginning of the twentieth century. Early knowledge of sign language allows deaf students access to their history and culture, which in turn engenders pride in who they are. Through a bilingual, bicultural approach, we should see elimination of what Johnson, Liddell, and Erting (1989) call 'the cycle of low expectations' - which they suggest is the primary cause of the failure of deaf education.

If the adults in the deaf child's environment do not know the local natural sign language, how can the child develop full sign language fluency? Parents trigger the language acquisition process, but they do not control its ultimate outcome. Instead, children acquire the language of their peers. The earlier the child is placed in contact with the natural sign language, the better the child will learn it. Strategies for accomplishing this contact include opportunities for the child to play with other signing children (deaf or hearing), signing babysitters, regular visits to the local Deaf clubs or schools, and other interactions with members of the Deaf community. Johnson, Liddell, and Erting (1989) provide a number of additional suggestions, many modeled after the successful programs for the Deaf in Sweden. The critical factor is that the child must be placed in an appropriate language learning environment. If the parents never become fluent in the natural sign language and can only just manage in signed English, so be it. The focus should not be on what the parents can or cannot do. Rather the focus should be on the child's education, which requires communication in a natural language, on which all advanced learning is built. Early knowledge of sign language is a critical part of the solution, not part of the problem.

References

Ahlstrom, K. (1972). On evaluation of the effects of schooling. In *Proceedings of the International Congress on Education of the Deaf.* Sveriges Laraforbund, Stockholm.

Allen, G. D., Wilbur, R. B. and Schick, B. S. (1991). Aspects of rhythm in American Sign Language. *Sign Language Studies, 72,* 297-320.

Atkinson, M. (1992). *Children's Syntax.* Oxford: Basil Blackwell.

Bahan, B. J. (1996). *Nonmanual realization of agreement in ASL.* Doctoral dissertation, Boston University.

Baker, C. and Padden, C. (1978). Focusing on the nonmanual components of American Sign Language. In P. Siple (ed.). *Understanding language through sign language research.* (pp. 27-57). New York: Academic Press.

Battison, R. (1974). Phonological deletion in American Sign Language. *Sign Language Studies, 5,* 1-19.

Bellugi, U., and Fischer, S. (1972). A comparison of sign language and spoken language: Rate and grammatical mechanisms. *Cognition, 1,* 173-200.

Bloom, P. (ed.). (1993). *Language Acquisition.* Cambridge, MA: MIT Press.

Bonvillian, J. D., Charrow, V. R. and Nelson, K. E. (1973). Psycholinguistic and educational implications of deafness. *Human Development, 16,* 321-345.

Charrow, V. R. and Fletcher, J. D. (1974). English as the second language of deaf children. *Developmental Psychology, 10,* 463-470.

Charrow, V. R. and Wilbur, R. B. (1975). The deaf child as a linguistic minority. *Theory into Practice, 14* (5), 353-359. (Reprinted in S. Wilcox (Ed.), (1989). *American deaf culture. An anthology* (pp. 103-155). Silver Spring, MD: Linstok Press.)

Coulter, G. (1982). *On the nature of ASL as a monosyllabic language.* LSA, San Diego, CA.

Fletcher, P. and Garman, M. (1986). *Language Acquisition: Studies in first language development (second edition).* Cambridge: Cambridge University Press.

Frishberg, N. (1978). The case of the missing length. *Communication and Cognition, 11,* 57-67. Reprinted in *Sign Language & Linguistics, 5-2,* 2002.

Gee, J. P. and Mounty, J. (1991). Nativization, variability, and style shifting in the sign language development of deaf children of hearing parents. In P. Siple and S. Fischer (eds.). *Theoretical Issues in Sign Language Research, volume 2: Psychology* (pp. 65-83). Chicago: University of Chicago Press.

Hakuta, K. (1986). *Mirrors of Language: The debate on bilingualism.* New York: Basic Books.

Hirsh-Pasek, K. and Treiman, R. (1982). Recoding in silent reading: Can the deaf child translate print into a more manageable form? *The Volta Review, 84,* 71-82.

Hoffmeister, R. (2000). A piece of the puzzle: ASL and reading comprehension in deaf children. In C. Chamberlain, J. P. Morford, & R. I. Mayberry (eds.), *Language acquisition by eye,* pp. 143-164. Mahwah, NJ: Lawrence Erlbaum Associates.

Hoiting, N. & Slobin. D. (2002). What a deaf child needs to see: Advantages of a natural sign language over a sign system. In R. Schulmeister & H. Reinitzer (eds.) *Progress in sign language research: In honor of Siegmund Prillwitz,* pp. 267-277. Hamburg: Signum.

Johnson, R. E., Liddell, S. K., and Erting, C. J. (1989). *Unlocking the curriculum: Principles for achieving access in Deaf education.* (Available from Gallaudet Research Institute, Gallaudet University, Washington, D.C.)

Klima, E., and Bellugi, U. (1979). *The signs of language.* Cambridge, MA: Harvard University Press.

Lane, H. (1992). The *Mask of Benevolence: Disabling the Deaf Community.* NY: Alfred A. Knopf.

Liddell, S. K. (1978). Non-manual signals and relative clauses in American Sign Language. In P. Siple (Ed.), *Understanding language through sign language research* (p.59-90). NY: Academic.

Liddell, S. K. (1980). *American Sign Language syntax.* The Hague: Mouton.

Lillo-Martin, D. (1993). Deaf readers and universal grammar. In Marschark, M. and D. Clark (eds.). *Psychological perspectives on deafness* (pp. 311-337). Edison, NJ: Lawrence Erlbaum.

Lillo-Martin, D. (1994). Setting the null argument parameters: Evidence from American Sign Language and other languages. In Lust, B. Hermon, G. and Kornfilt, J. (eds.). (1994). *Binding, Dependencies, and Learnability.* (pp. 301-318). Hillsdale, NJ: Lawrence Erlbaum Associates.

Lust, B. Hermon, G. and Kornfilt, J. (eds.). (1994). *Binding, Dependencies, and Learnability.* Hillsdale, NJ: Lawrence Erlbaum Associates.

Lust, B., Suñer, M. and Whitman, J. (eds.). (1994). *Heads, Projections, and Learnability.* Hillsdale, NJ: Lawrence Erlbaum Associates.

Meadow, K. (1966). The effects of early manual communication and family climate on the deaf child's early development. Ph.D. dissertation, University of California, Berkeley.

Meir, I. (1998). Syntactic-semantic interaction in Israeli Sign Language verbs. *Sign Language and Linguistics, 1,* 3-33.

Moores, D. (1971). *Recent research on manual communication.* University of Minnesota, MN: Research, Development, and Demonstration Center in Education of the Handicapped.

Moores, D. (1974). Educating the deaf: Psychology, principles, and practices. Boston: Houghton-Mifflin.

Newport, E. and Meier, R. (1985). The acquisition of American Sign Language. In Slobin, D. I. (Ed.). *The crosslinguistic study of language acquisition. Volume 1: The data.* (pp. 881-938). Hillsdale, NJ: Lawrence Erlbaum Associates.

Padden, C. and Hanson, V. (2000). Search for the missing link: The development of skilled reading in Deaf children. In Lane, H. and Emmorey, K. (Eds.). *The Signs of Language Revisited: An anthology to honor Ursula Bellugi and Edward Klima.* Hillsdale, NJ: Lawrence Erlbaum Associates.

Padden, C. & Ramsey, C. (2000). American Sign Language and reading ability. In C. Chamberlain, J. P. Morford, & R. I. Mayberry (eds.), *Language acquisition by eye*, pp. 165-190. Mahwah, NJ: Lawrence Erlbaum Associates.

Petitto, L. A. (1993). Modularity and constraints in early lexical acquisition: Evidence from children's early language and gesture. In Bloom, P. (Ed.). *Language Acquisition.* (pp. 95-126). Cambridge: MIT press.

Pinker, S. (1993). Rules of language. In Bloom, P. (Ed). *Language Acquisition.* (pp. 472-484). (Reprint of Pinker, S. (1991). Rules of language. *Science, 253,* 530-535.)

Power, D. (1974). Language development in deaf children: The use of manual supplement in oral education. *Australian Teacher of the Deaf, 15.*

Prinz, P. (2002). Crosslinguistic perspectives on sign language and literacy development. In R. Schulmeister & H. Reinitzer (eds.) *Progress in sign language research: In honor of Siegmund Prillwitz,* pp. 221-233. Hamburg: Signum.

Quigley, S. P. and Frisina, R. (1961). *Institutionalization and psychoeducational development in deaf children.* Washington, DC: Council on Exceptional Children.

Quigley, S. P. and Kretschmer, R. E. (1982). *The education of deaf children.* Baltimore, MD: University Park Press.

Quigley, S. P. and Paul, P. (1984). *Language and deafness*. San Diego: College-Hill Press.

Quigley, S. P., Wilbur, R. B., Power, D. J., Montanelli, D. S. and Steinkamp, M. W. (1976). *Syntactic structures in the language of deaf children*. Urbana, IL: Institute for Child Behavior and Development.

Radford, A. (1990). *Syntactic Theory and the Acquisition of English*. Oxford: Basil Blackwell.

Schiavetti, N., Whitehead, R. L., Metz, D. E., Whitehead, B. H., and Mignerey, M. (1996). Voice onset time in speech produced during simultaneous communication. *Journal of Speech and Hearing Research, 39*, 565-572.

Singleton, J. L., Supalla, S., Litchfield, S. & Schley, S. (1998). From sign to word: Considering modality constraints in ASL/English bilingual education. In P. Prinz (ed.), *ASL proficiency and English literacy acquisition: New perspectives. Topics in Language Disorders, 18*, 16-29.

Siple, P. (1978). Visual constraints for sign language communication. *Sign Language Studies, 19*, 95-110.

Slobin, D. I. (ed.). (1985). *The Crosslinguistic Study of Language Acquisition*. Hillsdale, NJ: Lawrence Erlbaum Associates.

Stevenson, E. (1964). A study of the educational achievement of deaf children of deaf parents. *California News, 80*, 143.

Strong, M. & Prinz, P. (1997). A study of the relationship between ASL and English literacy. *Journal of Deaf Studies and Deaf Education, 2*, 37-46.

Stuckless, R. (1981). Real-time graphic displays and language development for the hearing-impaired. *American Annals of the Deaf, 83*, 291-230.

Stuckless, R. and Birch, J. (1966). The influence of early manual communication on the linguistic development of deaf children. *American Annals of the Deaf, 106*, 436-480.

Supalla, S. J. (1991). Manually coded English: The modality question in signed language development. In P. Siple and S. Fischer (eds.). *Theoretical Issues in Sign Language Research, volume 2: Psychology* (pp. 85-109). Chicago: University of Chicago Press.

Vallduví, E. (1991). The role of plasticity in the association of focus and prominence. In Y. No and M. Libucha (Eds.), *ESCOL '90: Proceedings of the Seventh Eastern States Conference on Linguistics* (pp. 295-306). Columbus, OH: Ohio State University Press.

VanPatten, B. (1995). Cognitive Aspects of Input Processing in Second Language Acquisition. In Hashemipour, P., Maldonado, R., and van Naerssen, M. (Eds.). *Studies in Language Learning and Spanish Linguistics: in honor of Tracy D. Terrell*. New York: McGraw-Hill.

VanPatten, B. (1996). Input Processing and Grammar Instruction: Theory and Research. Norwood, NJ: Ablex.

Veinberg, S. C. and Wilbur, R. B. (1990). A linguistic analysis of the negative headshake in American Sign Language. *Sign Language Studies, 68*, 217-244.

Vernon, M. and S. D. Koh. (1970). Early Manual Communication and Deaf Children's Achievement. *American Annals of the Deaf, 115*, 527-536.

Whitehead, R. L., Schiavetti, N., Whitehead, B. H., and Metz, D. E. (1995). Temporal characteristics of speech in simultaneous communication. *Journal of Speech and Hearing Research, 38*, 1014-1024.

Wilbur, R. B. (1979). *American Sign Language and sign systems: Research and applications*. Baltimore, MD: University Park Press.

Wilbur, R. B. (1987). *American Sign Language: Linguistic and applied dimensions*. San Diego, CA: College-Hill Press.

Wilbur, R. B. (1990). Why syllables? What the notion means for ASL research. In S. D.

Fischer and P. Siple (Eds.), *Theoretical issues in sign language research: Vol. 1. Linguistics* (pp. 81-108). Chicago, IL: University of Chicago Press.

Wilbur, R. B. (1991). Intonation and focus in American Sign Language. In Y. No and M. Libucha (Eds.), *ESCOL '90: Eastern States Conference on Linguistics* (pp. 320-331). Columbus, OH: Ohio State University Press.

Wilbur, R. B. (1993). Segments and syllables in ASL phonology. In G. R. Coulter (Ed.), *Current issues in ASL phonology* (*Phonetics and phonology*, Vol. 3). (pp. 135-168). New York: Academic Press.

Wilbur, R. B. (1994a). Eyeblinks and ASL phrase structure. *Sign Language Studies, 84,* 221-240.

Wilbur, R. B. (1994b). Foregrounding structures in ASL. *Journal of Pragmatics, 22,* 647-672.

Wilbur, R. B. (1995a). What the morphology of operators looks like: A formal analysis of ASL brow-raise. In L. Gabriele, D. Hardison, and R. Westmoreland (Eds.), *FLSM VI: Formal Linguistics Society of Mid-America: Vol. 2. Syntax II and semantics/pragmatics* (pp. 67-78). Bloomington, IN: Indiana University Linguistics Club Publications.

Wilbur, R. B. (1995b). Why so-called "rhetorical questions" (RHQs). are neither rhetorical nor questions. In H. Bos and T. Schermer (Eds.), *Sign language research 1994: Fourth European congress on sign language research, Munich* [*International Studies on Sign Language and Communication of the Deaf, Vol. 29*] (pp. 149-169). Hamburg: SIGNUM.

Wilbur, R. B. (1996). Evidence for function and structure of wh-clefts in ASL. In W. H. Edmondson and R. B. Wilbur (Eds.), *International Review of Sign Linguistics* (pp. 209-256). Hillsdale, NJ: Lawrence Erlbaum Associates.

Wilbur, R. B. (1997). A prosodic/pragmatic explanation for word order variation in ASL with typological implications. In K. Lee, E. Sweetser, and M. Verspoor (Eds.), *Lexical and syntactic constructions and the construction of meaning* (Vol. 1). (pp. 89-104). Philadelphia: John Benjamins.

Wilbur, R. B. (1999a). Typological similarities between American Sign Language and Spanish. *Actas de VI simposio internacional de comunicacion social (Santiago de Cuba), 1,* 438-443.

Wilbur, R. B. (1999b). A functional journey with a formal ending: What do brow raises do in American Sign Language? In Darnell, Michael, Edith Moravscik, Michael Noonan, Frederick Newmeyer and Kathleen Wheatly (Eds.), *Functionalism and Formalism, Volume II: Case studies*, pp. 295-313. Amsterdam: John Benjamins.

Wilbur, R. (1999c). Stress in ASL: Empirical evidence and linguistic issues. *Language and Speech, 42.*

Wilbur, R. B. (2000a). The use of ASL to support the development of English and literacy. *Journal of Deaf Studies and Deaf Education* 5: 81-104.

Wilbur, R. B. (2000b). Phonological and prosodic layering of nonmanuals in American Sign Language. In Lane, H. and Emmorey, K. (eds.), *The signs of language revisited: Festschrift for Ursula Bellugi and Edward Klima*, pp. 213-241. Hillsdale, NJ: Lawrence Erlbaum.

Wilbur, R. B. (2001). Sign language and successful bilingual development of deaf children. *Journal of the Institute for Social Research [Društvena Istraživanja]* 56: 1039-1079.

Wilbur, R. B. and Allen, G. D. (1991). Perceptual evidence against internal structure in ASL syllables. *Language and Speech, 34,* 27-46.

Wilbur, R. B. and Nolen, S. B. (1986a). Duration of syllables in ASL. *Language and Speech, 29,* 263-280.

Wilbur, R. B. and Nolen, S. B. (1986b). Reading and writing. In J. V. Van Cleve (Ed.),

---

Gallaudet encyclopedia of deaf people and deafness (pp. 146-151). New York: McGraw-Hill.

Wilbur, R. B. and Patschke, C. (1998). Body leans and marking contrast in ASL. *J. Pragmatics, 30*, 275-303.

Wilbur, R. B. and Patschke, C. (1999). Syntactic correlates of brow raise in ASL. *Sign Language & Linguistics* 2: 3-40.

Wilbur, R. B. and Petersen, L. (1997). Backwards signing and ASL syllable structure. *Language and Speech, 40*, 63-90.

Wilbur, R. B. and Petersen, L. (1998). Modality interactions of speech and signing in simultaneous communication. *Journal of Speech, Language and Hearing Research, 41*, 200-212.

Wilbur, R. B. and Petitto, L. (1983). Discourse structure of American Sign Language conversations; or, how to know a conversation when you see one. *Discourse Processes, 6*, 225-241.

Wood, S. K. (1996). *Nose wrinkles in ASL: A discourse particle for co-construction.* Paper presented to the American Association for Applied Linguistics, Chicago, IL.

ŠTO ZNAMO O ZNAKOVNOM JEZIKU NAKON 40 GODINA ISTRAŽIVANJA?

Sažetak

Istraživanje znakovnog jezika dobiva zamah u cijelom svijetu. Korisno je dati pregled spoznaja do kojih se došlo dosadašnjim istraživanjima, jer to omogućuje istraživačima koncentraciju na detalje koji su specifični za njihov vlastiti znakovni jezik i isključuje nepotreban istraživački rad. Na primjer, danas znamo da postoje znakovni jezici koji su prirodno evoluirali, te da se oni razlikuju od pedagoških znakovnih sustava kojima je cilj upotrebljavati dominantni govorni jezik popraćen znakovima, te od tzv. "kućnih znakova". Ne postoji univerzalni, međunarodni znakovni jezik, iako postoji europski međunarodni znakovni jezik. Znakovni jezici koji su prirodno evoluirali ne ovise o strukturi dominantnog govornog jezika, iako se na taj način mogu predstavljati u nastavi; to ne znači da govorni i znakovni jezik ne mogu biti slični. Naša su istraživanja pokazala da postoji više sličnosti između njemačkog znakovnog jezika i austrijskog znakovnog jezika i njemačkog jezika, nego između američkog znakovnog jezika i engleskog jezika. Upravo zbog toga što znakovni jezici evoluiraju sami, uz sociolingvistički utjecaj dominantnog govornog jezika kroz sustav školstva, očekujemo da ćemo pronaći i sličnosti i razlike. Istraživači ne bi trebali dokazivati da određeni znakovni jezik jest jezik (osim ako je jasno da se tek razvija) i ne bi trebali dokazivati da je drugačiji od govornog jezika. Prirodni znakovni jezici proizvode se s više artikulatora: dvije ruke, glava, tijelo, gornji dio lica (uključujući obrve, pogled i treptanje očnih kapaka), nos, usta/obraze, bradu i jezik. Jezični signali s tih artikulatora mogu se pojavljivati istovremeno ne ometajući jedan drugoga već zajednički doprinoseći ukupnom značenju. Prirodni znakovni jezici ne ometaju usvajanje dominantnog govornog jezika. Istraživanja pokazuju da osobe koje uče znakovni jezik od rođenja (gluha djeca gluhih roditelja) imaju bolje rezultate od svojih vršnjaka koji kasnije počnu učiti znakovni jezik (gluha djeca čujućih roditelja) u gotovo svim mjerama jezične kompetencije, govora, čitanja, pisanja, socijalnog razvoja i akademskih znanja (npr. u matematici). Nema značajnih razlika u razvijenosti govora djece koja rano uče znakovni jezik i djece poučavane oralnim pristupom. Istraživači ne trebaju dokazivati da je učenje znakovnog jezika kritični faktor za ukupni uspjeh i postignuća gluhe djece, već se trebaju usredotočiti na strukturalne razlike između znakovnog i govornog jezika kako bi stvorili prikladna sredstva kojima će gluhu djecu koja već imaju usvojeni prvi (znakovni) jezik poučavati drugome (govornome) jeziku.

Ključne riječi: *znakovni jezik, prirodni znakovni jezici, gluhi, dvojezično obrazovanje*

ACQUISITION OF THE FIRST HANDSHAPES IN NATIVE LSC SIGNERS

Maria del Pilar Fernández-Viader & Josep Maria Segimon

University of Barcelona, Department of Developmental and Educational Psychology, Spain
ILLESCAT (Centre for the Study of Catalan Sign Language), Barcelona, Spain

Abstract

The aim of this research is to examine the processes of the acquisition of the first hand-shapes in LSC (Catalan Sign Language). We continued a research done by Fernández-Viader (1993-1996); Fernández-Viader, Segimon and Jarque (1996-2000). We studied the first productions in a LSC native signing girl. We analyzed the formational errors in the first handshapes of signing children, taking as a reference those of adult LSC signers. Our subjects were two deaf girls, native signers, with LSC as their first language. One of them has deaf parents and a younger deaf sister. The other girl has a deaf father and a hard of hearing mother, as well as a younger deaf sister. We videotaped the girls in a familiar context, in their interaction with their mothers in everyday situations: feeding, playing, drawing and telling tales. Each video recording is 45 minutes long (covering the time from the age of 15 months to the age of 24 months). We compared our results with the data obtained by Parkhurst (2000) about the first handshapes in a hearing child, LSE signer. We analyzed the handshapes of children's productions. For each handshape we took into account the exact number of correct occurrences and the number of each occurrence that each girl used in a given configuration as a substitution for the handshape used by adults. We considered it very important to focus on the errors in children's productions. We have observed that formational errors seem to be characteristic of the beginning of signed communication. Nowadays, with the obtained data, it is difficult to corroborate the hypothesis of four stages in the process of handshape acquisition (Boyes-Braem, 1973; 1990; McIntire, 1977). Based on the girls' ages, we can confirm the majority of the handshapes present in the first stage mentioned by both authors, but one of them has not been found in LSC (S configuration). It seems to be a consequence of secondary factors (nature of the feedback). The first data we have obtained leads us to accept the evidence of anatomic conditionings in the first steps of sign language acquisition and development, but we need to go deeper into the distinctive features of these languages and their impact on native signing children. The importance of the nature of the language to which a girl or a boy have been exposed becomes evident.

Key words: sign language, Catalan Sign Language, handshapes, acquisition of the first handshapes

Background

In the course of a research begun some years ago in the Developmental and Educational Psychology Department of the University of Barcelona, we have demonstrated the importance of gestures and signs in the communicative development of deaf children (Fernández-Viader, 1993; 1996). We have also proved the importance of deictic gestures in prelingual stages in deaf and hearing children (Fernández-Viader, 1992, 1993, 1996).

We could say that the origins of language and consciousness amount to the pointing signs. Different authors have gone deeper into the importance of these gestures and their functions regarding deaf children (i.e. Hoffmeister, 1977; Petitto and Marentette, 1991; Pizzuto, 1990; Fernández-Viader, 1992; Triadó & Fernández-Viader, 1994; 1999).

These results can be linked to biological, physiological, anatomical and neuronal constrictions that affect the organisation and development of the first hand movements and handshapes of children.

For the sake of understanding the acquisition processes and the handshape development in native signers, we considered it important to link these results to those of Boyes-Braem (1973; 1990).

In all babies, deixis and all holding movements characteristic of psychomotor development are the most used functions. However, it is true that for signing children those handshapes are not enough for sign language acquisition.

For sign language acquisition a previous acquisition of some specific motor abilities is needed, such as the independence of the group of fingers that is not involved in the holding movement, in other words, the weakest group - the middle, the ring and the little finger. According to Boyes-Braem (1973, 1990), the control of these fingers is acquired during at least two steps in the chronology of sign languages development:

   1a. Handshapes in which thumb and index finger are involved in forming a pinch;
   1b. Handshapes in which the whole hand is involved;
   2.   Handshapes in which other fingers are involved.

Boyes (1973, 1990) proposed four stages in the development of handshape acquisition in ASL native signers.

   1.   A S L bO 5 C G
   2.   B F O
   3.   I D Y P 3 V H W
   4.   8 7 X R T

These stages are articulated by means of the acquisition of some specific features that represent a system of anatomical factors which are applied to fingers to create different handshapes, from the handshape considered as unmarked A (holding hand with thumb straight close to index finger). These features are the following:

-   *Opposition:* It is only applied to thumb. Its application to the unmarked A handshape gives place to S handshape in ASL.
-   *Complete extension:* It is applied to fingers when they are partially straight. One or more fingers are bent. Handshapes C and G are examples of this handshape.
-   *Close:* Contact movement of contiguous fingers to the line that crosses the middle finger. If we accompany it with bending, it results in C handshape, if not, we get B handshape.
-   *Contact of the tips of fingers with the thumb:* it can be applied to any finger. bO handshape is an example of that.

- *Contact of the second joint of a finger with the thumb:* for instance, P handshape.
- *Thumb between fingers:* T handshape.
- *Crossing adjacent fingers:* it is applied to R handshape.

Boyes-Braem (1990) mentions other secondary factors that might influence the production of the first handshapes. They are the following:
- A child's *preference* for a *contact* between the index finger and fingertips;
- Nature of the *feedback*;
- *Complexity* of the sign or the movement needed to perform it;
- Anticipation and retention of the *adjacent handshape* in the chain of signs.

In this work we will try to find out if the development stages of the first handshapes proposed by Boyes-Braem (1973, 1990) and McIntire (1977) for ASL can be found in children signing in LSC (Catalan Sign Language).

Methodology

Our subjects were two deaf girls, native signers, of normal development and with LSC as their first language. The first girl, whose parents are deaf, has a younger sister, also deaf. The second girl is the daughter of a deaf father and a hard of hearing mother and has a younger deaf sister, too. Within this research each girl was observed from the age of 15 months to the age of 24 months. Due to geographical and cultural proximity we compared our results with the data obtained by Parkhurst (2000) about the first handshapes in a hearing child, LSE signer.

Procedure

We videotaped the girls in a familiar context, in their interaction with their mothers in everyday situations: feeding, playing, drawing and telling tales. Each video recording is 45 minutes long.

Analysis

We analyzed the handshapes produced by children. For each handshape we took the following into account:
- the exact number of correct occurrences;
- the number of each occurrence that each girl used in a given configuration as substitution for the handshape used by adults.

Results

We considered it very important to focus on the errors in children's productions. We have observed that formational errors seem to be characteristic of the beginning of signed communication.

Nowadays, with the obtained data, it is difficult to corroborate the hypothesis of four stages in the process of handshape acquisition (Boyes-Braem, 1973; 1990; McIntire, 1977). Based on the girls' ages, we can confirm most of the handshapes present in the first stage mentioned by both authors, but one of them has not been found in LSC (S configuration). It seems to be a consequence of secondary factors (nature of the feedback). Something similar occurs in the following stages; in some video recordings we found handshapes that might be considered as belonging to the following stages (i.e. V, H, 8, X).

The first data we have obtained leads us to accept the evidence of anatomic conditionings in the first steps of sign language acquisition and development, but we need to go deeper into the distinctive features of these languages and their impact on native signing children. The importance of the nature of the language to which a girl or a boy have been exposed becomes evident.

This research has been supported by a grant by Divisió d'Educació, University of Barcelona, Spain (Project 1999-RED-5037-2A).

References

Boyes-Braem, P. (1973) *A study of the acquisition of the dez in American Sign Language.* Berkeley, MS.

Boyes-Braem, P. (1990) A study of the handshape in American Sign Language: a preliminary analysis; in V. Volterra & C. Erting (eds.) *From gesture to language in hearing and deaf children* (Springer Series in Language and Communication; 27) Berlin, New York: Springer, pp. 107-127.

Fernández-Viader, M.P. (1992) Interacción social y comunicación preverbal en bebés. *Revista de Logopedia, Foniatría y Audiología, vol XII*, 1: pp. 10-18.

Fernández-Viader (1993) *Estrategias comunicativas del niño sordos en contexto familiar. Interacción comunicativa.* Tesis Doctoral. Universitat de Barcelona.

Fernández-Viader (1996). *La comunicación de los niños sordos. Interacción comunicativa padres-hijos.* Barcelona: Confederación Nacional de Sordos de España/Fundación ONCE.

Fernández-Viader, M.P., Segimon, J.M., and Jarque; M.J. (1996) Procesos de adquisición de los primeros formantes de la Lengua de Signos Catalana. En M. Pérez Pereira (ed.) *Estudios sobre la adquisición del Castellano, Catalán, Eusquera y Gallego.* Santiago de Compostela: Servicio de Publicaciones de la Universidad de Santiago de Compostela, pp. 113-126.

Fernández-Viader, M.P., Segimon, J.M., and Jarque; M.J. (2000) Adquisición de la Configuración en los Primeros Signos de la Lengua de Signos Catalana (LSC). *Revista Española de Lingüística de las Lenguas de Signos, RELLS, número 2*, pp. 19-34.

Hoffmeister, R.J.(1977) *The acquisition of American by deaf children of deaf parents: The development of demostrative pronouns, locatives and personal pronouns.* Minneapolis: University of Minnesota.

McIntire, M. (1977) The acquisition of American Sign Language hand configurations. *Sign Language Studies, 16*, pp. 247-266.

Parkhurst, S. (2000) Primeras Configuraciones de un Niño Oyente. *RELLS, número2,* 35-42.

Petitto, L. and Marentette, P. (1991) Babbling in the Manual Mode: Evidence for the Ontogeny of Language. *Science, 251*, pp. 1493-1496.

Pizzuto, E.(1990) The early development of deixis in American Sign Language. What is the point? In V. Volterra y C.J. Erting (eds.) *From Gesture to Language in Hearing and Deaf Children.* N.Y. Springer-Verlag, 142-152.

Triadó, C. y Fernández-Viader, M.P. (1994) Utilisation de la deixis par des parents entendants d´enfants sourds. *Colloque International Communication prélinguistique et linguistique chez l´enfant.* Paris.

Triadó, C. y Fernández-Viader, M.P. (1999) Interacción comunicativa padres-niños sordos. En Del Río, M.J. (ed.) *El desarrollo del lenguaje en personas con necesidades educativas especiales: Una perspectiva interactiva.* Barcelona: Martínez Roca, pp. 47-60.

PRVI OBLICI ŠAKA U IZVORNIH GOVORNIKA KATALONSKOG ZNAKOVNOG JEZIKA (LSC)

Cilj je ovog istraživanja ispitati pojavu prvih oblika šaka u LSC (katalonskom znakovnom jeziku). Analiziraju se tvorbene greške u prvim oblicima šake dviju gluhih djevojčica u dobi od 15-24 mjeseca, kojima je LSC prvi jezik, u usporedbi s odraslim govornicima LSC-a. Pokušat će se utvrditi može li se usvajanje prvih oblika šaka koje su utvrdili Boyes-Braem i McIntire u ASL-u naći i u djece koja koriste LSC. Djeca su snimljena u poznatom okruženju, u interakciji s majkom u svakodnevnim situacijama hranjenja, igranja, crtanja, pričanja priča. Svaka snimka traje ukupno 45 minuta. Usporedili smo rezultate s podacima Parkhursta o prvim oblicima šaka čujućeg djeteta koje koristi LSE. Analizirali smo oblike šaka koje su djeca izvodila. Za svaki oblik šake uzeli smo u obzir točan broj izvođenja, broj izvođenja koje je svaka djevojčica koristila kao "zamjenu" za oblik šake kojega koriste odrasli. Smatramo da je veoma važno obratiti pažnju na greške u dječjim produkcijama. Promatrali smo tvorbene pogreške koje se čine karakterističnima za početak znakovne komunikacije. Možemo potvrditi prisutnost većine oblika šaka prisutnih u istraživanjima spomenutih autora, iako se jedan od njih ne može naći u LSC-u (oblik šake S). Čini se da je to posljedica sekundarnih čimbenika (prirode povratne informacije). Rezultati istraživanja ukazuju na anatomsku uvjetovanost početaka usvajanja znakovnog jezika.

Ključne riječi: *znakovni jezik, katalonski znakovni jezik, oblici šaka, prvi oblici šaka*

RESEARCH ON CROATIAN SIGN LANGUAGE

Ninoslava Šarac
Zagreb, Croatia; Purdue University, USA
Tamara Alibašić
Zadar, Croatia; Purdue University, USA
Ronnie Wilbur
Purdue University, USA

Abstract

In this research we attempted to record and systematically examine the basic sign para-meters and nonmanual characteristics in Croatian Sign Language (HZJ). Through the analy-sis of four videotaped minutes of a Deaf couple's signed communication, we identified many elements of the structure of HZJ signs. This research, like many other studies of ASL and other sign languages, showed that HZJ has the same four basic manual phonological parameters: location of articulation, handshape, movement, and orientation. In addition, nonmanual characteristics (face, head, body) are a very important part of sign language linguistics and have been examined on the phonological, morphological, syntactic, semantic, and pragmatic levels. Seven groups of nonmanual characteristics were analysed: mouth shape, eyegaze, eyebrow position, eye blinks, head movements, head nods, body movements, and body leans. These nonmanual characteristics represent a fifth phonological parameter, with all of them participating in sign, carrying thereby additional linguistic context. The importance of these basic parameters of sign formation lies in the fact that any change in these parameters would lead to a change of the sign and, thus, of the meaning. The results show the systematic struc-ture of HZJ phonology, lending support for its recognition as a real natural language.

Key words: *sign language, Croatian Sign Language, linguistics, nonmanual characte-ristics, phonology*

A typical grammatical analysis of a language consists of five components: phonology, morphology, syntax, semantics, and pragmatics. The purpose of this research was to examine the phonology of Croatian Sign Language (HZJ). Phonology is a discipline that relates the concept of sound with the concept of phoneme. In other words, it studies the internal sound system of a language, i.e. a set of distinguishing features or phonemes. The phonological system of a language consists only of those sounds that have a distinguish-ing function (Simeon, 1969). On the basis of these elements of phonology, the linguistics of sign languages has found significance for this language component as well. Although

[1] The development of this work was supported by professional discussions with lect. Kovačević, Ph.D. and lect. Jelaska, Ph.D. and in cooperation with family Lušić, Tereza Szavai, the students of "Slava Raškaj" Educational Center, Iva Stastny and Ivan Laća. On this occasion we would like to thank all of them and all the colleagues and friends not mentioned here for their support and assistance.

Manuscript preparation was supported in part by NSF grant 0345314 'A basic grammar of Croatian Sign Language', R. B. Wilbur, PI.

derived from the Greek concept *"phonologia"*, which refers to the **study of sounds** (from "phone" - sound), the term phonology is also used in the linguistics of sign languages. The phonology of sign languages, just like the phonology of spoken languages, studies the smallest distinguishing formational units. Linguists study the manner in which these units are organized to make up the structure of signs. According to the American linguist Stokoe, signs consist of smaller distinguishing elements, called "cheremes" (from Gr. "cheir" - hand). These are elements without meaning that, when combined, form signs in the same manner as phonemes combine to form words in spoken languages (Valli and Lucas, 1992). Four basic manual parameters forming the signs of American Sign Language (ASL) are the location of sign articulation, the handshape, the movement, and the orientation. The fifth parameter, considered as belonging to the basic phonological characteristics, are nonmanual characteristics. Nonmanual characteristics comprise body and head movements, and facial expressions. Just like a change in one phoneme of a spoken word may bring a change in the meaning of the word (bi**d** - bi**t**), a change in any of the phonological parameters in a sign language may change the meaning of the sign. For example, Croatian signs for LAZY and SWEET differ only in the location of sign articulation. The first is articulated in the middle part of the face - the cheek, and the second in the lower part of the face - at the edge of the lips. Other characteristics are the same: handshape, movement, and orientation. "A sequence of sounds that contains a communication may be divided into smaller sequences having i) a relative freedom of being moved within the spoken chain, and ii) its meaning. A sequence of sounds obtained in this manner is a unit of language called the **word.**" (Barić et al., 1990). Words differ among themselves in the number of the same (or different) sounds. Likewise, the number of the same (or different) parameters determines different signs. When signs are considered within the rules applicable to spoken words, the use of the term "word" is justified in sign languages as well (Klima and Bellugi, 1979).

Interest in a linguistic analysis of HZJ started almost twenty years ago. In the manual from his course (1986), Zimmermann presented a part of the basic parameters in Croatian Sign Language, such as i) the shaping of the hand comprising finger setting, palm orientation, and finger direction, ii) the location of movement and iii) the manner of making the movement in terms of direction, speed, and type of movement.

Research objective and method

The objective of this research was to examine which components take part in word formation in Croatian Sign Language.

Subjects were a Deaf couple, who are users of HZJ. They were offered, in advance, a series of conversational topics that they could choose from. The conversation was recorded using video camera. From the entire recorded material a four-minute sequence was selected for analysis. The criterion for selection was the subjects' greatest spontaneity and relaxation during their conversation, so they would not be strained by the manner of communication (i.e., they might have used more speech that facilitates the hearing persons' understanding of signing, which we wanted to avoid).

The results were analysed on the level of descriptive statistics and expressed in the form of a description, as well as frequencies and percentages. All results were recorded by means of a transcription system, formed for the purpose of this research following existing models from other sign languages..

Results

In the analysed communication between the Deaf spouses, five groups of phonologically distinguishing characteristics were recorded. A change in any one of them may bring about a change in the meaning, i.e. the disappearance of that sign. This may, but does not have to, result in the emergence of a new sign. Signs differ among each other in at least one distinguishing unit. Four basic distinguishing components of the manual (hand) part of the sign are the location, handshape, hand movement, as well as palm and knuckle orientation. Nonmanual characteristics do not take part in the formation of all signs, but may take part in the formation of some signs and are, therefore, also considered as a sign component.

Below we describe some phonological characteristics of HZJ signs, including:
1) Location of sign articulation
2) Handshape
3) Hand movement
4) Palm and knuckles orientation
5) Nonmanual characteristics

1) Location of sign articulation
The first component of sign formation is the location of sign articulation, in other words, the place in the signing space where the signer produces a particular sign. The signing space may be defined as the space stretching like a balloon from the top of the head to the hips, as well as to the signer's left and right. Some signs are produced below the pelvis, and some above the head. It is interesting that the size of the signing space varies depending on the signer's characteristics, on the person the signing is addressed to, and on the reason for signing. Persons signing in their native sign language use a smaller, narrower signing space, unlike those who are signing in a foreign sign language. If a communication is intended to be secret - intimate, a narrower space is used, and if it includes a wider audience, a wider space is used.

Locations of sign articulation in HZJ are the following: neutral space (space in front of the signer), face or the entire head; top of the head; upper face, forehead or eyebrows; the middle part of the face, eyes and nose area; lower face, lips, chin; profile, cheeks, temple, ear; neck; shoulders; chest; armpit; belly; lateral parts of the body, hips; upper arm; elbow; forearm; wrist, hand in supination (palm turned upward); wrist, hand in pronation (palm turned down). The most frequently used location is neutral space.

When locations of articulation are recorded, two symbols may be combined in order to mark the place of articulation more accurately. For example, the sign THINK is articulated in neutral space, at the temple level, so the symbols f and É can be combined.

2) Handshape

Handshapes observed in HZJ were the following:

A   – hand A (as «a» in one-handed manual alphabet)
B   – hand B (palm straight; fingers joined and straight with the thumb spread away from fingers)
Bo – hand Bo (palm straight, all fingers joined)
B4 – hand B4 (as «b» in one-handed manual alphabet)
C   – hand C (uppercase C; as «c» in one-handed manual alphabet)
c   – hand c (lowercase C; as «c» in two-handed manual alphabet)
D   – hand D (fingers joined; all fingertips touch each other)
E   – hand E (claw; fingers spread and curved)
F   – hand F (small bird's beak; fist clenched, the tip of the thumb touches the tip of the index finger)
Fo – hand Fo (small bird's beak with other fingers spread)
G   – hand G (bird's beak U; fist clenched, the tip of the thumb touches the tip of the index finger and the tip of the middle finger)
Go – hand Go (bird's beak U with other fingers spread)
H   – hand H (large bird's beak, palm folded with the thumb below the other fingers)
I   – hand I (little finger; as «i» in one-handed manual alphabet)
J   – hand J (index finger; as «i» in two-handed manual alphabet)
K   – hand K (as «k» in one-handed manual alphabet)
Ko – hand Ko (middle finger; palm spread with the middle finger folded)
K1 – hand K1 (fingers straight, the nail of the middle finger touches the tip of the thumb form ing a circle)
L   – hand L (as «l» in one-handed manual alphabet)
Lo – hand Lo (thumb and index finger straight and touch each other, other fingers folded)
M   – hand M (palm folded; thumb straight and up, other fingers folded)
O   – hand O (uppercase O; as «o» in one-handed manual alphabet)
o   – hand o (lowercase O; as «o» in two-handed manual alphabet)
P   – hand P (caron (tick); clenched fist with the index finger curved)
R   – hand R (double caron (tick); clenched fist with the index finger and the middle finger spread and curved)
Ro – hand Ro (letter «r» in one-handed manual alphabet)
S   – hand S (clenched fist; as «s» in one-handed manual alphabet)
T   – hand T (pincers; clenched fist, the thumb and the index finger raised a little)
U   – hand U (as «u» in one-handed manual alphabet)
U3 – hand U3 (hand U with the thumb straight and spread away)
V   – hand V (as «v» in one-handed manual alphabet)
Z   – hand Z (spoon; palm folded and concave)
X   – hand X (clenched fist; the thumb straight and spread and the index finger half-curved)
Y   – hand Y (flying hand; as «y» in one-handed manual alphabet)
Yo – hand Yo (flying hand, but with the index finger straight)

W – hand W (as «w» in one-handed manual alphabet)
1 – hand 1 (thumb; as number 1)
3 – hand 3 (cock; as number 3)
4 – hand 4 (as number 4)
5 – hand 5 (palm spread; as number 5)
10 – hand 10 (as number 10, fingers straight, the tip of the middle finger touches the tip of the thumb)
E5 – hand E5 (hand relaxed; palm half-open, relaxed and spread)

The most frequently used handshape was hand 5. For some of the handshapes, it is uncertain whether they have a distinguishing function or not. For example, handshape E5 may be only a version of hand 5, B, or Bo, and most probably it is. Also, hand Lo may be a version of hand J. In order to be able to recognize and explain these phonological findings, more research is needed. Since this research was limited to four minutes of conversation, there might also be other HZJ handshapes that did not occur in that time.

3) Hand movement

Movement is the third parameter in sign formation, and it refers to a movement or movements of the hand(s) within the signing space. The majority of signs must be articulated by several different movements. Movements that take part in sign formation in HZJ are the following: upward; downward; upward-downward; upward bowlike; downward bowlike; right; left; right-left; diagonal; toward the signer; away from the signer; toward-away from the signer; behind the signer; parallel hand movement; upward palm rotation (supination); downward palm rotation (pronation); a 180-degree turn of the hand; nodding or bending; circular movement; bringing closer; spreading; touching; grabbing; crossing; entering; alternative hand movements; twitching; one repetition; two or more repetitions; pointing the index finger at someone or something; the index finger touches the thumb; the thumb touches the middle finger; bringing the hands closer and moving them away; fluttering the fingers; fluttering the hand; pulling; fingers of one hand touch each other (if this handshape does not include joined fingers); spreading the fingers of one hand (if this handshape does include joined fingers); wavelike movement; bending a finger/fingers at the finger joint; joining and spreading the fingers; hitting the hands together; opening the palm forwards; jerking downward movement of the hand.

The movement that occurred most frequently in sign formation of the analysed sample was the touching movement (contact).

4) Orientation

Hand orientation in sign formation is a very important parameter, comprising two types of orientation. The first refers to palm orientation and the second to knuckle orientation. 'Palm' orientation implies the direction in which the palm faces. There are six possible palm orientations: up, down, left, right, forward and backward. The orientation of 'knuckles' (the bones on the back of the hand ending in four "heads" visible when the fist is clenched) enables a more precise determination of hand orientation in signing. Two signs may be the same in palm orientation, but differ in knuckle orientation. Some authors use finger orientation instead of knuckle orientation, but the latter provides more precise description. There are six knuckle orientations as well: up, down, left, right, forward and backward.

The most frequent palm orientation in the analysed communication sequence was backward orientation, and the most frequent knuckle orientation was forward orientation.

5) Nonmanual characteristics

There has been worldwide recognition of the importance of nonmanual characteristics in sign languages. Nonmanual characteristics may be divided linguistically into nonmanual articulators on the lower part of the face, on the upper part of the face, and on the head/body (Wilbur, 1991). "Stokoe (1960) observed that the negative headshake in ASL (side-to-side movements of the head) has a grammatical role in signalling negation without negative signs (such as no, nothing, I don't know, etc.)" (Wilbur, 1987). Parts of the body above the neck may have many other roles. Eyebrows, eye gaze, blinking, nose wrinkles, various mouth and cheek positions, and head movements have morphological, syntactic, semantic, and intonational roles (Wilbur, 1987). However, nonmanual characteristics may also be an important element of sign formation. For this reason, this research has included nonmanual characteristics. Some signs cannot be correctly understood unless they contain the pertaining nonmanual characteristic. The sign NULA 'zero' is produced together with blowing with the lips pursed. If this nonmanual characteristic is not used, the sign may be misinterpreted as the sign TUŽAN 'sad'.

In this research nonmanual characteristics have been divided into eight groups, of which each group may appear in several possible forms. The main groups of nonmanual characteristics are the following: mouth shape (that may have lexical or non-lexical content); eye gaze; position of eyebrows; blink; head movements; head nods and head shakes (as in agreement or disagreement); body movement (left or right); body lean.

Conclusion

These phonological characteristics show that HZJ is comparable to other well-analyzed natural sign languages, such as ASL, British Sign Language, Austrian Sign Language, and German Sign Language, to name just a few. Future research will show that other linguistic components of HZJ are also similar to better studied sign languages.

References

Ahlgren, I., Bergman, B.& Brennan, M. (1992): Perspectives on sign language structure. The Fifth International Symposium on SLR 1, Spain.

Ahlgren, I. & Hyltenstam, K. (1994): Bilingualism in Deaf Education. Signum, Hamburg.

Babić, S., Finka, B. & Moguš, M. (1995): Hrvatski pravopis. Školska knjiga, Zagreb.

Barić, E., Lončarić, M., Malić, D., Pavešić, S., Peti, M., Zečević, V. & Znika, M. (1990): Gramatika hrvatskoga književnog jezika. Školska knjiga, Zagreb.

Frishberg, N. (1975): Arbitrariness and Iconicity: Historical Change in American Sign Language. Language 51, 676-710.

Gijn, I., Baker, A., Coerts, J. (1998): Structure, position and function of complex constituents in sign language of the Netherlands: preliminary results. University of Amsterdam.

Greenbaum, S.& Quirk, R. (1995): A student's grammar of the English language.

Longman Group UK Limited, Harlow.

Johnson, R. E., Liddell, S. G., Erting C.J.(1989): Unlocking the Curriculum: Principles for Achieving Access in Deaf Education. Department of Linguistics and Interpreting and the Gallaudet Research Institute.

Keller, Von Jorg: Mundbilder in europäischen Gebärdensprachen.

Kovačević, M. (1997): Jezik i jezične sastavnice. U: Ljubešić, M. (ur.) Jezične teškoće školske djece. Školske novine, Zagreb.

Kyle, J.G., Woll, B. (1993): Sign language, The study of deaf people and their language. Cambridge University Press.

Lyons, J. (1995): Language and linguistics. Cambridge University Press.Newport, E. L., Meier, R. P. (1986): The acquisition of American Sign Language. The crosslinguistic study of language acquisition 1. Theoretical Issues, University of Illinois

Petitto, L. & P. Marentette (1991): Babbling in the Manual Mode: Evidence for the Ontogeny of Language.

Pribanić, Lj. (1998): Jezični razvoj djece oštećena sluha (disertacija). Edukacijsko-rehabilitacijski fakultet, Zagreb.

Reilly, J. & M. McIntire (1980):. American Sign Language and Pidgin Sign English: What's the Difference. Linstok Press.

Simeon, R. (1969): Enciklopedijski rječnik lingvistčkih naziva. Matica Hrvatska, Zagreb.

Sinclair, J., Fox, G. & Bullon S. (1995): English dictionary. HarperCollins Publishers, London.

Stokoe, William C., Casterline, D. & Croneberg, C.G. (1976): A Dictionary of American Sign Language on Linguistic Principles. Linstok Press.

Veinberg, S. & R. Wilbur (1990): A Linguistic Analysis of the Negative Headshake in American Sign Language. Linstok Press.

Wilbur, R. (1987): American Sign Language, Linguistic and Applied Dimensions. College-Hill Press.

Wilbur, R. B. (1994): Foregrounding Structures in American Sign Language. Journal of Pragmatics 22: 647-672.

Wilbur, R. (1997): Body leans and the marking of contrast in American Sign Language. Journal of Pragmatics 30: 275-303.

Wilbur, R. (1990): Intonation and Focus in American Sign Language. Purdue University.

Wilbur, R. (1994): Eyeblinks & ASL Phrase Structure. Sign Language Studies 84: 221-240.

Zimmermann, A.(1986): Uvodni seminar o komunikaciji s osobama oštećena sluha: drugo prošireno izdanje (materijal samo za internu uporabu). Savez osoba oštećena sluha grada Zagreba.

ISTRAŽUJUĆI HRVATSKI ZNAKOVNI JEZIK

Sažetak

Ovim radom pokušalo se ispitati postoji li utjecaj osnovnih komponenti znaka i nemanualnih obilježja na oblikovanje znakova u hrvatskom znakovnom jeziku (HZJ) te sustavno zabilježiti sve te komponente. Analizirajući četiri minute komunikacije gluhog bračnog para zabilježen je niz elemenata koji čine strukturu znakova HZJ-a. Brojna istraživanja američkog i drugih znakovnih jezika, kao i ovo istraživanje HZJa, pokazala su da fonologiju znakovnog jezika čine četiri osnovna parametra, a to su: mjesto tvorbe znaka, oblik šake, pokret ruke i orijentacija dlana i kostiju šake. Nemanualne karakteristike pokazale su se kao vrlo važan dio lingvistike znakovnih jezika te se istražuju na fonološkoj, morfološkoj, sintaktičkoj, semantičkoj i pragmatičkoj razini. U ovom radu zabilježeno je osam skupina nemanualnih karakteristika: oblik usta, pogled očima, položaj obrva, treptaj, pokreti glavom, kimanje glavom, pomak tijela te naginjanje tijela. Neke od ovih nemanualnih karakteristika fonološki su parametar, a sve sudjeluju u znakovanju te nose određeni lingvistički kontekst. Važnost osnovnih parametara koji sudjeluju u oblikovanju znakova sastoji se u tome da se niti jedan od njih ne smije promijeniti jer bi time uzrokovao promjenu znaka, a time i značenja. Rezultati ovog istraživanja pokazuju sustavnost fonološke strukture hrvatskog znakovnog jezika te potvrđuju njegovo prihvaćanje kao jezika.

Ključne riječi: znakovni jezik, hrvatski znakovni jezik, lingvistika, nemanualne karakteristike, fonologija

DENOTATION OF SIGNS IN DIFFERENT REGIONS OF SLOVENIA

Stane Košir

School of Education, University of Ljubljana, Slovenija

Abstract

This research analyses the denotative space of signs in Slovenian Sign Language on three geographically defined sub-samples consisting of 92 deaf or hard-of-hearing persons. Statistically significant differences were found in the denotation of signs between different groups. Differences exist regarding the frequently used signs with a concrete meaning, as well as regarding the signs with an abstract meaning. It is concluded that, due to the meaning not being standardized, the regional colloquial language is being used simultaneously with the signs, which does not ensure a good information transfer. This has a negative effect primarily on the acquisition of academic skills. In this paper, the research, standardization and notation of sign language are supported, as well as its more frequent usage in communication, not only through direct conversation, but also through multimedia and video.

Key words: communication, deaf, hard of hearing, sign language

1. Introduction

In Slovenia there are two dictionaries comprising 1,600 signs of Slovenian Sign Language. There is a lack of knowledge particularly to the language structure, semantics, morphology and syntax of the Slovenian sign language. This situation impedes the correct information transfer as a requirement that is gaining importance in today's information society. Since we do not have the linguistic standard of the Slovenian Sign Language, we may challenge the unambiguousness of its individual sign as the principal communication element.

2. Objective

The objective of this research is to establish any differences in the denotative space of signs in terms of the area where the sign language speakers live.

3. Work methods

3.1. Measuring instrument

A visual test with 10 signs was prepared (Podboršek, Moderndorfer, 1984). Each sign was presented by 20 images that were in varying degrees included in the denominative space of the sign. They were used to organize the denominative space. The signs referred both to concrete and abstract concepts, all of them were very frequent, i.e. among 500 most frequent words of the Slovenian standard language (Hajšek-Holtz, 1986).

From among the images presenting a sign the respondents chose 3 to 5 images which in their opinion best described the content of that sign.

3.2. Subjects

The sample involved 92 persons of both genders with the loss of hearing between 40% and 100%, aged between 15 and 55. They were members of the Deaf Associations of Ljubljana, Celje, Nova Gorica, Kranj or Maribor, respectively. The sample was divided into the following three sub-samples: two "pure" geographical groups - Maribor and Ljubljana, and a group comprising all the others. The reason for such a division was a very intensive engagement of spoken language by one group (implying their small engagement of sign language) and the fact that the other group preferred the total approach to communication.

3.3. Data processing

Data were processed on the level of descriptive statistics, by calculating percentages, frequencies, selection rates, correlations and (χ^2 test, by use of SPSS software package. Selection rate is defined as the frequency of selection of a certain concept from among 20 concepts making the space of a sign. The significance of differences in the denotative space of the three groups of sign language speakers was analysed.

4. Results and discussion

4.1. Analysis of concrete concepts

For the first five meanings of the sign "mushroom" in all groups only the concepts cep mushroom and sewing pad are found. As for the other concepts, up to the fifth rate only two groups correspond with the concept fly agaric and the other two groups with the concept ice cream. The meaning of other concepts for a certain group still has a high rate, but the correspondence between the groups becomes smaller. The concepts to which an individual sign refers differ more and more from group to group.

We may see that for the sign "to write" for all the three groups the rate is highest for the following meanings: "signature", "office" and "quill". For two groups each also the

Table 1 *Denotative space of the sign "mushroom"*

	Maribor		Ljubljana		Others	
	% of selection	Rate	% of selection	Rate	% of selection	Rate
1 cover	7.1	6	7.3	6	10.3	4
2 sponge	1.4	14.5	8.7	4	4.5	9
3 sponge for washing	5.6	7.5	7.9	5	5.8	7
4 cup	4.2	10	2.8	11	8.4	6
5 ice cream	12.8	2	5.8	7.5	12.9	2
6 atomic mushroom cloud	5.6	7.5	5.8	7.5	4.5	9
7 drunkard	1.4	14.5	2.1	13	0	16
8 destroyed	2.8	12	1.4	15	1.9	14
9 rounded	1.4	14.5	0.1	16	3.3	12.5
10 cep mushroom	18.4	1	17.9	1	16.1	1
11 fly agaric	4.2	10	11.5	3	9.0	5
12 leprous	4.2	10	2.1	13	0.6	15
13 to cover	9.9	4	4.3	9.5	3.9	11
14 smooth	1.4	14.5	4.3	9.5	4.5	9
15 sewing pad	9.8	4	15.9	2	11.0	3
16 a lot	9.8	4	2.1	13	3.3	12.5

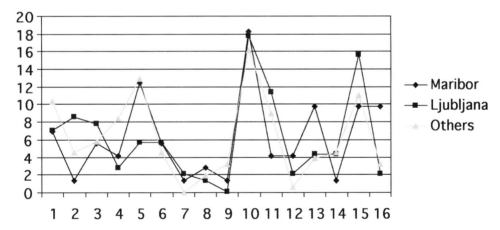

Figure 1 *Denotative space of the sign "mushroom"*

meanings "to draw", "letter" and "typewriter" are very important, while for the third group these meanings are less frequent; this is where the differences in the interpretation of signs among the three groups can be seen.

The correlation coefficient for the selection rate of the meaning of the sign "mushroom" between the Maribor and the Ljubljana groups of deaf persons is r = 0.47. The

Table 2 *Denotative space of the sign „to write"*

	Maribor		Ljubljana		Others	
	% of selection	Rate	% of selection	Rate	% of selection	Rate
1 typewriter	6.7	7.5	8.5	5.5	7.9	4.5
2 signature	18.3	1	13.5	2	15.9	1
3 notes	6.7	7.5	5.7	8.5	4.0	10
4 office	8.3	5.5	10.6	3	7.9	4.5
5 letter	11.7	3.5	9.9	4	6.0	7
6 desk	0	16	5.7	8.5	2.6	15
7 bicycle	5.0	9	1.4	14.5	3.3	13
8 to search	3.3	11	2.1	13	2.6	15
9 to turn the pages	3.3	11	2.8	12	4.6	8.5
10 to draw	15.0	2	8.5	5.5	11.3	3
11 quill	11.7	3.5	14.2	1	13.2	2
12 to erase	8.3	5.5	7.8	7	6.6	6
13 to introduce	3.3	11	1.4	14.5	3.3	13
14 braille alphabet	1.7	14	3.5	10.5	4.6	8.5
15 Morse code	1.7	14	3.5	10.5	2.6	15
16 cuneiform writing	1.7	14	0.1	16	3.3	13

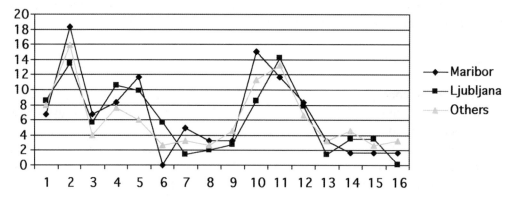

Figure 2 *Denotative space of the sign „to write"*

Table 3 *Correlations of the rates of selection*

	Mushroom	To write
Ljubljana – Maribor	0.47	0.75
Maribor – others	0.61	0.84
Ljubljana – others	0.82	0.83
Average of all deaf	0.63	0.81

selection rate correlation coefficient between the Maribor group and the other deaf is r = 0.61, and between the Ljubljana group and the others r = 0.82.

The correlation coefficient for the selection rate of the meaning of the sign "to write" between the Maribor and the Ljubljana groups of deaf persons is r = 0.75. The selection rate correlation coefficient between the Maribor group and the other deaf is r = 0.84, and between the Ljubljana group and the others r = 0.83. We can see that all correlations are high, but the lowest one is always between the Ljubljana and the Maribor deaf persons. This means that in the use of signs the greatest communication noise appears in the use of the signs "mushroom" and "to write" between the Ljubljana and the Maribor deaf persons, while the noise is smaller in communication between the Ljubljana and the other deaf.

Correspondence with concrete concepts is greater with verbs and smaller with nouns. It is also greater between the reference group and the individual group - Maribor or Ljubljana - than directly between the Ljubljana and the Maribor groups of the deaf.

The differences suggest that the sign "to write" or the sign "mushroom" provoke different ideas in persons with hearing impairments from different geographical regions of Slovenia. This is related to the specific experience in regard to a sign that is not used in communication identically by all groups. Language code is born by learning, by socialized usage in a given culture. Due to the low educational level of the deaf, conversations on concrete topics and thus the usage of concrete concepts are frequent in the communication of the deaf. Differences are probably due to the specific usage of signs in both geographical regions. The differences in the comprehension of the meanings of the signs may be a consequence of differences in the systems of communications used by the respondents of the three groups (the spoken language system of communications as the more frequent and the sign language system as the less frequent system in the Maribor group, in comparison to the other groups of respondents).

4.2. Analysis of abstract concepts

The defining concepts of the sign "time" are classes, history and second. However, the meaning and the rate of these concepts are different. Other defining concepts differ from group to group, and so does their meaning.

The analysis of the next abstract concept "to complain" also shows correspondence between the defining concepts on the level of the first and the second rates between all the groups, while in the following rates the groups increasingly differ.

Correlations of the rates of the defining concepts between the groups also show a very uneven comprehension of the signs "to complain" and "time". Correspondence is greater between the Ljubljana and the Maribor groups for the concept "time" and between the Ljubljana group and the others for the concept "to complain" than between the individual group and the overall (all-Slovenian) comprehension of the signs.

In defining abstract concepts, the correspondence between the groups is greater with verbs than with nouns as well. Of all the groups the correspondence is the greatest between the Maribor and the Ljubljana groups of deaf and their correspondence is smaller with the reference group of other Slovenian deaf. The reason for this is probably the fact that there are two strong rehabilitation centres there and due to this the signs for

Table 4 *Denotative space of the sign „time"*

	Maribor		Ljubljana		Others	
	% of selection	Rate	% of selection	Rate	% of selection	Rate
1 classes	11.8	3	15.2	1	13.7	2
2 history	13.2	2	12.3	3	11.6	3
3 rocket	3.9	11	3.6	11	8.9	4
4 Christmas tree	9.2	6	5.1	8.5	0	14
5 picker	10.5	4.5	5.1	8.5	4.8	7
6 scribble	6.6	7	11.6	4	0.7	12
7 past	5.3	8.5	4.3	10	7.5	5
8 future	10.5	4.5	6.5	6.5	4.8	7
9 vagabond	5.3	8.5	2.9	12.5	2.7	9
10 danger	3.9	11	6.5	6.5	2.1	10
11 second	15.8	1	13.0	2	17.1	1
12 money	2.6	13	8.7	5	0.7	12
13 joke	0	14	2.9	12.5	0.7	12
14 crush down	3.9	11	2.2	14	4.8	7

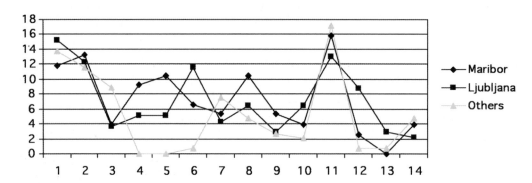

Figure 3 *Denotative space of the sign „time"*

abstract concepts are used more frequently and specifically than we might expect in other parts of Slovenia, where such centres do not exist. Otherwise, the overall correspondence between the groups in defining abstract concepts is smaller than in defining concrete concepts.

Differences between the three groups in comprehending the signs "mushroom", "time", "to complain" and "to write" are statistically significant. This shows that the groups use regional language varieties which, consequently, significantly differ from each other and therefore do not enable reliable mutual understanding. There is a need to define a standard Slovenian Sign Language.

Table 5 *Denotative space of the sign „to complain"*

	Maribor		Ljubljana		Others	
	% of selection	Rate	% of selection	Rate	% of selection	Rate
1 here	10.2	4	6.5	8.5	5.7	7
2 there	7.7	7	7.2	6.5	11.5	3.5
3 to ring	17.9	1	15.8	1	18.5	1
4 to sue	12.8	2.5	13.7	2	14.6	2
5 to knock	8.9	5.5	7.2	6.5	7.6	6
6 peeling	0	15	2.9	12	1.9	12.5
7 fair, market	3.8	9.5	3.6	11	1.9	12.5
8 louse	1.2	13	1.4	13	1.9	12.5
9 rust	2.4	11	5.7	10	5.1	8
10 ladybird	1.2	13	6.5	8.5	3.8	10
11 ant	1.2	13	0.1	14.5	1.9	12.5
12 frog	6.4	8	0.1	14.5	0	15
13 alarm clock	3.8	9.5	7.9	5	11.5	3.5
14 complaint	8.9	5.5	9.3	4	4.5	9
15 book of complaints	12.8	2.5	10.8	3	9.5	5

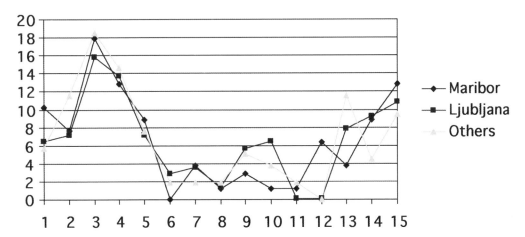

Figure 4 *Denotative space of the sign „to complain"*

Table 6 *Correlations of the rates of selection*

	to complain	time
Ljubljana – Maribor	0.68	0.78
Maribor – others	0.57	0.72
Ljubljana – others	0.35	0.90
Average of all deaf	0.53	0.80

5. Conclusion

The research shows significant differences in denotative spaces of the four signs between the three geographically defined groups of persons with hearing impairments. Differences exist both in regard to the signs denoting concrete concepts, which are very frequently encountered by deaf and hard of hearing, and in regard to the signs denoting abstract concepts. Diverse meanings of the same signs of the Slovenian sign language reflect regional specific qualities and are, as, such, a potential source of misunderstandings in communication and, in particular, hardly represent a good code for the transfer of academic knowledge. Research in the field of the linguistics of Slovenian sign language is required, as well as its linguistic standardization and the design of sign-language notation, which imposes rules and standards to a much greater extent than a "live" sign does.

From the point of view of successful communication, the diversity of denotative spaces should be particularly considered when new signs are invented for the semantic spaces for which today there are no signs in the vocabulary of Slovenian sign language. A pre-requisite for successful communication is an unambiguous transformation process of coding and decoding within the same language system. It would be rational to extend the logic of such an unambiguous transformation process from the language of the hearing to the national sign language, which would reduce noise in communication. This means that the sign would get the necessary centripetal basis. Such a decision has very far-reaching effects that will eventually be manifested in the logic, ethic and culture of the users of both languages, who will, thanks to this, not depart from each others due to the hermetic quality of the language systems. This would also ensure a better flow rate of information and help avoiding the fatal cultural and overall isolation of the deaf.

6. References

Bellugi, U. (1978): Studies in sign language. Psycholinguistics and total communication. The state of the art. American Annals of the Deaf, pp. 68-74.

Bellugi, U & Fischer S.A. (1972): A comparison of sign language and spoken language. Cognition, 1. pp. 173-200.

Bergman, B. (1990): Sign Language Dictionaries for Specific Subjects. Sign language Research and Application. Hamburg.

Brito Ferreira, L. & Langevin, R. (1986): Structure sublexical une langue de signes. Prepublication du laboratorie de topologie Universite de Bourgogne.

Bloom, L. (1970): Language development. Cambridge Mass. M.I.T. Press.

Brennan, M. & Hayhurst, A. (1980): The renaissance of British sign language. Supplement to The British Deaf News, 12, 1-5.

Goldin, M. S. & Mylander, C. (1990): The Role of Paternal Input in the Development of a Morphological System. Journal of Child Language; vol. 17, No. 3, pp. 527-563.

Goldin, M. S. & Mylander, C. (1984): Gestural Communication in Deaf Children: The Effects and Noneffects of Parental Input on Early Language Development. Monographs of the Society for Research in Child Development; vol. 49, No. 3-4, pp. 1-151.

Hajšek-Holz, M. (1984): Izbor najpogostejših slovenskih besed. Znanstveno raziskovalni center SAZU, Institut za slovenski jezik, Ljubljana.

Mounty, J. L. (1986): Nativization and Input in the Language Development of Two Deaf Children of Hearing Parents. Dissertation, Boston University.

Namir, L. & Schlesinger, I. M. (1978): The grammar of sign language. In Schlesinger, M.I. & Namir, L. (Eds) Sign language of the deaf. New York: Academic Press.

Podboršek, L. & Moderndorfer, M. (1984): Govorica rok. Zveza slušno prizadetih Slovenije, Ljubljana.

Prillwiz, S. (1982): Zum Zusammenhang von Kognition, Kommunikation und Sprache mit Bezug auf die Gehörlosenproblematik. Bundesminister für Jugend, Familie und Gesundheit. Stuttgart.

Prillwiz S. (1975): Analyse des primären Spracherwerbs normalsinniger Kinder als Orientirungsbasis für den Sprachaufbau bei Hörsprachgeschädigten. Psycholinguistik in der Sonderpädagogik. Berlin.

Schlesinger, H. & Meadow, K. (1972): Sound and Sign. Childhood Deafness and Mental Health. Berkeley.

Spile, P. (1972): Linguistic and psychological properties of American sign language: an overview. In: Spile, P. (Ed): Understanding language through sign language research. New York: Academic Press.

DENOTATIVNOST ZNAKOVA SLOVENSKOG ZNAKOVNOG JEZIKA U RAZLIČITIM REGIJAMA SLOVENIJE

Sažetak

U ovom istraživanju analiziran je denotativni prostor znakova slovenskog znakovnog jezika u trima geografski definiranim poduzorcima koje su sačinjavale 92 gluhe i nagluhe ispitivane osobe. Utvrđene su statistički značajne razlike u denotativnosti znakova između skupina. Razlike postoje kod vrlo čestih znakova s konkretnim značenjem i kod znakova s apstraktnim značenjem. Zaključuje se da se zbog nestandardiziranosti značenja upotrebljava regionalni razgovorni znakovni jezik koji, međutim, ne osigurava dobar prijenos informacija. To predstavlja štetu prvenstveno pri stjecanju akademskih znanja. U radu se ističe potreba istraživanja i standardizacije znakovnog jezika, njegove notacije i češće upotrebe u komunikaciji, neposrednoj i posredovanoj upotrebom vizualnih medija.

Ključne riječi: *komunikacija, gluhi, nagluhi, znakovni jezik, denotativnost*

ON THE CONFUSION OF TONGUES AND A SEARCH FOR ORDER

Milon Potmesil

The Institute for the Deaf, Beroun, Czech Republic

Abstract

The first dictionary of Czech Sign Language, containing around 3,000 sings, was issued in 1988. Other dictionaries are being prepared within a scientific project, too. The strongest impetus for starting this lexicographic project has been given by teachers from deaf schools who considered their stock of signs insufficient for teaching school subjects. The project goals are as follows: by analyzing school textbooks, single out Czech words necessary for teaching individual school subjects; create a basic corpus of Czech words for a general dictionary of sign language that would include all different sign varieties, brought about by differences in the geographic origin of respondents, collect the richest possible stock of signs, describe them, classify/analyze them and offer them for use to the group of people communicating in sign language. We consider that this project will also result in new findings in the field of grammar. This work presents the approaches, results and problems related to/faced with during the preparation phase of the project. We believe that we will create pre-requisites for the education of a new deaf generation which will be proud of its language.

Key words: sign language dictionary, Czech Sign Language, deaf, deafness

When the descendants of Noah decided to build a town and a tower there, a tower whose spire would reach the heaven, the God punished their presumption by a confusion of tongues. As a result, the people would open their mouths, would talk to each other but nobody would understand the meaning of what the others would say. This is what the Bible says. Our aim is not to argue about the probability of that event, we only wish to imagine such a situation and to reflect on it; to reflect on how we might describe it and analyse it from the point of view of the communication theory. We would probably say that the situation could not have been worse. The order seems to be lost.

We might imagine how the situation would develop, how the individual languages would be formed and what would happen with them. While wondering about these topics, we may realise a simple fact – the majority of languages have their written forms; this definitely is a feature that influences the development of languages. The written form enables not only research, but also working with a particular language relatively easily - we have in mind working with a language or special theoretical papers dealing with a language. These papers offer the language - described and researched - to users who might, apart from other things, learn to use it correctly, be taught in that language, and last but not least, accept it as a part of their own, usually national culture.

One of the linguistic research projects we have in mind and the one that actually is a reason for writing this paper is a whole range of activities connected with the preparation of sign language dictionaries. We have been preparing these dictionaries for four years and we are trying now to reflect on the approaches, results and problems we have been coming across throughout the preparation stage. What we are interested in is mainly a search for the system of the Czech Sign Language and the efforts to describe it.

The pioneer work in this field was accomplished by publishing the Dictionary of Sign Language[1] by D. Gabrielova, J. Paur and J. Zeman in 1988. According to the authors, the dictionary contains about 3 000 notions and is based on Prague Sign Language.

The demands of teachers from special schools for deaf and hard of hearing students became the first and the strongest impulse for launching this project of creating new dictionaries. We assume that, most probably, these teachers felt that their stocks of signs were insufficient for educational purposes, mainly for particular branches - school subjects. We believe that they were able - to a certain extent - to use the sign language in communication but needed some material for the enrichment of their professional sign language stocks. However, tutors from hostels of special schools and teachers from special kindergarten/pre-school institutions, where the "specialised" language needs are also obvious, expressed their demands, too. All the above mentioned calls suggested how vast the expected project might be.

We regarded these demands as a great challenge to start a piece of work, which was very interesting from the very beginning. We approached the preparation stage - mainly the theoretical part of it - with a great care and a lot of effort, however, we were also ready to face different difficulties that accompany similar projects quite naturally. It proved to be a good decision.

We tried to set our goals in such manner that they were reachable and, at the same time, allow us to present some partial results of our work or put them into practice gradually, not only after the whole project was carried out. Most valuable for us was the experience from Finland.[2]

We decided
-   to collect the stock of Czech words (based on primary school textbooks) for individual branches - school subjects[3] to create the basis for dictionaries intended mainly for hearing teachers and hearing parents of children and pupils with impaired hearing;
-   to create a basic corpus of Czech words for a general dictionary of sign language that would include all familiar varieties of signs, the variability being caused by different geographical origin of the interviewees;

---

[1] Gabrielova, D., Paur, J., Zeman, J.: Slovnik znakove reci. Horizont. Praha, 1988
[2] Savolainen, L.: Finnish Sign Language - Finnish dictionary: defining the head signs. Nordiske satudier i leksikografi III., 359 - 364, 1995
[3] We have decided to use rather the term branch than the term school subject since from the practical point of view it seems much more convenient to collect more complex topics according to branches than according to school subjects. A school subject is related to a particular grade of primary or secondary school and is limited by a syllabus. It would not be possible to maintain some flexibility and show how subjects are interrelated within a particular grade - given its content and needs. Of course, we can say that the stock of notions is characterised much better by a branch rather than by a school grade.

-   get the richest[4] possible stock of signs for the above mentioned fields, to describe it, classify/analyse and offer it for use to the group of people who use sign language for communication.

When working on the Czech language word stock for the individual branches[5] we asked teachers of particular subjects from special schools for deaf and hard of hearing students for help. The basic source were the textbooks themselves. In view of the fact that we were aware of the incomparability of the word stocks in textbooks for regular primary schools and in textbooks for deaf and hard of hearing pupils in special schools, we wanted to enrich the word stock of the latter to an extent that would exceed the prescribed amount of words. Gradually, we found tens of contributors who approached the task with all their individual experiences and thus this first part of the lexicographic project really includes more words than the present prescribed standard requires.

To collect the Czech part of the general dictionary was much more difficult, however, it was also much more interesting.

At first we had to prepare the part that includes the Czech language words. We have to point out here that the dictionary is intended for hearing users, for people for whom the sign language is not their first language. From the very beginning we had to consider and accept a well-known limitation based on a view that it is not possible to presume the existence of sign equivalents to all included words. As far as we could find out, there was no agreed process in the Czech Republic that would enable us to accomplish our task. We had to put aside the frequency dictionary of the Czech language[6], whose word stock and the frequency rates are rather out-of-date. At the same time it was apparent that we had no clue as to which words to choose from the frequency dictionary, those words that would serve as a basis for our planned dictionary. We designed our own procedure that was used and tested in this project. For collecting Czech words we used textbooks of foreign languages published in the Czech Republic and intended for people who study on their own; mainly the Czech parts of comprehensive vocabulary lists from each textbook. To get objective results based on a wider choice we used textbooks of the following languages - English, French, Chinese and Russian. We argued that the vocabulary lists for these textbooks must have been collected on the basis of some principles. More textbooks used in this tasks meant more principles (although not openly presented anywhere). The final collected list of words was revised later; in case of multiple occurrence the identical expressions were removed, and so were some words that seemed to occur only in individual foreign languages and often due to political or some temporary reasons.

After having modified the Czech part of the dictionary corpus to correspond to lexicographic demands, we started to collect the individual signs of the sign language and

---

[4] By richness we mean an effort to include the largest possible number of signs for one Czech equivalent (if at all translatable as: word = sign). That is why we have co-operated with the users of the sign language from different regions of the Czech Republic – to respect geographical varieties – dialects.

[5] e.g. Czech Language, Physics, History, Chemistry, Wood-processing, Sciences

[6] Jelinek, J., Becka, J.V., Tesitelova, M.: Frekvence slov, slovnich druhu a tvaru v ceskem jazyce. Praha, 1961 Gabrielova, D., Paur, J., Zeman, J.: Slovnik znakove reci. Horizont. Praha, 1988

to record them on a videotape in a "draft" version, that means, in a form that should serve only for storing the shape and form of the sign and, if needed, for commentaries. This "draft" version was made in VHS format and it was never intended as a material for any final products, written or digitised. We invited people with impaired hearing, mainly deaf people, who use the sign language, and preferably the second deaf generation in the family to help us. Another requirement was to get interviewees from different parts of the country in order to get the clearest possible picture in terms of geographical varieties.[7]

We managed to co-operate with people from Prague, Pilsen (Plzen) and Olomouc. We feel deeply obliged to these people (they are referred to as colleagues or interviewees).

The fact that the sign language users with impaired hearing who had already retired co-operated with us proved to be a precious contribution to the whole project and probably even for the projects to come. These people represent "a treasure" of signs and after working with them it was easy for us to disprove some claims that the sign language is poor.[8]

Any artificial changes - those we may sometimes see, probably made in an effort to show similarity of the sign language to the Czech language, to allow a word-for-word translation and thus to prove richness of the sign language, to support the sign language in a presumable competition fight for survival - proved to be unnecessary. We believe that hearing-impaired people whose mother tongue is the Czech language, but who manifest their identification with the deaf, might be interested in these artificial changes of the sign language. There was a period in the Czech history comparable to this in terms of competition - related to Germans and Czechs during the Czech National Uprising. Allow us one more remark, namely that no sign demonstrated was regarded as bad or

---

[7] We have to say that the co-operation with our interviewees was not easy. Of course, we would like to thank those who worked well, but they were only few. A lot of times the interviewees did not respond and it was very difficult to get representatives from different regions. We thought we would try to get in touch with people from some regional centres (where usually there are some special primary or secondary schools, or some clubs or other types of non-state organisations of people with impaired hearing). We asked for help in collecting the stock of signs. Since only few people were willing to help, we feel much has to be done in respect of educational activities, not only on the part of our institution, but also on the part of the special schools for children with impaired hearing. In these schools, children should meet the sign language and should learn to respect it, to acquire a positive attitude to it. The sign language is a part of the deaf culture. We know that our colleagues in other countries have the same experience. It took a couple of years before a "new" deaf generation - with the help of schools and some parents - became interested in their own language, became actively involved as organisers or initiators of projects, e.g. creation of dictionaries, preparing course syllabi, etc. We are very glad to say that in the majority of our special schools nobody argues about the justification of the sign language. The question is different today: when to start, how to teach. The next stage will probably be the following: the sign language will be taught, and also some specific features related to it, specific problems connected to external reality, relationships, historical heritage, etc. Formative features will become important in the same way as the educational ones, especially from the point of view of the language. We believe that the deaf students who study at different secondary schools and universities will become qualified, skilled and motivated people, not only for the field of pedagogy.

[8] We are convinced that this fact should be an impulse for an independent grant project. It may "only" be aimed at creating the video recording to record the signs, which might vanish with the people who use them and disappear forever. At present, we cannot afford such a project within our institution, it is the number of available people and, of course, money that matters. Perhaps, some students might pick up this topic for their written papers or diploma theses.

wrong by any of our deaf colleagues (with the exception of a few cases of misunderstanding the Czech words). Every demonstrated and accepted sign was used for enriching or enlarging the stock of signs in this part of the project.

The proposed methodology

For searching and including signs we decided to apply the following procedure:

1. A particular chosen word from the Czech word stock was assigned - by our colleagues with hearing impairment - one or more well-known signs which everybody would accept. These signs were recorded on the "draft" version of the videotape together with the information about the region of origin and some other important data. As far as word formation of the sign language is concerned, it was not always a sign that would „translate" the word; sometimes we would see metaphorical or classifier morphemes.
2. In the case that none of the interviewees knew the sign, they were asked to find out the sign among their relatives or friends and to „bring it back". If the reaction was positive, we moved to step no. 1. Later, these signs were processed in the same way and some data were included. Naturally, we were aware of the possibility that the sign would not exist.
3. If nobody was able to find the sign among the community of Czech people with impaired hearing - users of the sign language that our interviewees would know and meet, we would start searching the sign language dictionaries of foreign languages. If we found that sign, we would discuss it within the group of our interviewees and in case of their approval this sign would be included as an example of how to enrich the Czech sign language.
4. We assume that - if needed – the fourth, and the last logical step might be to ask our interviewees to agree upon the meaning of the Czech word and let them suggest or create one of the possible forms of an unknown sign and ask them to record it and describe it.[9]

With regard to the above mentioned procedure we have to say that the vast majority of 1 300 signs were recorded already after the first or – at maximum - the second step.

The "draft" video recording served as a basic material for creating a new digital video recording, which was produced with an almost professional equipment.

---

[9] Of course, this is particularly sensitive. One has to be very careful not to bring about bad changes in a language. We think that this is quite a common procedure when dealing with languages. What brought peace into our minds was the skill of language to "clean" itself, to remove any bad features in the same way a living organism does not accept anything heterogeneous, anything destructive. We have an example here, the artificial word "magnetoscope" (magnetoskop), only some older people would know it today. Twenty years ago this word was suggested as a name for video recorder, the users of the Czech language used to meet it but the language rejected it in the end.

[10] For all these types of notes a special system of notation was used. It was created and arranged for usage by professor Macurova in our institution.

Processing of recorded signs

Each sign was described and recorded in a file that contained the following data:
- a word in the Czech language
- the source of the word
- the branch (biology, mathematics, hobbies)
- an example of sentence usage
- a definition or explanation of meaning in the Czech language
- Czech synonyms
- related expressions in Czech – superordinate and subordinate
- sign notation + notes (comments, pictures, explanations)[10]
- the source of the sign
- notes
- the author
- the date when recorded

The main source of inspiration for this particular way of recording our data were the information and experience of our colleagues from Finland whose institution we visited. A team of experts from Helsinki, from the centre for the deaf called Lighthouse, had been preparing materials for the dictionary of Finnish sign language for ten years.

Gradually, we have been creating a basis of a larger piece of work, which - at this initial level - contains about 1 400 signs. It equals one half of the selected Czech words that were processed earlier. We have been trying to describe the signs according to the above mentioned structure as much as possible. The final videotape, digitally recorded, should serve as a material for creating the photographs of individual signs. These photographs have been accompanied by arrows to show the movement and a description - this is being done by our deaf colleague. Another version, a by-product of the above mentioned process, is the CD ROM version of the dictionary. The technical processing - one sign equals one individual file - enables a very simple access to the whole file system, e.g. in case some correction is needed or for gradual expansion of the dictionary corpus.

We hope that in the next, future stages of our work we will not only enrich the sign language stock in correspondence with the enrichment of the Czech language part of the general dictionary, but also enrich the school subjects or branches as it was suggested above. We believe that we will be able to create dictionaries of described signs for various branches and to offer these for use in special schools. At the same time, this may contribute to a better insight into the sign language from the linguistic point of view. Apart from the sign language stock description, we expect some progress in the field of grammar as well. Furthermore, we might expect some influence on the field of methodology of the sign language.

We believe that - from the language point of view - we will be able to create conditions for conscious education of a generation of people with impaired hearing, a generation of people who would highly esteem their language and use it with respect and who would care for its position among their own culture values.

If we are to compare our work with the dictionaries that have been completed in our country so far, we have to say that we have been trying (and this should be the primary approach to our work in the future) to collect the files of signs in such manner as to include more varieties of individual signs - dialects, to acquire notation and other relevant data for each individual sign, and, last but not least, to reflect the meaning of individual words as accurately as possible (some dictionaries in the Czech Republic disregard the latter feature).

We are currently also preparing a monolingual version which will offer the explanations of particular notions in the sign language. The creation of such a dictionary for the branch "Czech language" (explanations of some notions or phenomena are enabled) has approached its final stage. It is an experiment which is very demanding, not only as far as the content and the formal layout are concerned, but also in respect of the software part of it.

O ZBRCI MEĐU JEZICIMA I POTRAZI ZA REDOM

Prvi rječnik češkog znakovnog jezika izdan je 1988. godine i sadrži oko 3000 znakova, a pripremaju se i novi rječnici u okviru znanstvenih projekata. Najjači poticaj za započinjanje projekta izrade novih rječnika dali su učitelji iz škola za gluhe koji su smatrali da je njihov fond znakova s kojim raspolažu nedovoljan za poučavanje školskih predmeta. Ciljevi projekta su sljedeći: putem analize školskih udžbenika izdvojiti češke riječi potrebne za poučavanje pojedinih školskih predmeta; stvoriti bazični korpus čeških riječi za opći rječnik znakovnog jezika koji bi uključio sve varijante znakova, uzrokovane različitim geografskim podrijetlom ispitanika; sakupiti što bogatiji fond znakova, opisati ih, klasificirati/analizirati i ponuditi na uporabu grupi ljudi koji komuniciraju znakovnim jezikom. Smatramo da će ovaj projekt rezultirati i novim saznanjima u području gramatike. U radu su prikazani pristupi, rezultati i problemi koji su se javljali tijekom faze pripreme. Vjerujemo da ćemo stvoriti preduvjete za edukaciju nove generacije gluhih koji će biti ponosni na svoj jezik.

Ključne riječi: rječnik znakovnog jezika, češki znakovni jezik, gluhi, edukacija gluhe djece

WHY DON'T MY STUDENTS SIGN LIKE DEAF PEOPLE? SUGGESTIONS FOR SIGN LANGUAGE CURRICULUM DEVELOPMENT

Linda Lupton

Saint John's Health System, Anderson, Indiana, USA

Abstract

Sign language instructors struggle with the fact that their students do not produce native or even near-native like signing ability. This presentation will address some of the factors that contribute to sign language fluency. It will also focus on specific hands-on methods that can be used in teaching signed languages. Participants will be able to identify the factors that differentiate native signers from students, list the most salient features of fluency, iden- tify the components to a succesful sign language instructional program and abtain resource material for additional information.

Key words: *sign language, sign language instruction, sign language curriculum, ASL*

I have been teaching American Sign Language (ASL) for over 20 years and have always been interested in how students learn signed languages. In this paper I will focus on 3 projects that I have been involved with and provide suggestions for curriculum development in the area of sign language instruction.

The first project was one I worked on with Howie Zelaznik of Purdue University. It was reported in Sign Language Studies (1990). We looked at students enrolled in their first semester of sign language class. Using one of the first motion analysis systems for sign language study, the WATSMART system, we tracked the students' productions of specific signs at 3 different stages of the semester. We attached electrodes to their hands and plotted their movement displacement and rate. The students signed more quickly and uniformly as the semester progressed. We concluded that the students were able to produce the individual signs in an acceptable manner by the end of the semester.

Although students were able to produce the individual signs effectively, they still would not be considered fluent signers. This lead to a study that I did with Ronnie Wilbur, also of Purdue University, concerning this topic. This two-part project, report- ed in The Journal of Deaf Studies and Deaf Education (1998), focused on native signers and what constitutes fluent signing.

During the first part of the project we asked native signers to rate the fluency of six videotaped native signers as they signed a set of four paragraphs. The judges were actu- ally viewing two distinct groups of signers, one group who had been included in a pre- vious study as good exemplars of ASL and the other group who had been excluded because of their less than skillful productions. The judges provided numerical ratings of skill and descriptions of signing skill. Not surprisingly, their judgments fell into two categories for the two groups of signers. For the more skilled signing group the judges commented on such things as their use of facial expression, ability to ACT OUT the paragraphs and sign more ASL-like. For the less skilled signers the judges noted their excessive use of mouth movements, choppiness, bad posture and positioning, and poor eye contact.

For the second part we wished to explore which characteristics were most closely linked to fluent signing. For this we used a second group of judges and the 21 pairs of criteria gleaned from the first study. Judges were asked to rate each of the signers on a seven point scale for such characteristics as too much fingerspelling/not enough fingerspelling and signs too small/signs too large. Once again the two groups of signers were divided into two skill levels. When correlation coefficients were determined for the ranking of fluency and the actual criteria used, the top five criteria essential to fluent signing were: no mouth movement, good eye contact, signing in an ASL-like manner, being able to create a picture and having good posture. Interestingly, less crucial skills were the rate of signing, size of the signs, using the correct signs and the amount of fingerspelling.

This project led to the work on my PhD thesis (unpublished, 1993) concerning aspects of rhythm in ASL. I examined native signers, fluent non-native signers (like myself) and advanced students on various aspects of rhythm including; rate of signing, duration of lexical items, duration of transitions between signs, movement amplitude, phrase structure and pausing and how rate changes are accomplished.

By having the three groups of signers sign the same lexical items in isolation, in context of sentences and paragraphs and at different rates I was able to examine the continuum of signing skill that occurs with these signers. When the students produced the signs in isolation, their measurements of sign amplitude and duration were similar to those of both the fluent and native signer groups. On all other aspects studied there was a progression from student to non-native signer to native user. The native signers signed faster, with shorter transitions between signs and with smaller sign amplitudes than the other two groups. When asked to sign "fast" the native signers made their signs smaller and used co-articulation and assimilation of handshapes to produce the signs in a compact, efficient manner. The students' fast signing looked frantic with larger movements and poorer articulation of the signs, clearly a task they were unaccustomed to performing and unable to accomplish. The native signers signing rate when signing "slow" was still faster in terms of signs per minute than the students signing at their fastest rate.

So to answer the question, "Why don't my students look like native signers?", it would appear that the way the signs are produced is not the problem, rather the way in which they are put together into sentences and longer utterances. The factors of rate of signing, size of signs and the duration of the transitions between signs are all part of the answer.

This leads us to a discussion of how to teach ASL, or any signed language for that matter, such that the students sign in a more native-like manner. When I teach I focus on four areas: lexical items in context, Fingerspelling and numbers, linguistic concepts and Deaf culture and history. Here are some basic ideas for teaching ASL.

Lexical items in context

Generally speaking, the more fun students have in class, the more likely they are to remember and use what they have learned. For this reason, I tend to use games, objects, toys, pictures, and mini field trips as much as possible. This might entail a visit to the vending area or cafeteria when talking about food or use of a family of toys to teach signs for family members. I have recently begun using some rhythmic exercises to work on fluency. These take the form of a simple dialogue that the students perform while thinking in their head of a particular children's nursery rhyme or song. As my students are typically hearing, thinking of this "song" while performing an ASL dialogue helps them to produce the flow of signs in a rhythmic manner. One example is signed to the rhythm of the children's song, Row, Row, Row Your Boat, and goes like this:

GOOD MORNING HOW-YOU
FINE TODAY AND YOU
#OK NOW BUT YESTERDAY SICK HAVE #FLU

As a hearing instructor, it is tempting for myself and the students to talk in class. I limit this to questions at the beginning and end of class and strongly enforce a "no talk-ing rule" during class. I often have the students wear earplugs so that they cannot hear one another's murmurings.

Linguistic topics

Because of my interest in ASL linguistics, I include many aspects of this topic in the class. Some of the items I cover during the course of the first semester include: classi-fiers, loan signs, four parameters of signs, sentence types and use of the face for gra-mmar, dominance and symmetry conditions, noun/verb pairs and the notions of signs as iconic, transparent or opaque. These topics can easily be introduced during the lesson and reinforced throughout the course, i.e. is that sign iconic, transparent or opaque?, or in which parameters do those two signs differ?. Students seem to appreciate learning about these topics, especially as they relate to English. When discussing loan signs, I often point out how we borrow foreign words and force them into our phonology in English (e.g. gyros or croissant). These topics are generally introduced verbally, but can be reinforced via sign or fingerspelling during the rest of the semester.

Deaf culture and history

Because I am hearing, this is perhaps the hardest topic to cover effectively. I use videotapes, readings, use of an "expert lecturer" and class discussion to cover Deaf cul-ture and history. The students write a paper on some topic relating to this area and write short reaction papers to the Deaf culture videotape. We do cover rules of politeness such as interruptions, introductions and turn taking early in the semester. I introduce the class with a Deaf awareness quiz, which we discuss at length.

Where to get more information

There are a multitude of ASL curricula, videotapes, journals and catalogs from which to obtain ideas for teaching. Thanks to the Internet such items are now easily accessible.

References

Lupton, L. (1993, unpublished PhD): Aspects of Rhythm in American Sign Language, Purdue University.

Lupton, L., (1998): Fluency in American Sign Language, Journal of Deaf Studies and Deaf Education, 3:4, 320-328.

Lupton, L. & Zelaznik, H. (1990): Motor Learning in Sign Language Students, Sign Language Studies, 67, 153-174.

ZAŠTO JE ZNAKOVNI JEZIK MOJIH UČENIKA DRUGAČIJI OD JEZIKA GLUHIH OSOBA? PRIJEDLOZI ZA KREIRANJE PROGRAMA POUČAVANJA ZNAKOVNOG JEZIKA

Instruktori znakovnog jezika suočavaju se s činjenicom da njihovi učenici ne postižu u znakovanju razinu izvornih govornika ili razinu bliskoj onoj u izvornih govornika. U ovom radu razmatraju se obilježja flentnosti u znakovnom jeziku, čimbenici koji doprinose fluentnosti u znakovnom jeziku, metode koje se mogu koristiti u poučavanju te komponente kvalitetnog programa učenja znakovnog jezika kao drugog jezika.

Ključne riječi: *znakovni jezik, poučavanje znakovnog jezika, programi poučavanja znakovnog jezika, ASL*

SUGGESTIONS FOR SIGN LANGUAGE INSTRUCTION

Linda Lupton
John's Health System, Anderson, Indiana, USA

Abstract

The paper focuses on the practical aspects of sign language instruction. The framework of an American Sign Language curriculum is provided as well as ideas that have been useful in classroom settings. Issues like learning objectives, vocabulary instruction, fingerspelling and numbers, linguistic factors and deaf culture and history are considered. A list of available ASL curricula is included.

Key words: *sign language, sign language teaching, ASL, sign language instruction*

Sign language instruction for second language learners is a multi-faceted undertaking. While there are many curricula that have been developed for American Sign Language, there is no curriculum that does it all. At the very least, a well structured program should include the following components: vocabulary building, fingerspelling instruction, linguistic structure, Deaf culture and history of the language. Ideally, each of these components should be incorporated into each lesson. What follows is a compendium of ideas on what to teach and how to teach it based on the author's 20 plus years of experience as a sign language instructor. It should be pointed out that while these ideas may work for American Sign Language, they may not work for other signed languages. Many of these ideas are adapted from established American Sign Language curricula (credit given in the references).

Vocabulary instruction

Whenever possible provide an experience with the lesson, e.g. if you are talking about food, go to the vending area, cafeteria or a restaurant. What follows is a list of suggestions for a variety of vocabulary topics. The more creative and fun the activity, the better the students will remember it.

1.   Family members:

- build a family with the class members to introduce vocabulary such as mother, father, boy, girl, daughter, son-in-law, married, single, divorced, babies etc. Review often to show that the students understand the relationship every time a new person is added to the family. For example, a girl becomes a woman, a wife, a mother, a mother-in-law and a grandmother as new family members are added
- have students bring in pictures of family and friends and have them explain the pictures as they circulate among one another
- use dolls, toys & overheads to review relationships among family members

2. *Food*

- bring in pictures of food or food toys (make friends with a speech therapist to provide you with these)
- visit the vending area or cafeteria and review what is in each machine or in the food line
- for more advanced students make the last class a visit to a restaurant and have one person be the spokesperson and everyone else sign his or her order
- bring in empty boxes, bottles and other containers of food items
- have students fingerspell their favorite food or foods they dislike
- have students sit in a circle, fingerspell these same items and the next person in the circle must produce the sign for the fingerspelled item

3. *Giving directions*

- take a tour of the building asking students to tell you how to find the phone, library, cafeteria, office, bathroom, vending area, water fountain etc.
- draw a map on the blackboard and show how to give directions from the signer's perspective
- ask students how to find known locations outside of the building, bookstore, dormitory, restaurant, parking lot, etc.

4. *Housing & vehicles*

- draw pictures of dwellings on the blackboard e.g. an apartment, a house, a dormitory, a tent and a trailer (the worse your artwork, the more the students enjoy it)
- ask students to talk about their keys and what they go to (e.g. apartment, mother's house, bicycle lock, office). This is also good for number practice.
- use pictures of the above locations to stimulate discussion
- have students circulate and introduce themselves and ask where they live (this is a good time for creativity, e.g. live in a doghouse, in a tree, or on a boat)
- after introducing the vocabulary of vehicles (using pictures of a car, boat, train, plane, helicopter, bus, cab etc.) have students circulate and ask each other how they come to class (this can be quite hilarious if creativity is encouraged)

Fingerspelling and Numbers

- working in small groups is best, have students fingerspell closed set items, e.g. fruits and vegetables, car types, where they grew up, where they want to live, states, countries, famous people
- create a list of unusual letter combinations (e.g. bn, pl, gn, ps) and have students think of words that have these combinations in them and then practice the words
- use sentences that contain all the letters of the language, e.g., "The quick brown

fox jumped over the lazy dogs", this can be used as a receptive as well as an expressive activity

- sitting in a circle, a student fingerspells a word and the next student must sign it
- put short first names on pieces of paper with the first letter on the outside, the students circulate and try to guess the other person's name
- play children's number games such as "Buzz" where they take turns counting until they come to a number with seven in it or a multiple of seven and they that person must fingerspell "buzz" or he/she is out of the game
- have students create the quiz for the day by fingerspelling tricky words
- use children's songs such as the "Alphabet Song" to hum along as they produce the letters of the alphabet

Linguistics

Because I have studied ASL linguistics, I find this a fascinating topic to incorporate into the lesson plan. The students seem to appreciate discussions comparing English to ASL. Some of these ideas may be inappropriate for other signed languages. I will merely list some topics I cover in the introductory courses.

- parameters of sign (handshape, movement, location, orientation) and how signs can be described using these parameters
- the difference among iconic, transparent and opaque signs
- loan signs
- how compounds are formed
- sign order, grammatical use of the face
- phonological rules such as the dominance and symmetry conditions

Deaf Culture & History

For the Introductory classes, Deaf culture is best taught either by a team of a hearing and a Deaf person or with a Deaf lecturer and voice interpreter. There are many excellent videos that discuss the topic of Deaf culture in American Sign Language. Additionally, outside reading or experiential assignments are beneficial.

Similarly, the history of the language or the Deaf experience can be taught through lecture, videos & readings. Activities may include:

- visiting a play, lecture or sporting activity at a school for the Deaf
- small group discussions after viewing a videotape
- writing a reaction paper to a video tape
- classroom lecture about the evolution of signs (e.g. moving from two-handed to one-handed signs, or how new signs enter the mainstream)
- guest lecturer who is a faculty member or respected member of the Deaf community

Resources

Curricula

American Sign Language, Cokely, D., Baker, C., 1980, T.J. Publishers, 817 Silver Spring Avenue, 365-D, Silver Spring, MD, 20910

Basic Sign Communication, Newell, W., 1983, NAD Press, 814 Thayer Avenue, Silver Spring, MD, 20910

Beginning American Sign Language VideoCourse, with Billy Seago, 1993, Sign Enhancers, Inc., 1320 Edgewater Street, N.W. Suite b-10, Salem, Or, 97304

Signing Naturally, Smith, C., Lentz, E.M., Mikos, K., 1988, Dawn Sign Press, 2124 Kitteridge Street, 107 Berkeley, CA, 94704

Signing with your Clients, Vold, F. C., Kinsella-Meier, M.A., Hughes Hilley, M.C., 1990, Gallaudet University Press, Washington, D.C., 20002

Catalogs

Academic Communication Associates, Publication Center, Dept. 21 A, 4149 Avenida de la Plata, P.O. Box 4279, Oceanside, CA, 92052-4279, 760-758-9593, www.acadcom.com (some children's books and materials to work with developmentally delayed children)

ADCO Hearing Products, Inc., 5661 South Curtice Street, Littleton, CO, 80120, 800-726-0851 (V/TTY), www.adcohearing.com (books, sign language related gifts, software)

Dawn Sign Press, 6130 Nancy Ridge Drive, San Diego, CA, 92121-3223, 800-549-5350, www.dawnsign.com (books, videos)

Gallaudet University Press, 800 Florida Avenue, N.E., Washington, D.C., 20002, 800-621-2736 (V), 888-630-9347 (TTY), http://gupress.gallaudet.edu (a wealth of materials including books, videos, & research materials)

Sign Enhancers, 10568 SE Washington, St., Portland, OR 97216-2809, 800-767-4461 (V), 888-283-5097 (TTY), signenhancers.com (curricula, videos, books, games)

NEKI PRIJEDLOZI ZA POUČAVANJE ZNAKOVNOG JEZIKA

Ovaj rad bavi se praktičnim aspektima poučavanja znakovnog jezika. Dat je okvir programa tečaja američkog znakovnog jezika kao i neke sugestije koje su se pokazale korisnima u praksi. Razmataju se ciljevi učenja jezika, poučavanje rječnika, ručne abecede i upoznavanje brojeva, lingvističke spoznaje u kontekstu tečaja te sadržaji vezani uz kulturu i povijest zajednice gluhih. Navedeni su i neki od programa poučavanja američkog znakovnog jezika koji su se pokazali efikasnima u SAD-u.

Ključne riječi: *znakovni jezik, poučavanje znakovnog jezika, američki znakovni jezik, ASL*

HOW HARD IS IT TO PREDICT SUCCESS IN SIGN LANGUAGE ACQUISITION?

Richard A. van Royen

SLN Interpreter & Teacher Training College, University of Professional Education, Utrecht, The Netherlands

Abstract

After four years of education, students at our Interpreter & Teacher Training College for Sign Language of the Netherlands (SLN) must have a thorough command of this sign language. It concerns SLN acquisition as a foreign language. We prefer to select only those candidates who are expected to have the potential for learning SLN within four years on a near-native level. We expected that there are several aspects that can be used as a predictor of success in SLN acquisition. Two important aspects are the following: success in a test of visual discrimination and success in a SLN test. This paper concerns the research on the quality of these tests and the predictive value of the tests in regard to the success in SLN acquisition.

Sign languages are visual languages, and in many sign language curricula the training of visual discrimination skills is an important subject. It is expected that candidates with better visual discrimination skills are more successful in sign language acquisition. One part of the instrument that was used to select students concerns visual discrimination skills.

Another part of the instrument is the SLN test. In a short lesson the candidates learn to sign ALSTUBLIEFT (REQUEST), to use the correct handling classifier with the sign GEVEN (GIVE) and to use the correct movement. Afterwards the students are tested. It is expected that students with higher scores on this test will have a higher success rate in SLN acquisition after the four years of education.

Unfortunately, our expectations were not confirmed. Neither test can be used as a predictor of SLN acquisition due to very weak correlations between test scores and scores on the SLN exams during the schooling. More research on aspects that can be used to predict success in the acquisition of sign language as a foreign language is needed.

Sign language of the Netherlands

The sign language used in the Netherlands is called the Nederlandse gebarentaal (NGT). In English: Sign Language of the Netherlands (SLN). In the Netherlands there are 17,500 potential users of SLN (this also includes the hearing users). There are approximately 12.000 users of sign language interpreters. In 1997 there were only 90 professional SLN interpreters employed.[1] These numbers tell us that there is a shortage of professional SLN interpreters in the Netherlands. It was expected that in 2002 the Dutch government would accept SLN as a real language, next to Dutch and the Friesian language. This would have important consequences. First, the number of requests for a

---

[1] Commissie NGT (1997). Méér dan een gebaar: rapport van de commissie NGT. Den Haag: Sdu Uitgevers.

SLN interpreter would increase. Secondly, different groups of people would like to (or have to) learn SLN for personal or professional reasons. More professional SLN interpreters and teachers must be trained in the near future to fulfil this demand.

SLN interpreter & teacher training college

In 1998 the University of Professional Education started the SLN Interpreter & Teacher Training College[2]. 95 students were selected to participate in the first group. Deaf, hard of hearing or hearing students learn SLN (as a second language) at a near-native level, learn about deaf culture and practice interpreting or teaching skills. Deaf and hard of hearing students are trained to be SLN teachers. Hearing students can choose between the following two professions: SLN interpreter or teacher. The education lasts for four years, which is normal for all higher education in the Netherlands.

Table 1 Selection aspects & tests

Aspect	Test
Attitude towards the college, profession and deafness	Questionnaire
Spoken Dutch skill (interpreter only)	Observation
Summarizing (deaf/hard of hearing/hearing)	Written or signed test
SLN skills	Visual discrimination task SLN task Observation

Both professions have a resemblance concerning the language and deaf culture. Therefore, the first two years of the education for both professions are similar. After two years the curriculum specializes for the chosen profession.

Selection of candidates

Each year we have to select students for our college. We prefer to select only those students who are expected to have the potential for completing the education in four years, have the potential for being a SLN interpreter or teacher and who are capable of learning SLN within four years on a near-native level. In the selection process we use several tests to measure the students on several aspects. This is shown in Table 1.

In Van Royen (2000) all the aspects and instruments are explained[3]. In this paper we will focus on the SLN skills of hearing students only.

---

[2] Seminarium voor Orthopedagogiek (1996). Tweedegraads leraren en tolkenopleiding NGT. Utrecth: FEO, HvU
[3] Van Royen, R. A. (2000). Selectie voor toelating. De kwaliteit van het selectie-instrument voor het toelaten van kandidaten tot de opleiding leraar/tolk NGT. Utrecht: FEO, HvU.

SLN acquisition

It is difficult to learn a foreign (spoken) language in four years on a native speaker level. Jacobs (1996) states that learning a sign language is as difficult as learning Arabic, Chinese of Japanese[4] (for an English speaking person). Not everybody is able to learn a foreign language in four years.

We prefer to select only those students who are capable of learning SLN in four years. But what aspects can be used as a predictor for this? We expected that the following skills could be used as a predictor of success in SLN acquisition:

- Visual discrimination skills;
- SLN skills.

Visual discrimination skills

Sign languages are visual languages. Our brain receives a lot of stimuli when signing. Every stimulus must be given a meaning in a very short time and we must be able to distinguish that stimulus from other stimuli that may be very similar. In sign language a small difference in one of the five parameters of a sign can result in the total change in its meaning.

We expect that students with better visual discrimination skills and visual memory will acquire SLN faster or better.

For our selecting tests we developed three visual discrimination tasks.

- 7 identical or different shapes

On videotape the signer creates a

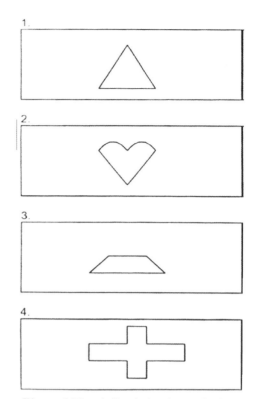

Figure 1 *Visual discrimination task: draw shape on paper*

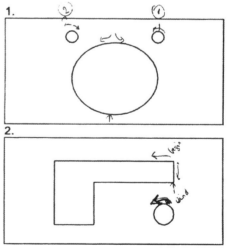

Figure 2 *Visual discrimination task: draw shape in the air*

[4] Jacobs, R. (1996). Just How Hard Is It To Learn ASL, The case for ASL as a truly foreign language. In Lucas, C. (ed.). *Multicultural Aspects of Sociolinguistics in Deaf Communities.* Washington: Gallaudet Unyversity Press.
[5] Cokley, D. & Baker_Shenk, B. (1980). American Sign Language. A teachers' resouce text on Curriculum, Methods, and Evaluation. Washington: Clere Books, Gallaudet University Press.

shape in the air twice. These shapes are the same or are different on one of the parameters. Students have to recognise if the shape is different or the same. For every correct answer (identical or different, and, if different, on which parameter?) the students receive a point.

- Draw 5 shapes in the air (copy the signer on tape)

The signer on tape creates a shape in the air. These shapes are symmetrical or non-symmetrical.

Students see the shape twice. They have to create the same shape in the air. This is taped. Figure 1 shows some examples of these shapes. The student receives a point for every correct shape in the air.

The shape is correct when the student copies the behaviour of the signer on tape. When the signer starts on the right side of the shape, the students also have to begin on the right.

- Draw 10 shapes on the paper

The signer on tape creates a shape in the air. These shapes are symmetrical or non-symmetrical. Students see the shape twice. Then they draw the shape on the paper. Figure 2 shows some examples of these shapes. For every correct shape the students receive a point. Students are able to score a maximum of 22 points on this visual discrimination test. We expected that students with a higher score on this test would be better at SLN acquisition than people with a lower score. When this is indicated this visual discrimination test can be used as a predictor of success in SLN acquisition.

To prove this hypothesis, we gathered information about SLN acquisition during our students' first year of the study. Students received a total of 800 hours of education in SLN in four units/modules and two units focused on SLN grammar. Each unit ends with an exam. These SLN and SLN grammar exams are a reliable measure for success in SLN acquisition (after standardization, r = .92).

It was expected that students with a higher score on the visual discrimination task have a higher score on the exams. Table 2 is the result of the correlation analysis.

We expected that there would be a correlation between the scores on the visual discrimination task and the result on the SLN exams. We were surprised that the correlations were weak and not significant. Because of this weak correlation we decided not to continue the regression analysis. The hypothesis has been falsified. The visual discrimination task is not able to predict success in SLN acquisition.

Table 2 Visual discrimination tasks (rS, two sides)

Identical/different shapes	.09
Draw shapes in the air	.18
Draw shapes on the paper	-.02

[6] Anderson, J. R. (1995). Cognitive psychology and its implications. 4th ed. New York: W.H. Freeman and Company

SLN skills

Someone is a quick learner when he/she is flexible with his/her knowledge. This means that a learner can receive and understand information quickly and, more importantly, can use the information in other situations. This is the principle of the transfer of knowledge[6]. Students have to learn a complete new language in four years. Therefore, a student must be able to learn quickly and must be able to use the information in new situations. For this reason we developed a SLN lesson. The goal of this lesson is to use the sign ALSJEBLIEFT (REQUEST), to use the grammar rule of the correct handling classifier with the verb GEVEN (GIVE) and to use the INDEX correctly.

There are several objects in the classroom: a book, a flower, a paper, a box and a cup. The SLN teacher teaches the different sign for each object. Then the SLN teacher picks up the book (for example) and gives it to one of the students. Then the teacher asks the student to give the book to another student (in SLN):

ALSJEBLIEFT INDEX2 BOEK 2GEVEN (Q5-cl) INDEX3a
(PLEASE INDEX2 BOOK 2GIVE (Q5-cl) INDEX3a)

Every object uses a different handling classifier. If you give a book, the hand has another shape (Q5-cl) than if you give a flower (Tcl). It is important that students ask to give the object to the correct person (and make the correct movement, INDEX). In this SLN lesson the teacher gives feedback. Each student receives the same amount of attention of the teacher. After the lesson a SLN task is given. In this task we want to know if students are able to use the information in other situations.

The content of the SLN task is similar to the SLN lesson. Students must ask a person to give an object to another person. The objects are different from those that were used in the lesson. The task contains five requests. These requests are taped. For each correct request the students receive three points (maximum 15 points). A request is correct if the sign ALSTUBLIEFT (REQUEST) is correct, if the student uses the correct handling classifier and makes the correct movement.

It was expected that students with a higher score on this SLN task would be better or faster in the acquisition of SLN. Again we looked at the correlation between the scores on the task and the SLN exams. Table 3 shows the result.

This table shows a very weak and even negative (not significant) correlation. This was totally unexpected. Unfortunately, this means that the SLN lesson and the SLN task cannot be used as a predictor of success in SLN acquisition.

Table 3 *SLN skills (r_s, two sides)*

SLN task	-.05

Conclusion

This paper started with a question: how hard is it to predict success in SLN acquisition? I hope this paper made clear that it is very difficult to predict this success.

Cokely & Baker-Shenk claim that visual discrimination skills and memory are crucial for the acquisition of visual sign language. However, Poizner, Klima & Bellugi (1987) indicate that the left hemisphere is specialized in language, including sign language. The right cerebral hemisphere is dominant for perception and processing of spatial patterns, relations and transformation[7].

The visual discrimination skills are skills that are more organized in the right hemisphere. Our discovery that the visual discrimination task cannot be used as a predictor for success in SLN acquisition confirms the findings of Poizner, Klima & Bellugi. We decided to delete the visual discrimination task from the selecting tests.

We were very surprised by the result concerning the SLN task. We expected that the SLN lesson and task could tell us if a student is capable of learning SLN. Unfortunately, this is not the case.

We decided to keep the SLN task, because the SLN lesson gives our SLN teachers some idea about the student: is the student capable of learning SLN? Our SLN teacher mentioned that you could feel if someone is capable or not. Now we are trying to make this intuition measurable.

More research on the aspects that can predict sign language acquisition is needed. For validating the tasks we used the exams of the first year only. In 2002 our first students will receive their diplomas. By that time students must have reached a near-native SLN level. Then we will repeat this research and look at the correlation between the tasks and SLN exams over four years. We hope to find better results.

---

[7] Poisner, H., Klima, E.S., & Bellugi, U. (1987). What the Hands Reveal About the Brain. Massachusetts: MIT Press.

KOLIKO JE TEŠKO PREDVIDJETI USPJEH U UČENJU ZNAKOVNOG JEZIKA?

Nakon četverogodišnje edukacije, studenti našeg studija za edukaciju tumača i učitelja za nizozemski znakovni jezik (SLN – Sign Language of the Netherlands) moraju solidno vladati znakovnim jezikom. To se odnosi na uporabu SLN-a kao stranog jezika. Većinom uzimamo samo one kandidate koji imaju potencijal da u četiri godine nauče SLN na razini koja je blizu razine izvornog govornika. Mislimo da postoji nekoliko aspekata u predviđanju uspjeha u učenju znakovnog jezika. Dva su važna aspekta: uspjeh na testu vizualne diskriminacije i uspjeh u testu SLN-a. Ovaj rad odnosi se na istraživanje kvalitete tih testova i njihove prediktorske valjanosti u odnosu na učenje SLN-a. Znakovni je jezik vizualni jezik, te je u mnogim znakovnim jezicima vrlo važna vizualna diskriminacija. Kandidati s boljom vizualnom diskriminacijom lakše uče znakovni jezik. Prilikom odabira studenata jedan dio ispitnih zadataka odnosio se na vještine vizualne diskriminacije. Drugi je dio test SLN-a. U kratkom predavanju kandidati nauče riječ na znakovnom ALSTUBLIEFT (ZAHTJEV), nauče koristiti ispravni klasifikator pri produkciji znaka GEVEN (DATI) i ispravno izvoditi pokret. Očekivalo se da će studenti s boljim uspjehom na ovim testovima nakon 4 godine edukacije za tumača imati bolji uspjeh u savladavanju SLN-a od onih s lošijim uspjehom. Nažalost, naša predviđanja nisu potvrđena. Rezultati niti jednog od testova ne mogu se koristiti kao prediktori uspješnosti u učenju SLN-a. Potrebna su daljnja istraživanja o čimbenicima na temelju kojih se može predviđati uspješnost učenja znakovnog jezika kao stranog jezika.

Ključne riječi: *znakovni jezik kao drugi jezik, nizozemski znakovni jezik*

References

Commissie NGT (1997). *Méér dan een gebaar: rapport van de commissie NGT*. Den Haag: Sdu Uitgevers.

Seminarium voor Orthopedagogiek (1996). *Tweedegraads leraren en tolkenopleiding NGT*. Utrecht: FEO, HvU

Van Royen, R. A. (2000). *Selectie voor toelating. De kwaliteit van het selectie-instrument voor het toelaten van kandidaten tot de opleiding leraar/tolk NGT*. Utrecht: FEO, HvU.

Jacobs, R. (1996). Just How Hard Is It To Learn ASL, The case for ASL as a truly foreign language. In Lucas, C. (ed.). *Multicultural Aspects of Sociolinguistics in Deaf Communities*. Washington: Gallaudet University Press.

Cokely, D. & Baker-Shenk, B. (1980). *American Sign Language. A teachers' resource text on Curriculum, Methods, and Evaluation*. Washington: Clerc Books, Gallaudet University Press.

Anderson, J.R. (1995). *Cognitive psychology and its implications*. 4th ed. New York: W.H. Freeman and Company.

Poisner, H., Klima, E.S., & Bellugi, U. (1987). What the Hands Reveal About the Brain. Massachusetts: MIT Press.

WHY IS DEAF CULTURE IMPORTANT?

Paddy Ladd

University of Bristol, United Kingdom

Abstract

This paper traces the efforts made by Deaf people and their allies to colonised Deaf co-mmunities over the last 120 years. It follows the path liberate themselves from the medical concept of deafness which has taken by Deaf people towards that liberation and finds that in the UK there were 8 stages of development in the last 20 years. Each has produced a small amount of change, but in some ways and some areas, these have come up against what may be the 9th stage, and the final barrier of them all. This 9th stage I identify as Deaf culture. To accept that Deaf people have a culture is to finally acknowledge that they have a collective view of the world, rooted in over 200 years of history, and that this view should be given primacy in Deaf related affairs. Since this is the ultimate argument for decolonization, it is not surprising that it is resisted. At the same time there has been a backlash from the colonisers - Oralism has gained new life with the advent of cochlear implants and the genetics movement. When they are opposed by Deaf communities, they find that Deaf arguments are framed in terms of Deaf cultural disagreement. Thus the concept of Deaf culture has become the final battleground for either the renaissance or the survival of Deaf communities.

Key words: *deaf, Deaf, Deaf culture, Deaf community*

Outline

Before explaining the importance of the concept of Deaf culture, I want to describe the general patterns of development of Deaf issues in the West over the past 100 years, so you can compare them with your own, and see if the similarities and differences are important.

Put simply, we experienced a period between 1780 and 1880 where Deaf schools were established using sign language and Deaf teachers. In this period also, many of our Deaf clubs were set up. We then experienced 100 years where Oralism took over and where Deaf teachers were banished (Lane 1984). In that time also, Deaf clubs and services were taken over by hearing people.

From about 1980 onwards, there have been 10 stages of what I call the Deaf Resurgence (Ladd 2003):

(i)   The setting up of radical Deaf organisations or groups in some countries, insisting of Deaf self-government.

(ii) Campaigns for partial change in Deaf education - known as 'Total Communication' - usually resulting in forms of 'Signed English' etc

(iii) The recognition of sign languages as real languages.

(iv) A second wave of campaigns for situating Deaf communities as linguistic minorities, and for bi-lingual, bi-cultural education.

(v)   The emergence of Deaf TV programmes.

(vi) The emergence of Interpreters and new openings in professional jobs for Deaf people.

(vii) The recognition of the importance of Deaf History, and the growing acknowledgement of the damage done to the community (i.e. not simply to the individual person) by Oralism.

(viii) The development of university courses in Deaf Studies and increased university access in general.

(ix) The beginnings of the re-emergence of Deaf arts.

(x) The realisation that the Deaf culture exists and underpins all of the above.

These positive changes (and there are others too, but time is short here) have been held back or threatened by the following :

(i) The emergence of mainstreaming. This threatens the existence of the Deaf community by severing Deaf children from their community and culture (Lee [ed] 1991).

(ii) The emergence of cochlear implants. This is an immense danger to Deaf communities and Deaf culture because it is closely tied to the old oralist movement, and can bring it to a new lease of life and thus serve to stop work on Deaf Studies and bilingual Deaf education. Acceptance of Deaf communities and their languages is retarded in favour of technological so-called 'miracle cures', which do not accept Deaf people as they are, with all that they can offer the world. Furthermore, the physical, social and psychological effects of implants are not only unresearched, but actively discouraged. Deaths of Deaf children are occurring and going unrecorded, as well as many other negative effects. Moreover there is an immense financial investment in these implants which is not being recouped by profits per se. It would appear that some unnamed powerful multinational bodies are funding this work, and for aims that have nothing to do with Deaf children. One possible explanation is that these children are just a staging post in what may be a giant military-industrial experiment. Such vast resources may explain why the media is so compliant in following the wishes of the experimenters, and why dissenting Deaf and hearing voices are not only silenced but persecuted. (Lane 1993).

(iii) The threat of genetics. Much of what has been said above may also apply here to these attempts to manipulate genes and remove 250 of the world's languages from the earth.

It is my task here to explain how the Deaf culture concept not only underpins the first 10 points and the second 3 points, but how it is in fact the logical extension of all those developments, and all that Deaf people have been saying for the past 250 years.

2. Resistance to deaf culture

Through each of the stages above, we have tried to persuade those in power of the Deaf 'point of view'. We have tried many different concepts - linguistic minority, human rights, child abuse, even genocide (NUD 1982, Lee [ed] 1991). We thought at every stage that once the concept we were putting forward was accepted, that the rest of our arguments would be accepted. For example, you would have thought that recognition of sign languages would be enough to convince people that there was a collective Deaf viewpoint. But this has not happened.

There is a strong resistance in fact to the idea that Deaf people as a collective group have several key beliefs which are shared by almost all the community.

(i)   One reason for this is that Western societies are, or have become cultures which are based on individualism (Mindess 2000). They find it hard to believe that 70 % of the world's cultures are in fact based on collectivism, where group values and responsibilities are almost primary, and take precedence over individual desires. Where such communities exist inside Western societies, they are mis-understood for that reason, let alone the other cultural differences.

(ii) Of course there are other reasons also, not least that by definition members of a culture are largely unaware that their beliefs and values are simply products of their culture - in many cases people think that theirs is the natural way to behave, and that all others are either odd or misguided. So they have done little thinking about the concept of culture itself.

(iii) Then of course we have the unique situation of Deaf communities - that only 10% of its members at most have Deaf parents, so that it is hard for the parents of the other 90% to believe their child is a member of a different culture. And of course we have the medical model of deafness as a disability, which makes it hard for people to accept that these defective people have something positive going for them.

But of all these, the individual-collective cultural difference is one of the biggest hurdles we face. Policies are constructed with the indidividual in mind - so that if one talks of discrimination, or campaigns for access, it is always thought of in terms of enabling the individual to participate in mainstream society. *But if a people belong to a collective society, then damage to the individual also damages the quality of life in that society.* For example, if a Deaf school-leaver cannot read, that is not simply an indivi-dual tragedy, but one which affects the future running of Deaf clubs and organisations. If a person is psychologically damaged, then the quality of the community he or she joins in 'lowered' in order to cope with that person. And so on.

This is how we know in the end that Deaf peoples' struggles are more like linguistic minority struggles than disability struggles. Because in the West, disabled people seek as individuals to join the mainstream, not set up their own society. But linguistic minori-ties seek to establish high quality of life for their own peoples *as a group,* not only as individuals. We also notice that one of their primary concerns is control of their own education system, so that their children can be educated in their own language - and their own culture (Ladd 2003). And, people are prepared to go to war for these principles.

Why, then, should Deaf communities with their own languages be any different?

And yet, even when Deaf communities' sign languages are recognised, even in bilingual movements, the idea of Deaf culture is still resisted.

From my own years of research, it is clear to me that there is one other reason for resistance. And that is - that the moment one concedes that Deaf culture exists, then one has to concede that there exists also Deaf ways of seeing the world, Deaf ways of thinking, which might be different from your own. That there therefore exists Deaf values, beliefs, norms, Deaf epistemolgies even.

And that frightens people. Perhaps some of it is fear of the unknown. But often it is simply a fear around power. Somehow, many who believe in sign language in Deaf education think that all they have to do is learn to sign and things can go on as normal. But they cannot. Because Deaf education, Deaf welfare services, Deaf TV, Deaf organisations then have to become 'Deaf centred' in order to be effective. And in order to achieve that, the obvious next step is Deaf control of those fields (Ladd 2003).

No wonder people fear the Deaf culture concept, because if its existence is admitted, then all the other walls begin to crumble....

However, if people are able to take the necessary steps to face their fears, we will find that the Deaf culture concept is actually a truly positive tool for meaningful change that can benefit everyone in the end.

3. Useful cultural parallels

In order to understand where the cultures of Deaf linguistic minorities fit into the broader picture, it is helpful to look at other equivalents.

Many linguistic minorities seek independence to remove the imperialism or colonialism that rules them, and to control their own destinies. But the strength and confidence of each one varies widely. There are three basic types of examples.

(i) In Spain, the Catalan and Basque people have the normal percentage of able and qualified professionals to carry out the changes they desire - it is only the lack of political power which constrains them.

(ii) Then there is a middle group, with a smaller number of professionals and resources and a huge underclass legacy from colonialism, such as Black South Africans, African Americans and so on.

(iii) And then there is another group, such as Native Americans, Aborigines in Australia, and other First Nation tribes and societies, where the professional class is minimal.

In each type of example, the reconstruction which is involved in carrying out liberation or independence takes very different forms and requires very different approaches.

In the first type, the language and culture are relatively strong, and do not experience much residual psychological inferiority.

In the second, inferiority has been deeply ingrained, and the professional class is caught between attempting change based on a Western model (which of course they have already been trained in), and trying to reclaim what exists of their former cultures and to integrate these into the Western political structure which they have been forced to utilise.

In the third, the culture has been virtually destroyed and requires a huge effort to preserve it. They have also been almost completely marginalised by the majority society. These two factors together mean that for them enclaves of self-government to give them the time and space to rebuild are a priority. Therefore, development of Western political structures is much less important.

Where do Deaf communities fit into that schemata? In the majority of Western examples, they come into the second type, although the way they are perceived often has more in common with the third type. Some of the characteristics of that second type are:

(i)   There are at present very few Deaf professionals who can step into the holes which have been breached in the walls of oppression which they have inherited.

(ii) Moreover, they face the same classic dualism - blindly adopting 'hearing' professional values, or attempting to explore their own culture, locate their own particular values and to bring those into the professional arena.

(iii) Because their own culture has been oppressed for so long, there is a priority to first of all overcome psychological inferiority connected to their own ways of thinking. Then there is the task of exploring themselves, trying to ascertain which parts of the two cultures they have absorbed, (majority 'hearing' society and Deaf), are acting on them in any given situation, and to try and make decisions as to which features to support and encourage, and which to reject.

The best model for this kind of process is the Black Consciousness Movement founded by Steve Biko in South Africa (Pityana et al [eds] 1991).

But what we can learn from approaching things in this way is that the task of Deaf reconstruction is a 'Long March', and one that will take 10 to 20 years to achieve in some countries. In Scandinavia, this process is well under way, of course. But in other countries, the colonialist process is far from being over, and often Oralism still holds sway.

4. Application to deaf cultures

The process is still a complex one to unravel. Most of the minorities mentioned above at least have the culture of their own homeland to use as a reference tool. Even African-Americans are able to look to Africa to attempt to understand who they have become in reference to whom they once were (Karenga 1993). For Deaf cultures this is much harder. We might be able to identify some cultural features which are Deaf, and some which are Croatian. But it is a third group that is hardest to pin down, namely those Croatian features which the Deaf culture has absorbed, adapted into their own ways, and are thought to be 'Deaf ways', when really in fact they are 'hearing ways'.

A good example from the UK lies in cultural features such as the amount of criticism which is seen as part of the 'Deaf way'. It does not take that much analysis to locate this pattern as a legacy or Oralism - but we have to be willing to make that analysis in the first place, which is what my research has tried to do.

Another example I found was in the oppressive ways that certain power holding sections of the what we have called the 'Old Guard' operated. After analysis, it was found that they were Deaf cultural adaptations of the hearing directors, missioners, or welfare officers' ways. If more radical Deaf people, who had picked up different ideas from extensive socialising in bars with hearing people criticised them, they were dismissed as having 'hearing ideas'. The difference between the two was that one wished to enlarge the sense of what it meant to be a Deaf person, and the other sought to maintain it at a diminished level.

A third example is one where we see Deaf people in one country divided against each other by race or religion. The largest Deaf Way, if you like, is the one that sees Deaf people as forming a global people, which recognises that divisions do not serve them well, and which traces those divisions correctly to the divisions instigated by hearing people. This is not said to pretend that Deaf people are innocents in the process, but simply to aid reconstruction by striving to locate the largest positive vision. By following this, for example, white Deaf people can learn to discard their oppression of Black Deaf people in their own countries, and similarly with Protestants and Catholics.

Deaf culture and deafhood

It is to solve this kind of cultural problem that I have devised the term Deafhood. What this does for us is to 'draw a line under' Deaf culture as it presently exists, and say 'what we have now can be termed Deaf *traditions*. What we have to seek lies in two directions. One is towards the future, to seek to build the largest Deaf self that is possible. The other is back deep in the past, to locate what might be termed existential Deaf values, or those which existed prior to Oralism. This search is what I term the search for Deafhood, and it this we use, not just to rebuild our own communities, but also to bring into Deaf education, to give a powerful example.

If in Deaf education we are to create a Deaf-centred environment, then we realise that we are faced with reclaiming a responsibility we once had - that is, to shape the moral and ethical and social development of Deaf children into first class Deaf citizens. Building on this base, we have to lay down paths by which they can then move towards becoming proud bilingual and bicultural members of the societies in which they live. In working with hearing colleagues to achieve this, we have to realise that we must put aside many of our reactions which are based on past pain - for example resentment towards hearing parents. This process is of course two-way, and is profoundly challenging but also profoundly rewarding.

Let me end by giving you a powerful example. One of the most profound experiences that Deaf people have comes with their ability to communicate across any nation or race, to physically show that we are truly a part of a global community. This experience sets an example to all other hearing people across the globe as a model of what we can offer them as such a living example. It's not always easy to do this of course. In order to do so, one has to put aside as many features of the hearing nation they come from as possible. Sign language communication has to become one which does not carry features of the national sign language which are either related directly to the alphabet, or to concepts in sign based on them. Instead, other, deeper and more 'universal' features have to be used.

It would be big mistake to think of these simply as gesture - they contain many grammatical features. But in undergoing this process, going for this deepest Deafhood, the Deaf international experience is an awesome one. We can go to any country in the world if need be, and live there not as tourists, but at the native level. The collective sum of 5,000 of these experiences interacting at any one place and time produces a profound psychological experience which verges on the spiritual.

And indeed, when reconstructing Deaf communities, if we work from this larger spiritual dimension, we cannot go far wrong. Work with Deaf people has been for so long now bedevilled by the childishness of paternalism, the seeing and treating Deaf people as infantile. Our knowledge about Deaf affairs is so minimal that most of our academic work, in medical fields, in education fields and so on, is also impoverished and diminished compared to the sophisticated depths found outside it in sociology and psychology to give but two examples. It is time to accept that we have reached a watershed, a time to move into adulthood if you like, and finally take on adult challenges in this field. Exploring and understanding Deaf culture, and restructuring all our misguided social policies around those understandings is a truly adult challenge. And the beginning of a new century and millennium is as good a time to start as any!

References

Karenga, M. (1993): Introduction to Black Studies. Los Angeles CA. University of Sankora Press

Ladd, P. (2003): Understanding Deaf Culture. Cleveden, Multilingual Matters

Lane, H. (1984): When the Mind Hears. New York, Random House

Lane, H. (1993): The Mask of Benevolence. New York, Random House

Lee, R. [ed] (1991): Deaf Liberation. Feltham, National Union of the Deaf

Mindess, A. (2000): Reading Between the Signs- Intercultural Communication for Sign Language Interpreters. Yarmouth ME : Intercultural Press

Pityana, B. et al. [eds] (1991): Bounds of Possibility – The Legacy of Steve Biko and Black Consciousness. Cape Town: David Philip

National Union of the Deaf (1982): Charter of Rights of the Deaf. London. National Union of the Deaf

ZAŠTO JE KULTURA GLUHIH VAŽNA?

U radu se daje prikaz napora Gluhih i njihovih suradnika u kolonijaniziranim zajednicama Gluhih tijekom proteklih 120 godina. Prati se put oslobađanja od medicinskog modela gluhoće kojega su poduzeli Gluhi u Velikoj Britaniji. U posljednjih 20 godina možemo pratiti 8 razvojnih faza. Svaka je faza donjela male pomake, a neke od njih rezultirale su onim što bismo mogli nazvati devetom fazom i posljednjom preprekom. Ta faza može se identificirati kao kultura Gluhih. Prihvaćanje činjenice da Gluhi imaju svoju kulturu znači konačno prihvaćanje činjenice da imaju kolektivni pogled na svijet, ukorijenjen u 200 godina dugoj povijesti, kojemu bi se trebao davati prioritet u rješavanju pitanja koja se tiču Gluhih. Budući da je ovo ultimativni argument dekolonizacije, nije čudo da cijeli pokret nailazi na otpor. U isto vrijeme kolonizatori razvijaju novi zamah - oralizam je ojačao pojavom kohlearnih implantata i razvojem genetike. Zajednice Gluhih tomu se protive te koncept kulture Gluhih postaje mjesto posljednje bitke koja će rezultirati ili renesansom ili pukim preživljavanjem zajednica Gluhih.

Ključne riječi: gluhi, Gluhi, kultura Gluhih, zajednica Gluhih

DEAF CULTURE IN CROATIA

Angel Naumovski
Deaf Theatre, Visual Arts and Culture – DLAN, Zagreb

Abstract

As one of the founders of the Deaf Theatre in Zagreb, playwrighter, actor and an active representative of the Croatian deaf community, the author of this paper describes his experiences with literature and performing arts in the deaf community, particularly in relation to the birth of the first play in Croatian sign language, «The Planet of Silence», performed for the first time on the occasion of the international symposium «Sign Language and Deaf Culture» in 2001 in Zagreb. He also describes his view of Deaf culture in general.

Key words: *Deaf culture, Deaf theatre, Deaf arts, sign language*

Four months before the international symposium "Sign Language and Deaf Culture", the Organizing Committee entrusted me with the organization of and preparations for a *play in sign language*. I accepted the task without hesitating, not knowing that this was, in a way, going to shape my destiny (and, I believe, the destiny of many deaf persons).

I set to write a synopsis, which I enjoyed the most. Many of my experiences and thoughts about deafness, reactions of my parents, sister, hearing and deaf friends and, finally, my wife, who has gone though a lot due to my deafness, could come to light. The synopsis was completed in the twinkling of an eye and was followed by that part of the job I was not familiar with - the preparation of the play. With the assistance of Ms. Vesna Ivasović, M.Sc., I got in touch with a Croatian actor Kristijan Ugrina - Kiki, and prof. Vojin Perić from the Theater of the Blind. We had several meetings in which we designed the stage, tone and light and chose music. An audition followed, done by 40-50 deaf persons, but only the most persistent and brave remained, fourteen of them. We had rehearsal after rehearsal, but the uncertainty was not getting smaller. I worried about the outcome, but at the dress rehearsal at the theatre "Gavella", with music and lights, I was amazed at what it looked like. At that moment I fell in love with theatre. I am grateful to the Organizing Committee for entrusting me with this task, to Vesna for helping me realize my ideas, to Kiki for introducing me to the world of theatre, to my wife Duda who had so much love and understanding for my dreams!

The premiere was a success ... my plans were accomplished ... I touched a nerve with both the deaf and the hearing (especially my parents). The hearing were not able to understand the play, i.e. the sign language, which meant that my plan succeeded. This was, to be sincere, my sweet revenge. The hearing felt just like me, who could not go to theatre because I could not follow and understand the words.

After the premiere of "The Planet of Silence", we gave another performance for those who did not see the premiere. Soon after that we, deaf actors and the hearing colleagues who helped with the performance, met and talked about what next. And here we are, we founded the Association "Deaf Theatre, Visual Arts and Culture - DLAN". So far we have had seven shows. At the moment we are planning guest performances in Split and London. Theatre is not the only activity of the Association. We also have poetry in sign language (which is little known among us, but we are slowly gathering experience), organize art workshops, seminars and workshops on Deaf culture and sign language, storytelling in sign language, sign dance (combination of sign language and dance), etc.

What made me found the Association? There are many reasons, but I will quote the one that will be more or less acceptable to everyone: there was not a single Deaf theatre in Croatia, nor an association engaging in similar activities. I can proudly state that our theatre is the first theatre that gives performances in sign language. Thanks to the Deaf Theatre, the long suppressed wishes of many deaf are now coming true. We have had many wonderful experiences and are now, full of motivation, moving on into a new life, the world of Deaf art and culture. At the earlier mentioned Symposium I learned and discovered a lot about Deaf culture. Many times I had found myself in a dilemma, many times I had discussed Deaf culture with the deaf and the hearing, many times I had fought and provoked disapproval of some people who had been working with the deaf for years in the field of speech and hearing rehabilitation. I will never forget the words of a women who had been working with the deaf for 40 years and was proud of her work: "If I knew that my unborn baby is going to be deaf, I would not have him." She said that to my face, just like that, as if I was not worth living. And the sad thing is that I did not say anything, I just kept nodding. That is something I will never forgive myself. And I wish to say to this lady that she has missed her profession and should do something else in life.

After all this, I wish to say that the concept of Deaf culture is still unknown to the Croatian public, even to our deaf community. Some suggest that there is no Deaf culture in Croatia and there has never been. However, Deaf culture exists, has always existed, ever since civilization was born. By definition, culture is language, customs, tradition, usages of the community. Each culture is primarily determined by language. For the deaf it is the sign language - the most beautiful language in the world! We, the Deaf, have fostered our tradition for years, have our customs, habits ... We have our Olympics, contests, international festivals, conferences on the rights of the deaf and sign language, myriad events (youth festivals, gatherings of campers, theatre festivals, pantomime festivals, exhibitions of renowned artists, masked balls, organized summer and winter vacations ...). We marry among ourselves, have deaf children, have our social clubs where the old and the young gather to exchange experiences, socialize, attend lectures ... It seems that the hearing have no idea about us and that we are not aware of our culture. Why is that so? Because the awareness of Deaf culture in Croatia is at a minimum and we do not know how to express our customs and needs. If we wish to obtain more understanding and support of the authorities - ministries, local government, etc. - for our needs and wishes, we should say clearly and publicly what we really need. In order to get what we really need, we should revive our Deaf culture and show proudly to everyone that we exist and do not wish our sign language and culture to be obliterated, to die out, disappear.

Based on the experiences of Western and other countries where sign language is officially recognized, I believe that we will greatly benefit from by the recognition of sign language in Croatia. An empty stomach is an enemy of common sense, but sign language will be the moving water powering the mill, and the mill will give flour that will feed the deaf. I breath like my deaf breath and love what is mine - my language and culture, and this is what powers the mill in me. I still patiently wait (I do not know until when I will be waiting) and live for the day when they will give us the right to a free choice: oral or bilingual approach to school education, lipreading or sign language ... I emphasise: a free choice!!! For today I am not a free man, we the deaf are not free because we have no choices but are always imposed something. No one asks us anything (probably because no one knows how to ask).

And, finally, what can one say? We have everything: top sports results, our beautiful language, recognizable poets, renowned artists, professors and other highly educated deaf ...

I believe that we the deaf are slowly beginning to realize and discover our values. I hope that also the others - the hearing - will soon recognize them and stop ignoring our language and culture - the Deaf culture.

DEAF CULTURE IN CROATIA

Kao osnivač kazališta gluhih u Zagrebu, pisac kazališnih komada, glumac i aktivni predstavnik zajednice gluhih u Hrvatskoj, autor iznosi svoja iskustva vezana uz literarno i scensko stvaralaštvo u zajednici gluhih, a posebno ona vezana uz nastanak prve predstave na znakovnom jeziku «Planet tišine» u sklopu simpozija «Znakovni jezik i kultura gluhih». Također iznosi i svoje poglede na koncept kulture gluhih općenito.

Ključne riječi: *kultura gluhih, scensko stvaralaštvo, gluhi, znakovni jezik*

"OUR" VS. "THEIR" LANGUAGE: THE PROBLEMS OF CROSS-CULTURAL UNDERSTANDING

Alena Macurová

University of Prague, Czech Republic

Abstract

The cross-cultural understanding between the hearing and the deaf Czechs has been coming into existence slowly, step by step. No wonder. One of the basic preconditions of understanding in general is not fulfilled here: the languages involved in the intercultural communicative acts are not shared by the participants of the communication. The hearing majority has no access to the "real" Czech sign language, the deaf minority has no first-rate access to written Czech. The paper discusses the sociolinguistic factors that contribute to this situation, esp. the attitudes to language / languages. The paper also addresses the question of the "world view", the linguistic picture of the world - and tackles the topic of the "common world" of the deaf and the hearing. Considering these problems, the cross-cultural understanding is connected to the context of cognitive linguistics.

Key words: *sign language, sociolinguistic, cross-cultural understanding*

Hearing and deaf Czechs live – geographically and in the physical sense of the word – in one country; their "home" is the Czech Republic. However, they are not "at home" in one language. Hearing Czechs "live" in the Czech language, deaf Czechs from deaf families live in Czech sign language (CzSL). Nevertheless, under certain conditions and with the necessary prerequisites fulfilled, users of different languages are able to communicate and mutually understand each other.

One of the conditions necessary for such understanding is that both (all) communication participants share the same language. This, of course, applies for communication between hearing and deaf Czechs, too – they can share either (written) Czech and/or CzSL. As for the Czech situation, we are still a long way from sharing a language or languages. Hearing Czechs usually do not have (and until recently did not have at all) access to the "real" CzSL, and deaf Czechs have no access to written Czech. This fact considerably complicates mutual communication.

The present situation is evidently connected with the deeply set, traditional attitudes of the hearing majority towards deafness, towards the deaf and especially towards their language. The prejudices of the past are reproduced even at present, at a time of open borders and heading for an open society.

The present-day Czech society ascribes an unequivocally lower status to CzSL. It is reflected in different ways. For example, it is inferred that signed language is not applicable to teaching communication, because it has "a small vocabulary" and "no grammar". In fact, the majority of hearing Czechs has no idea of what CzSL is (and can not have it). In the Czech context, CzSL is usually confused with what is referred to as "signed speech". Within "signed speech courses" lists of individual (manual) "signs" and their usage in the word-order structure of Czech sentences are taught hand in hand. The ideal, then, is the equivalence of "one word = one sign". This way, hearing Czechs can become, at most, acquainted with frozen manual signs – they will not get to know anything about the productive morphology or grammar of Czech sign language – or did not get to know them until recently. So generally it is a rule that hearing Czechs cannot share sign language with their deaf fellow-citizens; for them CzSL is something "strange", "unfamiliar", "unintelligible", even in these days.

For deaf Czechs, written Czech is similarly "strange", "unfamiliar", "unintelligible" (Macurová, 1998). The reasons are obvious: The teaching of Czech is mostly based on the "knowledge" of spoken Czech and, moreover, it is built upon the precondition that a deaf child understands the relation between phonemes and graphemes. The structures of (written) Czech are not correlated in any way with the structures of CzSL (nor is it possible when hearing teachers of the Czech language have no idea of CzSL). The meta-linguistic reflection of the language/languages is not developed. A language is – again – reduced to its vocabulary (the opinion that "the deaf do not know Czech since they have a small vocabulary" is widespread and diffused). CzSL is not even used as a means for teaching communication during the teaching of Czech. The language deficiency of those deaf children (usually from hearing families) who only had learnt to articulate several Czech words in the period before the written language has not been considered at all. Nor is the social and cognitive deficit of the deaf, as well as the deficit of information, taken into consideration, despite its being essential for the acquisition of written Czech (compare, e.g. inference ability). In this situation, deaf Czechs obviously cannot share written Czech with the hearing ones.

The situation where languages are not shared is changing very slowly, perhaps also with a contribution from Czech linguistics, which began to take an interest in communication of the deaf only in 1993. Even then it was obvious that deaf communication poses many interesting problems for both linguistics and the related disciplines. To designate these problems, determine their origins and the extent of their effects, or possibly to decide about the order of their urgency, is not so easy (and is often not a problem of linguistics only).

The optimal situation would obviously be to grasp and describe communication of the deaf in all its extents and forms. Two extensive fields can be identified here. The first includes (1) intra-cultural communication (among the deaf) and inter-cultural communication (the deaf with the hearing). It transverses the second one, where (2) "signed" communication (or possibly also a "rival" spoken one) and written communication are established.

A clearly outlined "assignment" is of course complicated, above all by attitudes. The attitudes of "hearing" linguistics and the attitudes of the community of the deaf itself (attitudes towards CzSL and attitudes to its description) enter the fray. Both these types of attitudes cloud the demarked range of problems and complicate a seemingly clear assignment.

I think that there were no such opinions in Czech linguistics compared to those formulated in Slovakia at the beginning of the 1990s, during the period of Czechoslovakia, which held: "It shall be necessary to try to create a Slovak sign system – signed Slovak

– in order to match its language organization to the Slovak of the speaking population" (Groma - Dočkal, 1992). Czech linguistics does not want to "create a signed system", nor to adjust it to the "Czech of the speaking population" – and it prefers description to prescription. Nevertheless, Czech linguistics also has to pose the question as to what should be described at all (and maybe, sometime in the future, shall be described).

The answer seems to be simple at first glance: CzSL should be described. What is more complicated is an answer to the question: And what is CzSL at all? It is well known that the structures and the function of every signed language are, to a great extent, determined by the fact that it is a minority language existing in the hearing world, in close proximity to the "stronger" majority language. It is also well known that the variability of signed language, especially in grammar, is closely connected with the means of its existence.

The phenomenon of diglossia (the existence of two or more separate varieties of the same language specialized for formal and informal functions and distinguished by linguistic and social characterizations - dictionary, phonology and grammar, usage, prestige, acquisition, standardization) has been mentioned in connection with American Sign Language by Stokoe (1969). I am deliberately leaving out "post-Stokoe" opinions, where the so-called "diglossic continuum" is considered and where features typical for pidgin are identified in the intermediate varieties of the continuum or where the so-called post-Creole continuum is considered, etc. (compare Woodward, Lawson, Fischer, etc.). The precondition of the existence of (only) two varieties of signing ("high" and "low") will clearly differentiate the attitudes that the Czech deaf take toward them.

There exist, of course, the Czech deaf who do not think about CzSL at all - and there are more than a few of them. Among the handful of those that think about their language, two clear-cut attitudes clash at present. Taken in a simplified way, these attitudes are as follows:

Some of the Czech deaf represent, with their attitudes towards signing, a direct pattern of the "diglossia situation". The variety closer to the majority language (manual Czech?) is considered by them to be superior (to CzSL), the variety further away from the majority language is considered by them to be "inaccurate", "ugly" articulation. When being asked about the structures of CzSL different from Czech, they admit that "some deaf people use them", but they do not consider them to be "correct". What is referred to by this group of the deaf as "inaccurate", or "wrong", is evidently that which keeps signing apart from the majority language, for example, simultaneous constructions or the constructions using space in the service of grammar – and actually everything where the equivalence "word-sign" does not work. Nevertheless, the language attitudes and opinions expressed by these members of the deaf community are neither always nor consistently in agreement with their real language behavior – they do not use - always and methodically - higher varieties of signing themselves, not in the least within intra-cultural communication.

Younger and somewhat linguistically educated deaf people (since 1998, in the program of the Faculty of Arts and Philosophy – Czech in the communication of the deaf) have especially rejected the contact varieties between CzSL and Czech and their attitude to "higher" signing (to manual Czech?) is unequivocally negative. Not even their language attitudes are – and cannot be, considering their "oral" past – consistent with their actual language behavior. Similarly, their usage of language tends to be in conflict with their attitudes to language, in inter-cultural communication in particular they often use the higher varieties, even though they refuse them in their proclamations.

Nevertheless, the proclaimed "positive" attitudes of the Czech deaf towards CzSL themselves carry a certain weight. Through the reflection of the language as a value, they indicate a gradual change in the self-reflection of the Czech deaf, their seeking of an identity in the hearing world.

Within this world everything that is already standard in some other countries is pushed forward very slowly. Only step by step does CzSL become respected as a language embedded in the minor culture. Only gradually do its dissimilarities from the majority language become accepted and only step by step is it being admitted that CzSL could be comparable with Czech from the viewpoint of its functions. Even in this "period of changes" it is clear that linguistically informed native users of CzSL, more than anyone else, can contribute to changing the attitudes of the hearing majority. More than anyone else they can also contribute to the "discovery" of their own language.

Native users cannot be replaced in another, wider context, this is only now being established in the Czech Republic, step by step. The issue is not only the discovery of CzSL or about the understanding based on the sharing of language. It is also the sharing of everything that is "under" the language, what in the language refers to culture, to the world (and how this process works). In other words, it is a matter of the problems that cognitive linguistics focuses on (and which are opened within Czech linguistics, also in regard to the context of the phenomenological philosophy by Vaňková, 1999, 2001).

Up to this time sign linguistics has been concentrated on describing the language from two aspects: structural linguistics has described language as a structure, a system of hierarchically arranged levels; linguistics focused on communication has concentrated on language as a means of communication, as a requirement for fulfilling the intents of communication and reaching the aims of communication. Cognitive linguistics lays emphasis on a different aspect: on the interconnection of a language with thinking (and understanding), on the human conceptions of the world closely connected with language (or languages) and articulated through it (for details, see Vaňková, 2001).

In connection with signed languages, the cognitive-linguistic aspect highlights a number of questions; in many respects these questions are completely different from those posed so far. I shall mention only some of them here – although I cannot answer them.

How does the CzSL conceptualize reality – and how does it interpret this reality? What world view is constructed with CzSL and in CzSL? To what extent is the linguistic picture of the world in the Czech community of the deaf comparable to the linguistic picture of the world of hearing Czechs?

In some respects it shall undoubtedly be the same: generally it is thought (Johnson, 1987; Lakoff-Johnson, 1980) that every human creature's relation to reality is given partly by his or her very being ("the body in the mind"), partly by his or her ability to imagine ("the metaphors we live by"). In something it shall differ – e.g. in the different perceptual experience of hearing and deaf human beings. Based on different perceptual experiences, the difference in constructing the so-called mental spaces shall unwind, because: "Mental spaces are constructed from human perceptual experience and are extended through imaginative mapping processes. The three most significant processes are metaphor, metonomy, and blends." (Janda, 2000, p. 12). And what about these imaginative mapping processes themselves? Shall they agree with both the hearing and the deaf?

Similarly, how are the basic types of metaphors - orientational, ontological, structural metaphors – exhibited in CzSL? To what extent is e.g. the nature of the orientational metaphor (which is the extension of orientations such as IN/OUT, UP/DOWN, FRONT/BACK to non-spatial domains) different in CzSL? Is the spatial organization of signed language of any importance in this context? It is certainly necessary to take the structural and functional roles of metaphor into account, i.e. its part in productive morphology (Brennan, 1990). Apart from that, the metaphor also represents a way to grasp the world in the sense illustrated by an analysis of the English phrase *falling in love*. It uses all three types of metaphor: "an orientational metaphor extending the use of *in,* an ontological metaphor identifying love as a place, and a structural metaphor that maps our understanding of physical falling onto our understanding of an initial encounter with love" (Janda, 2000, p. 12). A matter of the same interest is e.g. the correlating of source and target metaphor domains. Are time, emotions and states of being the usual target domains also in CzSL? Or, similarly: how are different metaphor types used in Czech sign language grammar – and are they used (maybe?) in a different way than in Czech grammar (where e.g. an orientational metaphor is connected with cases, prepositional constructions, prefixes)?

Another large circle of questions is connected with the problem of categorization: How does CzSL categorize? How are the (linguistics and/or cognitive) categories motivated by a "prototype", how are they organized "around it"?, and so on and so forth.

These all are questions that interest, in relation to Czech, the other side, the Czech deaf, as well. Many things are surprising and completely new for them – e.g. the Czech hearing world view presented in Czech phraseology or the ways of grasping abstract concepts in Czech.

For example, one of the possible "Czech" conceptualizations of fortune (described by Vaňková, 2001): "…it is a living being (a female being – compare personified fortune – Fortune), who is beautiful, but *changeable, fickle,* and so on. Fortune can give us a *smile –* or even *smile at us,* we can *grasp fortune by the hair,* it can *meet* us or *turn us its back, leave* us, and so on. (And sometimes we say: *As fortune goes around, sometimes it sits on a moron*)." A question, of course, comes up in this context: what is the situation in conceptualizing fortune in CzSL? This we can learn only from native speakers of CzSL – the linguistic picture of the world is "built" on their (and only their) conception of the world.

The conceptualization of fortune in Czech was surprising for the Czech deaf. Many things from this field shall be quite surely new and surprising for hearing Czechs – provided that we start to care methodically about the linguistic picture of the world among the Czech deaf and that we learn – via native speakers of CzSL – something about it.

The "detection" of the cognitive structures hidden under both languages, CzSL and Czech (and every signed language and relevant spoken language) will result in our stronger mutual understanding – an understanding of people living in two different languages, people with a dual cultural background, people living in two different worlds: in one of them, meanings are carried by sound, and in the other not.

Bibliography:

Brennan, M. (1990): Productive Morphology in British Sign Language. Focus on the Role of Metaphors. In: Prillwitz, S. - Vollhaber, T. (eds.): Current Trends in European Sign Language Research. Proceedings of the Third Congress on Sign Language Research. Hamburg, July 26-29, 1989. Hamburg: Signum-Verl., p. 205-228.

Groma, M. - Dočkal, V. (1992): Posunková reč nepočujúcich. Psychológia a patopsychológia dieťata 26.. Príloha k č. 2, s. 1-15.

Janda, L. (2000): Cognitive Linguistics. Http://www.indiana.edu/~slavconf/SLING2K//pospapers/janda.pdf.

Johnson, M. (1987): The Body in the Mind. The Bodily Basis of Meaning, Imagination, and Reason. Chicago - London: University of Chicago Press.

Lakoff, G. - Johnson, M. (1980): Metaphors We Live By. Chicago - London: University of Chicago Press.

Macurová, A. (1998): Naše řeč? Naše řeč 81, s. 179-188.

Stokoe, W. (1969): Sign Language Diglossia. Studies in Linguistics, vol. 20, s. 27-41.

Vaňková, I. (1999): Člověk a jazykový obraz (přirozeného) světa. Slovo a slovesnost 60, p. 214-224.

Vaňková, I. (2001): Domov v řeči. Mateřský jazyk jako (společný) obraz světa (in print).

"NAŠ" I "NJIHOV" JEZIK: PROBLEMI RAZUMIJEVANJA MEĐU KULTURAMA

Međusobno razumijevanje kulture čujućih i kulture gluhih Čeha pojavljuje se polako, korak po korak. Nije ni čudo kad jedan od glavnih uvjeta svakog razumijevanja nije ispunjen: sudionici komunikacije ne dijele zajednički jezik. Čujuća većina nema pristup "pravom" češkom znakovnom jeziku, gluha manjina nema potpun pristup pisanom češkom jeziku. U radu se govori o sociolingvističkim faktorima koji doprinose ovoj situaciji, pogotovo o stavovima prema jeziku/jezicima. Također, u radu se govori o pitanju "svjetskog gledišta", lingvističkog prikaza svijeta - i dotiče temu "običnog svijeta" gluhih i čujućih. Razmatrajući te probleme međukulturalno razumijevanje nalazi mjesto u kontekstu kognitivne lingvistike.

Ključne riječi: *znakovni jezik, sociolingvistika, međukulturalno razumijevanje*

DIVERSITY AND IDENTITY: IMPLICATIONS FOR DEAF EDUCATION

Ila Parasnis

Department of Research, National Technical Institute for the Deaf,
Rochester Institute of Technology, Rochester, NY, USA

Abstract

The educational experiences of deaf students can be enhanced if teachers, counselors, and other professionals provide a supportive environment that respects individual differences as well as sociocultural differences within the deaf student population. The sociocultural model of deafness views deaf people as a bilingual-bicultural minority group in a hearing society. In this paper the advantages and limitations of this model will be reviewed briefly. The impact of diversity on the development of the self-identity and group-identity of deaf people will be discussed. In particular, the stages of identity development in racial/ethnic minority group members and issues related to bilingual-bicultural identity development will be discussed to show how this information can be useful in conceptualizing Deaf identity development. The role educators can play as agents of change along with the concept of hearing and deaf professionals as allies will also be discussed.

Key words: *deaf, identitiy, group-identity, self-identity, minority group*

Introduction

We need to take an interdisciplinary approach in understanding the experiences of deaf people. Information from disciplines other than deaf education such as minority education, multicultural education, communication studies that focus on cross-cultural research and inter-cultural communication, psychology, sociology, cultural anthropology, and sociolinguistics is directly relevant to the issue of effective accommodation of diversity in the educational process. I believe we need to knit together information from these disciplines so that we can appreciate the complex issue of how diversity influences identity and the educational experience.

We need more communication and a wider platform for presenting the many issues and diverse perspectives in our field. The common bond that unites us professionally is our attempt to enhance the educational experiences of deaf people. We need to remind ourselves of that common bond as our field continues to diversify. Many of us are frustrated by what we see as fragmented information. We have to remind ourselves that our field is multi-disciplinary in its approach and unless we try to weave together a meaningful pattern, a common thread will not easily emerge. We have to collectively put time and energy into determining where the points of connection and departure are in our diverse teaching and research interests in order to deepen our understanding of deaf education as a coherent educational process.

Later on I will discuss the specific role teachers can play as agents of change. It is also applicable to counselors, researchers, and other professionals involved in educating deaf people. I am using the term teacher in a very broad sense as someone who facilitates the educational process.

Sociocultural Model of Deafness

There has been a small revolutionary shift in deaf education away from the medical model of deaf people as disabled to the sociocultural model of deaf people as a minority group with its own language and culture (e.g. Johnson, Lidell, & Erting, 1989). Several books have been published discussing the sociocultural context in which deaf people live and its relevance for deaf education (e.g., Lane, 1992; Parasnis, 1996a). In general there is a growing interest in the field of deaf education in treating deaf children as bilingual-bicultural minority children although there is no clear consensus on what functional roles the Deaf community and American Sign Language (ASL) can play in the psychosocial development of deaf children and how relevant these are to deaf education. The heterogeneity of the deaf community, the diversity of the educational and social experiences of deaf children, and differing philosophical perspectives regarding the use of a spoken language in teaching deaf children are some of the factors that contribute to the dissent among the educators. Perhaps, there is no one representative concept of a deaf child that can satisfy everyone's concerns. But then again, there is no fundamental need to have one in these increasingly pluralistic times.

The crucial question is not whether all deaf children can be viewed as bilingual-bicultural minority children, but whether many can be viewed as such, and whether this construct has any explanatory power that is different from the construct of a deaf child as a disabled child. For example, the strong deaf community ties and the pride in ASL that many deaf people develop are not easily explained by the disability model but make sense with the sociocultural model.

As I have noted before (Parasnis, 1997), this model is often contrasted sharply with the medical model and the debate centers around the question of whether hearing status should be considered an innate physical characteristic exhibiting variation such as race or color, or whether deafness should be viewed as a disability. This debate creates an unnecessary and artificial dichotomy because issues of medical management or social support services are made to appear orthogonal to issues of minority status and minority rights. Deaf people may need to utilize adaptive equipment and special services such as hearing aids, FM systems, and ASL interpreters to overcome the barriers to spoken communication used by the majority of the society. However, this does not mean that they don't have a legitimate right to be considered a culturally and linguistically diverse group. Alternative means are often used to overcome communication barriers such as providing interpreters at an international conference without questioning the sociocultural identity of the speakers.

The advantage of using the sociocultural model of deafness to guide educational and research activities rather than a disability model is that it emphasizes the documentation of differences rather than deficiencies. Deafness is seen within this model as a variation rather than as a pathology. I have discussed elsewhere the importance of using a sociocultural model of deafness in deaf education in more detail (see Parasnis, 1996b;1997;1998; Samar, Parasnis, & Berent, 1998).

Diversity

Let us examine the issue of diversity in understanding the experiences of deaf people. Diversity leads to multiple group affiliations. These group affiliations influence how we interact with each other, perceive ourselves and are perceived by others. People who have multicultural or multilingual backgrounds often belong to more than one group and feel marginalized as they move between several groups. Marginalization is a process that occurs when you do not hold a core membership in a group. As a sociological term it does not imply negative consequences but it is often seen as having negative consequences because each group trying to preserve its identity defines what is normal for that group and generally believes that their way is superior compared to others. People who move in and out of different groups are conscious of these differing group values and group-identity requirements.

Many deaf people belong to more than one cultural group. Since 90% of deaf people are born to hearing parents and many acquire sign language and Deaf culture later in life it is easy to argue that many of them are affiliated with at least two groups: the Deaf culture and the Hearing culture. Many of them will thus be marginalized in both cultures (Glickman & Carey, 1993).

What needs to be pointed out here is that psychological hurt can occur when people realize they cannot be the core members of a group they admire. Sometimes they cannot be core members of any group such as deaf children of hearing parents.

When a group is as heterogeneous as deaf people are, we have to stop and ask ourselves what we mean by core membership in the first place. For example, considering the evolutionary history of Deaf culture and ASL use in the US, deaf native ASL signers appear to be the correct group for defining the core of the Deaf group. However, in planning educational programs and policies this definition of the core group characteristics is limiting because the majority of deaf people seeking education, who are not born to deaf parents and are not native ASL users, are then marginalized. What is the best way to conceptualize a representative deaf student? There is no easy answer to that question. However, I wish to point out that the question is similar to what any multilingual multicultural society faces.

Identity Development

Self-identity and group-identity
Let us now examine the general issue of identity development in deaf people. We all develop self-identity and group-identity. For some of us identity issues have not been well articulated. For some of us these issues have been in the forefront of our struggle to receive equal opportunity and equal rights. Self-identity is not a static concept. It is a dynamic concept influenced by psychological, situational, and relational variables.

An exercise often used in multicultural workshops is to ask the participants to define who they are in one sentence each (Adams, Bell, & Griffin, 1997). The point of this exercise is to show how difficult it is for some of us to define who we are. It is a sociopolitical statement and it has a psychological impact on many of us. Whether you belong to the dominant majority culture or whether you belong to a minority group apparently influences the ease with which you can state your identity.

According to Steele (1990), Tatum (1997) and Cross (1991), group-identity is something you are often aware of when you belong to a minority group. What happens is that you carry within you the knowledge that you have an individual identity but you are also a representative of your minority group to the rest of the world. Many minority group members use a hyphenated identity to refer to themselves such as African-Americans, Asian-Americans or Deaf-Americans. People use such a label when they feel that one group-identity does not capture who they are. It is not a fragmented identity. It is in fact an assertion that the individual is more than his or her local cultural group.

In different situations at different times different people have different identities. All of those multiple identities are valid and they need to be recognized. As educators of deaf people, we have to be aware that identity is a complex issue. It is not static. By labeling a person's identity as belonging to one group, you may not capture the complexity of what they go through in their daily lives when they interact with different people.

Identity development is influenced by many factors such as hearing status, language use, race/ethnicity, socioeconomic status, gender, sexual orientation, and religion. These factors also influence how other people perceive us.

Hearing status is an important factor in development of the Deaf identity. However, hearing status is not solely determined by hearing loss. One's attitude toward deafness and not necessarily one's degree of hearing loss is very important in determining hearing status, as Padden and Humphries ((1988) have illustrated.

Language use is another important factor. Again it is not necessarily fluency in ASL, but the acceptance of ASL use or of sign language use in daily life that seems critical in developing a Deaf identity (e. g. Kannapell, 1994). Attitudes toward speech and spoken languages, language used at home, and parental hearing status are also considered important in the development of Deaf identity.

Minority Identity

Race and ethnicity play a large role in identity development. However, race and ethnicity have been considered less important in the identity development of Deaf people. The common belief is that the Deaf community considers being deaf as the primary determinant of their group-identity. However, according to Arumboro (1989) and Brooks (1996), Black American deaf people perceive themselves as Black first and Deaf second. Similar findings were reported by Honda (1999) for Black, Asian and Hispanic Deaf Americans. Again, the question of identity is not simple and has several layers.

There are various models of identity development in ethnic-minority children (e.g. Cross, 1991; Tatum, 1997) that are applicable in understanding the diversity of the Deaf experience. Here I will mention the model originally developed by Atkinson, Morgan, and Sue (1979) and discussed by Sue & Sue (1990). This model suggests that there are five stages of identity development: Conformity, dissonance, resistance, introspection, and synergy.

Yacobacci-Tam (1987) and Holcomb (1997) have applied this model to the bicultural experiences of deaf children. It has definite implications for counseling a culturally diverse deaf child. It should be noted though that the model does not predict how and when an individual will progress through these stages. More research is needed to understand how deaf children develop their identities.

Let me note here in passing that accepting racial/ethnic or Deaf identity is a complex issue and it is related to the issue of perceived oppression. Labeling a student by his/her racial/ethnic group or by his/her hearing status can turn out to be detrimental for student's success as it can create a "stereotype threat". Claude Steele and his colleagues (Steele, 1999) have shown that Black students do worse on IQ tests when they are told that the test will test their abilities. This information is quite useful for teachers who may consider labeling students as a positive step for celebrating their diversity.

Bilingual-bicultural Identity

Along with racial and ethnic identity, there is also a bilingual-bicultural identity that a person can develop. One important experience many deaf people have, particularly deaf people born to hearing parents, is that they become bilingual as they grow older and come in contact with the larger deaf community. This experience has important implications for their identity development. Many deaf people can be considered bilingual and bicultural if we follow Francois Grosjean's definitions of bilingualism and biculturalism (Grosjean, 1982).

Grosjean (1982) defines bilingualism as the regular use of two or more languages in everyday life. The strength of this definition is that it presents bilingualism on a continuum that includes people varying in their linguistic knowledge, fluency, and the age of acquisition. It also recognizes that bilinguals acquire and use each language for different purposes, with different people, and in different domains of life. Grosjean (1982) defines biculturalism as coexistence and/or combination of two distinct cultures. The strength of this definition is that it recognizes that people live in two or more cultures, adapt to each culture to some extent, and sometimes blend aspects of each culture. Formal knowledge and acceptance of each culture or being born bicultural are not considered to be necessary criteria.

I suggest that we use these definitions in understanding the experiences of deaf people as a bilingual-bicultural minority group.

I also suggest that we consider defining a Deaf person as one who has both a self-identity and a group-identity as a Deaf person. This definition at first glance seems tautological but it is not. The strength of this definition is that it allows us to examine a broad range of culturally and linguistically diverse experiences deaf people have because it s not tied to the age of acquisition of ASL, the age of onset of deafness, parental hearing status, educational background, or the severity of hearing loss. It is tied to the acceptance of a Deaf identity by the person and the acceptance of his/her identity in the Deaf community. This definition of a deaf person allows us to validate and support the identity struggle of a variety of deaf people. It is inclusive and psychologically empowering.

Similarly, I suggest that we view Deaf people as having a co-culture, a concept often used in the field of multicultural education. Co-cultures are social communities that exhibit communication characteristics, perceptions, values, beliefs, and practices that are different enough to distinguish them from other groups, communities, and the dominant culture. This concept allows us to move away from the discussion of whether deaf people belong to a culture, or community or sub-culture, etc.

Deaf people display bilingual and bicultural behavior documented in hearing people such as code switching, lexical borrowing, making language choices when discussing different domains, having discourse style differences based on language choice, and choosing appropriate non-verbal gestures specific to that language. They also display bicultural behaviors such as adapting to different cultural expectations and blending both cultures. Research on bilingualism-biculturalism in hearing people related to the issues of cognitive advantages, metalinguistic awareness, valorization, language learning and language teaching is directly relevant and applicable to many issues in deaf education. The bi-bi approach to deaf education will be enhanced by considering this body of literature (e.g. Cummins, 1984; Hall & Hall, 1990; Hamers & Blanc, 1990, Parasnis, 1996a).

Challenges for Deaf Education

Acknowledging the complexity of the situation for providing optimal educational experiences to diverse students is the first step we need to take in deaf education to change institutional policies and practices. A common reaction is to consider the diversity issue as a political issue or a minority issue that does not have direct day-to-day relevance in the classroom for the business of imparting objective knowledge. However, education is also a process of enculturation of children. We generally transmit the traditional established knowledge passed from generation to generation that is heavily influenced by the dominant culture in which it is taught and learned. We also reflect the attitudes of the dominant culture toward that knowledge in the teaching-learning process.

What we have to remember is that students who come from minority groups within a dominant culture learn different sets of rules of behavior to function successfully and educators need to develop an understanding that cultural differences do exist and can influence learning styles, communication and relational styles. Cultural differences are also well documented in non-verbal communication (see Samovar, Porter, & Stefani, 1998) such as body behavior including postures, gestures, facial expression, eye contact, gaze, and touch. There are also cultural differences in understanding the concepts of personal space, perception of time, and how to interpret silence (Hall & Hall, 1990).

There are some common barriers to understanding different cultures or co-cultures. One is that it is often difficult to distinguish between individual differences and cultural differences when dealing with an individual student. Is someone shy because he or she comes from a different culture? Or is it just a personal idiosyncrasy? It is often difficult to determine how cultural values have influenced a specific behavior in a specific individual. Another barrier is our own ethnocentricity in interpreting our and other people's behavior. What we consider as objective often turns out to be defined by the subjective perspective of the group we identify with. A third major barrier is the language and dialect differences that exist among people that make cross-cultural communication often difficult to accomplish.

Although these barriers are difficult to overcome, educators of deaf people have to become invested in acknowledging and addressing cultural differences. Otherwise, many deaf students will feel marginalized as they go through the educational system and may not realize their optimal potential for success.

Teachers on an individual level can guard against their ethnocentrism by becoming aware that different behaviors have different connotations in different cultures and that major communication differences exist among different cultures.

However, an institutional commitment to such an agenda is needed to bring about a significant change in educational policies and programs related to diversity in deaf education. Unless there is a supportive institutional environment that accepts diversity, individual efforts to provide services to deaf students will have limited effectiveness.

Teachers as Agents of Change

I suggest that teachers and other professionals involved in deaf education act as agents of change. We need to consciously adopt a multicultural perspective in designing and implementing educational policies and services so that diversity becomes an integral part of curricular activities, co-curricular activities, and research. There are various ways by which this goal can be accomplished and various frameworks within which the change can occur.

One way teachers can begin is by knowing ourselves as instructors (Adams, Bell, & Griffin, 1997). Awareness of our social identities, confronting our own biases, acknowledging that we have doubts and ambivalence about our own competence, and a need for learner approval are some of the steps we can take to become more sensitive about diversity and its impact on us and the students we teach. Personal disclosures and using our own experience as example as well as negotiating authority issues are some of the strategies we can use in dealing with diverse students. Some other critical strategies are to consider the teaching-learning process as a continuum where a teacher is a master learner while a student is a novice learner, to use technology to facilitate communication and learning, and finally to empower students by discussing issues related to diversity with them honestly and openly. Becoming proactive allies is a powerful strategy to bring about change,

What is an ally? An ally is a person who takes a stand against social injustice directed at target groups. An ally takes responsibility for learning about their own and the target group's heritage, culture, and experience. An ally also listens to and respects the perspectives and experiences of target group members.

I suggest that we consider this concept which is used in the field of multicultural education for conceptualizing the contributions of hearing and deaf people in deaf education. It is an alternative to the usual in-group/out-group debate surrounding who should study the in-group and the hard feelings the debate creates on both sides. Note that this concept still allows us to maintain the in-group/out-group distinction commonly made in cross-cultural research (e.g. Banks, 1998) but simultaneously redefines this distinction in such a way that bridges can be built between researchers in the two groups. The ally concept has the advantage of having members of different groups work in harmony.

Conclusions

I conclude with two quotes that sum up for me this discussion.

"Not everything that is faced can be changed. But nothing can be changed until it is faced."
James Baldwin as quoted in Tatum (1997).

"The unity of civilization is not to be sought in uniformity but in harmony.....The faith of the future is in cooperation and not identification, in accommodation to fellow men and not imitation of them, in toleration and not absolutism."

S. Radhakrishnan as quoted in Parasnis (1996b).

References

Adams, M., Bell, L. A., & Griffin, P. (1997). Teaching for diversity and social justice. New York: Routledge.

Atkinson, D. R., Morten, G., & Sue, D. W. (1979). Counseling American minorities: A cross-cultural perspective. Dubuque, IA: William C. Brown.

Banks, J. A. (1998). The lives and values of researchers: Implications for educating citizens in a multicultural society. Educational Researcher, 27(7), 4-17.

Brooks, D. (1996). In search of self: Experiences of a postlingually deaf African-American. In I. Parasnis (Ed)., Cultural and language diversity and the deaf experience (pp. 246-257). New York: Cambridge University Press.

Cross, W. (1991). Shades of black: Diversity in African-American identity. Philadelphia: Temple University Press.

Cummins, J. (1984). Bilingualism and special education: Issues in assessment and pedagogy. San Diego, College-Hill Press.

Glickman, N. S., & Carey, J. C. (1993). Measuring deaf cultural identities: A preliminary investigation. Rehabilitation Psychology, 38, 275-277.

Grosjean, F. (1982). Life with two languages: An introduction to bilingualism.

Cambridge: Harvard University Press..

Hall. E. T., & Hall, M. (1990). Understanding cultural differences: Germans, French, and Americans. Yarmouth, ME: Intercultural Press.

Hamers, J., & Blanc, M. (1990). Bilinguality & bilingualism. Cambridge: Cambridge University Press.

Honda, H. (1999). Ethnic deaf identity. Unpublished doctoral dissertation. Columbia University.

Johnson, R., Lidell, S., & Erting, C. (1989). Unlocking the curriculum: Principles for achieving access in deaf education. Gallaudet Research Institute Working Paper 89 (3). Washington, DC: Gallaudet University Press.

Kannapell, B. (1994). Deaf identity: An American perspective. In C. J. Erting, R.C. Johnson, D. L. Smith, B. D. Snider (Eds.), The Deaf Way: Perspectives from the international conference on Deaf culture. Washington, D. C.: Gallaudet University Press.

Lane, H. (1992). The mask of benevolence: Disabling the deaf community. New York: Alfred A. Knopf, Inc.

Padden C., & Humphries, T. (1988). Deaf in America: Voices from a culture.

Cambridge: Harvard University Press.

Parasnis, I. (Ed). (1996a). Cultural and language diversity and the deaf experience. New York: Cambridge University Press.

Parasnis, I. (1996b). On interpreting the Deaf experience within the context of cultural and language diversity. In I. Parasnis (Ed.), Cultural and language diversity and the Deaf experience (pp. 3-19). New York: Cambridge University Press.

Parasnis, I. (1997). Cultural identity and diversity in deaf education. American Annals of the Deaf, 142, 72-79.

Parasnis, I. (1998). Cognitive diversity in deaf people: Implications for communication and education. Scandinavian Journal of Audiology, 27 (Supple 49), 109-115.

Samar, V. J., Parasnis, I., & Berent, J. (1998). Learning disabilities, attention deficit disorders, and deafness. In M. Marschark and M. D. Clark (Eds.), Psychological perspectives on deafness, Vol. 2 (pp. 199-242). Hillsdale, NJ: Lawrence Erlbaum.

Samovar, L., Porter, R., & Stefani, L. (1998). Communication between cultures (3rd Ed.). Albany, NY: Wadsworth Publishing Company.

Steele, S. (1990). The content of our character: A new vision of race in America. New York: St. Martin's Press.

Sue, D., & Sue, D. (1990). Counseling the culturally different: Theory and practice (2nd Ed.). New York: John Wiley and Sons.

Tatum, B. D. (1997). Why are all the black kids sitting together in the cafeteria? And other conversations about the race. New York: Basic Books.

Yacobacci-Tam, P. (1987). Interacting with the culturally different family. The Volta Review, 89 (5), 46-58.

RAZLIČITOST I IDENTITET: SMJERNICE ZA EDUKACIJU GLUHIH

Obrazovna iskustva gluhih učenika mogu se poboljšati ukoliko im nastavnici, savjetnici i drugi stručnjaci osiguraju pružanje podrške poštujući individualne i socio-kulturalne razlike koje postoje unutar populacije tih učenika. Socio-kulturalni model gluhoće poima gluhe pripadnicima bilingvalne-bikulturalne manjinske skupine u čujućem društvu. U radu su ukratko izložene prednosti i ograničenja ovog modela. Razmatra se i utjecaj raznolikosti na razvoj osobnog i grupnog identiteta u zajednici gluhih. Razmatraju se stadiji razvoja identiteta članova rasnih/etničkih manjina i pitanja povezana s razvojem dvojezičnog-dvokulturalnog identiteta, kako bi se ukazalo na način na koji se ove informacije mogu iskoristiti i za koncipiranje razvoja identiteta gluhih te uloga stručnjaka u tom pogledu.

Ključne riječi: osobni, grupni identitet, sociološki/kulturološki model gluhoće, manjinske skupine

ISSUES IN SIGN BILINGUAL EDUCATION

Susan Gregory

School of Education, University of Birmingham, UK

Abstract

Sign bilingual education can be described as 'an approach to the education of deaf children in which the language of the Deaf community (sign language) and the language of the hearing community (spoken and/or written language) are used. In the case of children from minority ethnic groups it is more appropriate to use the term "sign multi-lingualism" in order to recognise the position of additional home languages'. Sign bilingualism, as an approach the education of deaf children, was first introduced in the UK over ten years ago. A number of special and resourced schools now use this approach, although the decision as to whether it is adopted is made by the Local Education authority. This paper will look at the main features of sign bilingual education, the reasons it came about, and aspects of current practice. These will include issues relating to the use of sign language and the need for an appropriate assessment and curriculum, the teaching of literacy in a sign bilingual approach, the development of the curriculum and materials, working with families, and the training needs of staff. It will consider issues raised for the sign bilingual approach by developments in current educational practice, including the impact of cochlear implantation programmes with deaf children. It will also look at the changing nature of the Deaf community and the impact that this has on deaf education.

Key words: *sign language, bilingual education, deaf children, deafness*

Introduction

In this paper, I will describe and define sign bilingual education, discuss why it has come about and consider the goals of this approach. I will also talk about issues that arise in its implementation.

Sign bilingual education can be described as

An approach to the education of deaf children in which the language of the Deaf community (sign language) and the language of the hearing community (spoken and/or written language) are used. In the case of children from minority ethnic groups it is more appropriate to use the term 'sign multi-lingualism' in order to recognise the position of additional home languages.

Adapted from Pickersgill and Gregory 1998

We have chosen to call this approach 'sign bilingualism' rather than 'bilingualism' because we feel it differs in some significant ways from spoken language bilingualism. (Pickersgill and Gregory op cit)

Reasons for development of sign bilingual education for deaf pupils

1. Recognition of sign languages as full languages

Before the late 1960's and early 1970's, sign languages were not seen as proper languages but as crude system of mime and gesture. This is despite the fact that these languages had been used for many years by deaf people, see, for example, the description by Augustine AD 354 – 430. The first documentation of sign language in the UK was by Bulwer 1644. Recognition came first in the USA, in the 1960s, through the work of Stokoe, and Mary Brennan coined the term British Sign Language or BSL in 1976 for the sign language used by the Deaf community in the UK. This recognition meant that for the first time, the use of sign language in education became a possibility.

2. Poor attainments under the oral approach

At the time that sign languages were being recognised as true languages, oralism was the dominant approach in the education of deaf children. However, dissatisfaction with oralism was growing. Many countries reported studies showing the poor attainments of deaf pupils.

In the UK, the most important study was carried out by Conrad who looked at a cohort of deaf school leavers in the 1970's. He found that deaf pupils leaving school had a median reading age of 9, poor speech intelligibility and lip-reading skills no better than those of the hearing population, despite their training in this area. (Conrad 1979) Such poor achievements were also demonstrated in other studies from other countries.

A recent interview study by myself and two colleagues, of a non-selected sample of deaf young people, found that 1 in 7 did not have adequate linguistic skills in any language to participate in an interview. These were all young people born in the late 1960's and educated under the oral system. (Gregory, Bishop and Sheldon 1995)

3. Success of deaf children of deaf parents

In research into the attainments of deaf pupils, carried out in the 1970s and 80s, a number indicated that deaf children of deaf parents were more successful academically than those with hearing parents. These results emerged in studies of reading, writing and academic achievement and, in some instances, spoken language. Attributing this to the early use of sign language in these families lead to the conclusion that sign language could be beneficial in the education of deaf children.

The issue is, of course, more complex that this. For example, some have argued that this greater achievement could be because the deafness of deaf children of deaf parents was due to genetic, rather than other causes which were more like to be associated with other additional disabilities. Alternatively, or in addition, it may be that deaf parents are better at establishing the general pre-linguistic skills that are essential for later language development and this facilitates higher levels of attainment. However, at very least it can be said that the early use of sign language with deaf children does not **inhibit** intellectual and linguistic development.

4. Preferred language of deaf school leavers

In the study of young people already mentioned, it was shown that at the time they were interviewed, 38% used British Sign Language (BSL) as their preferred or only language demonstrating a significant role for this language in their lives.

5. Changing ideas of bilingualism in general

In many countries, in the 1960s, bilingualism was seen as a disadvantage rather than an advantage. Pupils who used more than one language were seen to be under additional pressure, or in a confusing situation. For example, in the UK in the1960s, there was a rise in immigration of families with a range of different first languages, and the initial reaction was to assert that the mother tongue or home language was a disadvantage which could confuse and inhibit development. The children were labelled as 'non-English speakers' and research seemed to show poorer attainments in pupils from other language using communities.

However, this finding was overturned by the work of a number of researchers including Cummins in Canada. He showed that for children using French and English bilingualism could be an advantage. Language development was not inhibited and greater cognitive flexibility was achieved in some tasks (Cummins 1978). This changed the dominant view of bilingualism as a disadvantage.

Goals of bilingual education

1.   To enable deaf children to become linguistically competent
2.   To provide access to a wide curriculum
3.   To facilitate good literacy skills
4.   To provide deaf pupils with a positive sense of themselves and of their own identity

These goals are probably the same as those for education for deaf pupils in general, but have a greater emphasis on self-esteem and identity.

Issues in bilingual education

Sign bilingualism was first introduced in the UK in 1989, and more places have adopted the approach since then. At first, teachers were delighted to have pupils with whom they could communicate easily. It seemed to offer greater possibilities for the education of deaf pupils in terms of literacy development and access to the wider curriculum.

However, many people now realise that it is not that straightforward, that sign bilingual education raises complex issues of educational practice, training and administration that need to be addressed. This is not an expression of the failure of the bilingual approach or of the need to dilute it, but recognition of the work needed to progress further.

I will mention eleven issues that occur to me, some in more detail than others. These arise from both research and practice. In discussing these, I shall draw on the study we carried out at the Open University which followed 25 children of 7 - 9 years of age over a period of one year. The researchers in that project were Sandra Smith and Alison Wells and the participating groups were the Deaf and Hearing-Impaired Support Service, Leeds, and the Royal School for the Deaf, Derby.

Theoretical concepts

1. Critical periods for language development

One of the arguments for sign bilingualism derives from the fact that there may well be a critical period for language acquisition, that if language is not acquired at a particular time it will never develop fully. The discussions around critical periods are complex, but certainly exposure to language during the early years of life would seem essential for the development of full linguistic competence. Results from cochlear implantation with young children may well illuminate this topic further.

2. What is transferred in sign bilingual education?

The basic premise in sign bilingual education is that knowledge of L1 (the first language) can facilitate the development of L2, (spoken/written language). This notion arose from work of Cummins among others - the linguistic interdependence model.

But when we consider the bilingual development of deaf pupils, questions arise as to what is transferred. Where there are two spoken languages it is argued that the speech skills in one language facilitate the development of speech skills in the other or, more unusually, literacy skills in one language facilitates the development of literacy skills in the other. Bilingual education with deaf children assumes there can be a transfer of skills from signing in, for example BSL, to reading and writing in the spoken /written language, English, but there is no evidence from other languages to suggest that such transfer is possible.

However that is not to suggest that transfer cannot take place. There could be a general linguistic competence such the early development of language is itself important regardless of modality. There is informal evidence for, as previously described, deaf children of deaf parents are reported as having better language skills than deaf children of hearing parents. This could imply some linguistic transfer is possible.

Issues arising from the use of sign language

3. Facilitating sign language development in children

Our research project suggested that, in a sign bilingual approach, pupils achieved good communication in sign language but not all were developing the linguistic structures necessary to address the more complex concepts of higher level education.

When we consider the language models available this may not be surprising. Most young deaf children have hearing parents, thus they acquire their sign language from people who are themselves still learning it. At school most of their teachers will be hearing and thus, although they may have good signing skills, they are not native users of the language. In addition, those deaf people, who work in schools and are native users of the language, may adjust their signing to take account of the hearing people with whom they work. In addition, the other children with whom they come into contact are mostly in the same position and thus they do not always provide good models of the language.

In the past, we have assumed that exposure to sign language was enough and the fact that pupils picked it up so quickly endorsed that view. However, if we are to develop deaf pupils signing to a high level in order that they may have access to the complex ideas within the curriculum we may need to develop specific teaching methods for the teaching of sign language. It is salutary to compare the attention paid to teaching BSL to deaf pupils, with that paid to teaching English to hearing pupils in school in the UK.

4. The sign language curriculum

In order to facilitate the development of sign language and to teach it effectively, we need a sign language curriculum, but this needs to be based on research which currently does not exist. In the UK, we do not know enough about the normal process of BSL development in children, although recent work by Bencie Woll and her colleagues at City University is contributing to our understanding in this area. We need to know this in order to develop a curriculum, to stretch BSL skills, and to correct errors appropriately.

Research in this area is complex as a proper research project would be based on children who were native users of sign language learning from native users of sign language, which means we are looking for two if not three generations of deafness in the family. This must be a priority when we are looking at the research required to support bilingual education.

5. Assessing sign language development

In order to facilitate the acquisition of sign language skills in children, we must also have ways of assessing their development. This too is dependent on research which charts the normal development of the sign language of deaf children acquiring it as a first language from native users of the particular language.

Currently, in the UK, much assessment that is carried out is inevitably based on procedures for considering pupils' English language skills but this is not appropriate. We know, for example, that English assessments often focus on use of tense or prepositions but these are realised differently in BSL and may well have a different place in the development of the language.

In the UK, assessing BSL development is not only important in developing children's skills but in order to demonstrate the progress of children in sign bilingual education. At times, the major significant development of pupils in a period is in their use of BSL. Unless we have evidence of this we cannot expect their progress to be recognised either within the system, or in the formal inspection and appraisal assessment systems that are currently in operation.

6. Intervention in the early years

If we are to achieve age appropriate language we must start with children as young as possible. Our research showed that most pupils arrived at school with limited skills in both BSL and English and the initial work with them had to focus on basic language development. Inevitably this set them behind their hearing peers. Our aim should be to achieve age appropriate language on school entry so that deaf pupils can fully access the curriculum.

In the UK, there are now a few initiatives in pre-school provision for deaf children. These are all slightly different in emphasis but represent a growing concern about the early years period. Research from other countries indicates similar concerns and currently pre-school work is the focus of new developments in a number of places including Holland and Russia.

7. Working with parents

Art of the work in the pre-school period must be working with parents to develop early language skills. When the parents are hearing and the language is sign language particular issues can arise. Working in Bristol Young studied the way in which deaf adults were introduced into homes to facilitate the development of BSL. One of the important questions she considered was the appropriate language expectations of hearing parents whose children are being educated bilingually. She suggested that it is not BSL skills per se that were seen by the deaf tutors as critical but the overall attitude to deafness and communication (Young, 1995).

Curriculum and assessment issues

8. Reading, writing and speech

It seems clear to me that the main way in which sign bilingual education will be assessed is in terms of achievement in the dominant spoken/written language, and particularly literacy which makes this a crucial area for these programmes.

Our research suggested that for the pupils it was easier to focus on writing rather than reading at the early stages. There seems a possible explanation for this observation. For a deaf child whose first language is sign language, writing allows them to think in their first language and control the use of the second as they choose the elements to be written down. Reading on the other hand means that they have to work from their second language where they have not direct control over the material, and they translate back into their first language. Of course, many approaches to reading recognise this and ensure that the child's first reading is of material he or she has prepared themselves.

In our research, our analysis of English written work suggested that many of the errors deaf children made related to the structure of BSL suggesting that this had an influence on this skill. Rather than seeing this as a disadvantage or problem, we suggested that it could be facilitative in that the first language, BSL, may be used to discuss and develop the second language, English (Gregory, Wells and Smith 1995).

Reading raises a number of questions as to what language should be used, is the use of voice essential, can a child read directly in sign language or must they produce some form of the written language first.

Within the development of some sign bilingual programmes, speech has, in the past, been given a low profile. Some approaches prefer an emphasis on general communication skill with hearing people, where speech is one of a range of strategies to use with hearing people. However in the UK, more consideration is now being given to the role of speech and how it should be encouraged and taught. Discussion of speech skills is easier, as pupils have command of BSL and thus a language in which to discuss the issues around voice and speaking. The impact of increasing numbers of children with cochlear implants in schools has raised issues in this area, which are likely to result in more systematic approaches to the development of speech.

9. Developing curriculum areas and resources

For hearing children, the vast majority of materials to support the curriculum are available in written form, although increasing use of computers and associated technology may change this. Sign bilingual programmes need to consider how the resources to support the curriculum can be developed. This is likely to require the development of materials on video or CD ROM which pupils can access and use themselves.

10. Assessment of bilingual children

Once the right of deaf pupils to be educated in sign language, which for some of them will be their preferred language, has been recognised, it follows that some will request or require to be assessed in sign language at all levels of their schooling, including public examinations. This may well involve the use of video and the marking of video presentations.

This raises a number of questions. How should sign language be used in assessments and how can its use be evaluated? Is it appropriate to use it at the higher levels as most resources at this level are in written language and students will need written language competence to access the majority of the material which supports this curriculum?

Training issues

11. Training to work in bilingual settings

In order for sign bilingual education to continue to develop, the number of courses which train people to work in a bilingual way will need to increase. However, in many countries it remains difficult for deaf people to enter the teaching profession.

There is also a need for further clarification on the training that is needed for assistants and support workers in the classroom, both deaf and hearing.

Evaluation of bilingual programmes

There has been little evaluation of bilingual programmes in the UK and only limited research from those countries who have had bilingual programmes for longer. Both Sweden and Denmark have carried out some evaluation which suggests that bilingual education is successful in developing literacy skills as well as the sign language of their community. However, in he UK and other countries, there are a number of difficulties of evaluation in deaf education. Control groups not feasible where it is not possible to compare groups of pupils in bilingual programmes with groups in different programmes. Often the reason they are in the various programmes (for example they may only be placed in sign bilingual settings if they have failed in oral settings), means they are likely to differ from each other in significant ways that could affect the results of the study. There is a further problem in that the aims of bilingual education may differ in emphasis from oral/aural education and social and emotional aspects may be given more status.

Current challenges

1.Inclusion

The move to the inclusion of all pupils with special educational needs into mainstream schools is taking place throughout Europe and beyond. In the UK, over 90% of deaf pupils are now educated in mainstream schools. It is much more difficult to provide full sign bilingual education in such settings, particularly if the number of pupils involved is small. For example, for sign language to develop, I would suggest that children must be exposed to at least two native users of that language in regular conversation, otherwise, how can linguistic structures such as pronouns develop fully. In terms of both deaf identity, and full participation in the classroom involving interaction with other pupils, I feel that there needs to be a significant number of deaf pupils to allow this to happen, and this is not always the case in inclusive settings.

2. The impact of cochlear implants

Traditionally, cochlear implants are seen as a threat to sign bilingualism. The Deaf Community in many countries has been vociferous in its criticism of implants, for a number of reasons, some valid, others with less basis.

I think it is important to point out that firstly, implantation is here to stay and that implanted children are drawn from the same group, profoundly and severely deaf children, as are those in sign bilingual programmes. However, secondly, I would argue that there are reasons for sign bilingual programmes to welcome cochlear implantation.

These are firstly, the access to environmental sound that implants provide. Secondly, implantation can facilitate the development of spoken language, which is an important part of sign bilingual development, and probably very important for literacy. Lastly, implant programmes, as a consequence of their high cost, have been required to demonstrate they are effective, which has improved the assessments available for all deaf children.

Some implant programmes are already suggesting that signing prior to implantation is an advantage, that those children make better progress in acquiring spoken language after their implants (McCormick 1997) . However, most programmes are ambivalent or even hostile to the use of signing after implantation, and I feel we need to be clear about the advantages sign language can bring for these children, who remain deaf even though implanted.

Conclusions

Bilingual education is in a state of evolution. Its continued development will depend on its relationship with the wider education system. There is a need for much more research, especially into the development of sign language. However, sign bilingual education offers deaf pupils an opportunity to develop their linguistic competence in both sign language and written/spoken language, to have access to an appropriate curriculum, and to develop notions of identity and self worth.

References

Conrad, R. (1979): The deaf schoolchild. London, Harper Row.

Cummins, J. (1978): Bilingualism and the development of metalinguistic awareness. J Cross-Cultural Psychology, 9, 131-49.

Gregory, S. Bishop, J. and Sheldon, L. (1995): Deaf young people and their families. Cambridge, Cambridge University Press.

McCormick, B. (1997): Paediatric audiology and cochlear implantation in the UK: taking off in the fast lane. British Journal of Audiology, 31, 303-307.

Pickersgill, M. and Gregory, S. (1998): Sign bilingualism: a model. Leeds, A Laser publication.

Young, A. (1995): Family adjustment to a deaf child in a bilingual bicultural framework. PhD these submitted to the University of Bristol, October 1995.

ZNAKOVNO DVOJEZIČNO OBRAZOVANJE GLUHE DJECE

Znakovno dvojezično obrazovanje može se opisati kao 'pristup u obrazovanju gluhe djece u kojem se koriste jezik zajednice Gluhih (znakovni jezik) i jezik čujuće zajednice (govorni i/ili pisani jezik)'. U slučajevima djece koja su iz manjinskih etničkih skupina, prikladniji je termin "znakovna višejezičnost", kako bi se prepoznao položaj dodatnih jezika koji se govore kod kuće. Znakovna dvojezičnost, kao pristup u školovanju gluhe djece prvi puta uveden je u Velikoj Britaniji prije više od deset godina. U brojnim posebnim i redovnim školama koristi se taj pristup, a odluku o njegovu uvođenju donosi lokalna školska uprava. U radu se razmatraju glavne osobine znakovnog dvojezičnog školovanja, razlozi zbog kojih se ono uopće pojavilo, te praktični aspekti dvojezičnog obrazovanja gluhe djece, uključujući pitanja vezana uz upotrebu znakovnog jezika, potrebu za dijagnostičkim instrumentarijem, obrazovnim programima i didaktičkim materijalima, rad s obitelji, kao i pitanja edukacije nastavnog i drugog osoblja. Razmatraju se i pitanja koja proizlaze iz razvoja područja edukacije gluhih, uključujući pojavu kohlearnih implantata. Razmatraju se i promjene prirode zajednice Gluhih i utjecaj koji ta činjenica ima na edukaciju gluhih.

Ključne riječi: *gluhi, edukacija gluhih, dvojezična edukacija, znakovni jezik*

CREATING A "DEAF-FRIENDLY" ATMOSPHERE FOR DEAF CHILDREN

Roger J. Carver
Deaf Children's Society, Burnaby, Canada

Abstract

What makes development and learning more conducive, or "Deaf-friendly", to deaf children? This presentation, based on the results of a recent nationwide survey of parents of deaf children, Deaf adults, and early intervention and educational programs across Canada offers important insights and useful suggestions. This survey resulted in the development of a "Deaf-friendly" child care model. All three major survey samples were in strong and unanimous agreement that the key to the successful education and development of deaf children is the implementation of a "deaf-friendly" environment. Most parents decried the lack of choices and the deep polarization and politicization in the field of deafness, which forced them into an "either-or" situation. There were calls for significant changes in how early intervention and information on deafness are provided to deaf children and their families as well as a paradigm shift in attitudes on the parts of professionals and the deaf community towards communication options available to these families. The paramount issue then is the right of deaf children to development and education in an environment that meets and integrates their needs - social, linguistic, emotional, cognitive, and educational.

Key words: deaf children, deaf community, education of the deaf, literacy, academic skills, communication of the deaf

Approximately 95 percent of children who are deaf have hearing parents (Annual Survey of Hearing Impaired Children and Youth, 1987) in consequence of which the children are deprived from birth of the opportunity to access spoken language. This deprivation, which may be prolonged if the loss of hearing is not identified early or if the parents do not use sign language to engage the child's visual orientation. The deaf child will enter a child care or educational setting with little, if any, language.

The famed deaf-blind activist, Helen Keller said that her blindness cut her off from things whereas her deafness cut her off from people. How can we ensure that children who are deaf are not cut off from their age-appropriate peers and caregivers or teachers? Do the children's special needs require a specialized setting with additional supports and services for the children to grow and develop optimally? How may deaf children engage in meaningful activities and communication with children with normal hearing in a regular setting? What should be taken into consideration when planning a program that is "deaf-friendly"? With these questions in mind, the Canadian Association of the Deaf (CAD) decided to undertake and develop a research project that would investigate the current situation and the conditions that create a "deaf-friendly" environment for the purpose of developing such a model for child care and education for young deaf children. I was engaged by the CAD to conduct this study.

To complicate matters, the field of deaf education is highly politicized and polarized with biases and emotions running deeply on all fronts (Moores, 1996; Rodda & Grove, 1987). These biases stem mainly from the well-known and age-old manual-oral controversy.

Data were obtained through personal interviews and mail questionnaires from three major stakeholder groups across Canada: Deaf adults, parents of deaf and hard of hearing children and early childhood and educational programs. Their responses, while varied in nature, showed remarkable agreement among themselves as to what "deaf-friendly" meant. Six areas of strong agreement emerged from these groups: 1) access to communication, 2) importance of early diagnosis and intervention for young deaf and hard of hearing children and their families, 3) importance of positive self-concept and identity, 4) the need for deaf children to interact with other deaf children, 5) development of literacy and academic skills, and 6) knowledgeable and skilled staff. In addition, deaf adults placed a high premium on access to sign language and deaf adult role models.

Access to communication

There is no question at all that this is the overriding need of all children, regardless of their hearing status. Communication leads to language, and language to identity and education. In the case of hearing children, communication access is built into their family environment through the sense of hearing, and it occurs naturally without effort on the parts of the children and their families. However, in the case of young deaf and hard of hearing children, it becomes problematic, not only in the home environment but also in the child care and educational environment as well. Communication is not, however, and does not have to be, contingent only on hearing, but on sight as well.

The vast majority of deaf adults in the survey emphasized the importance of sign communication to the development of young deaf children. This is also a fact that has been recognized and supported by a large majority of parents in the study. A common complaint by parents is that they did not have the means and wherewithal to learn sign language in order to effect communication with their deaf children from the earliest age possible. The value of such visual communication to young deaf children is immeasurable as it provides them with the quickest and easiest access to communication and language in the shortest possible time, a crucial consideration in the scheme of the child development when the optimum time for a child's brain to become "wired" for language occurs prior to the age of five (McCain & Mustard, 1999).

What of child care and educational programs that accommodate deaf and hard of hearing children? Do they provide effective access to communication? As the responses from all three groups indicate, access to communication is the most crucial feature of any child care or educational program when it comes to accommodating deaf and hard of hearing children. As the respondents indicated, the best kind of communication occurs when there are other deaf children and adults around and when caregivers and educators are skilled at communicating with them.

Early diagnosis and early intervention support

Health authorities such as hospitals and clinics are the first to be involved with parents upon diagnosis of their children's deafness. They are also the first to provide information. The questions become - what is the content of this information? Just how accurate is this information? Does this information present all the options in an equitable fashion? Judging from parents' comments, there appears to be considerable unhappiness with the information they received.

Another factor complicating the process is the training of medical and clinical professionals that condition them into focusing on and prescribing medical/therapeutic approaches. Deafness is much more than a medical condition: it is a social condition, and such professionals tend not to be adequately equipped to deal with or make recommendations that focus on non-medical issues. It is a well-known fact that medical and health professionals have a tendency to be hostile toward, or, at least highly skeptical of, "non-traditional" (translation: non-medical) approaches. In other words, they deal with deafness the way they had been trained to. Yet, this raises a troublesome question: are families receiving the complete information from them to enable a fully informed decision on behalf of their deaf and hard of hearing children? The evidence suggests otherwise.

In order for families to obtain information that is complete, factual, and free of bias, they need to deal with a team that would include a variety of disciplines such as social workers, other parents, psychologists, educators of the deaf, deaf professionals, and so on, in addition to medical and clinical professionals.

A strong case had been made throughout this survey for the inclusion of deaf adults in early intervention and education. Their very presence lies at the heart of what makes a program "deaf-friendly". It is worth repeating here a comment made earlier by a program respondent in this survey: "In order to make early childhood programs truly 'deaf-friendly' deaf persons must be employed in significant roles as equal partners…they can see through deaf children's eyes as they were deaf children once, and they know what these children need and how they feel." Not only do they have the value in making such programs more sensitive to the needs of such children, but also they are positive role models to young deaf children and their families. They also bring a sense of balance and reality to these programs and families. I quote Carol Padden and Tom Humphries (1988, p. 120): "When deaf children are denied connections with Deaf people…, they lose access to a history of solutions created for them by other people like themselves."

Positive self-concept

Ninety-four percent of the parents in this study have identified this area as the top developmental priority. Positive self-concept enhances the development of the child. Yet, deaf and hard of hearing children are at a higher risk for low self-esteem and poor identity development than children with normal hearing (Health Canada, 1994; Meadow & Trybus, 1979). Disruptions in family dynamics, poor self-concept, and feelings of powerlessness can adversely impact the deaf child's cognitive and academic development, especially literacy (Carver, 1989). Unless young deaf and hard of children are given greater opportunities for healthy, optimum personality development, the outcome is usually poor.

Of course, at the root of it all is communication: the ability to express one's feelings and to be understood. The greater the communication flow occurring between the deaf child and the adult, the better it is for the child's emotional development. It is crucial that the parent and the child develop a communication bond as quickly as possible, not only for mental health reasons but also for personal safety reasons such as protection against sexual abuse, being able to describe pain, understanding safety instructions, and so on. Justice Thomas Berger notes in his report to the Attorney General of British Columbia concerning the claims of sexual abuse at Jericho Hill School for the Deaf.

If children are going to be less vulnerable, they must acquire a sense of values, they must have confidence in themselves, and they must be given the means to communicate with their teachers, doctors, nurses, and social workers, and especially with their parents.

It is vital that hearing parents of deaf children and hearing brothers and sisters of deaf children learn sign language, if deaf children are to develop a set of values and have that measure of protection which family membership ought to bring, they must be able to communicate with family members from an early age.... it is intolerable for a society to countenance a situation in which children can't communicate with their parents. (Berger, 1995, p.37)

It means the deaf and hard of hearing child must have access to a communication system that they can quickly master from the earliest possible age. To delay or to prolong the language development process significantly places them at greater risk socially and emotionally.

The value of deaf adults in the emotional and social development of young deaf children is incalculable. Linda Cundy (1988), in her study of the impact of deaf teachers on deaf children identified communication as the most important factor: the ease of two-way communication between the deaf child and deaf adult "invites children to open up and share information; hence their ability to share information in a classroom setting is enhanced" (p. 61). Deaf and hard of hearing adults bring with them a sense of balance and reality to families and programs with deaf and hard of hearing children in a variety of roles such as sign language instructors, mentors, teacher aides and educators. They also fill in the gaps in the training obtained by hearing persons in professional training programs. This is supported by what I have heard from my students at the University of British Columbia where I teach a course on sign language and deaf culture to students learning to become teachers of the deaf or speech-language pathologists. They keep telling me over and over again over the years that, of all the courses they have taken during their training, they learned the most about the needs of deaf children from my course.

Peer interaction

Deaf adults, both oral and signing, in the survey, were unanimous in their opinion that other deaf children should be present in preschool or educational programs whenever a deaf child is enrolled. Peer interaction provides children a rich opportunity to develop language and social skills. James Roots (1999), in his study of the political socialization of the deaf child, notes that signing deaf children in deaf school settings display a greater level of social maturity than their oral deaf children counterparts. He believes that the reason for the greater immaturity of oral deaf children is that their internalization of inappropriate standards is intensified by their relationship with their hearing peers. In other words, young deaf children in integrated settings do not have the same opportunities as children with normal hearing to develop appropriate social skills; they are not able to overhear conversations between hearing children which would have provided tidbits of important social and cultural information and allowed them to correct their own behavior so as to fit in better. In other words, they simply base their behaviors on what they see, and little else.

In order to have satisfactory peer interaction, children must have a shared communication system, or at the very least, a shared experience base. Joanne Cripps (2000), a Deaf expert on the rights of deaf children, makes note of this fact: "Deaf children need to have friends with the same interests. They need to make friends, play sports and interact with others. In order to do this, there must be a shared language base so inner and outer conflicts can be identified and solved. Deaf peers provide the necessary social interaction to help the Deaf child become aware of him or herself." (p. 6).

Development of literacy and academic skills

Deaf adults in the survey picked this as one of the top developmental priorities (100%) for young deaf children. This is quite understandable, being based on their own personal experiences, as well as those of their deaf peers. Most of them have problems with literacy and experienced frustrations in school in terms of academic skills. Many of them have blamed these shortcomings on the inordinate emphasis on speech and language training during their school years. Indeed their sentiments have been echoed by the Canadian Association of the Deaf which declared that literacy should take precedence over speech development in education of the deaf, noting that "literacy is the crucial access point for Deaf Canadians to all aspects of the hearing world" (CAD, 1994c).

It is imperative that early intervention and educational professionals assign a high priority to the development of literacy and academic skills in young deaf and hard of hearing children as they are crucial to their well-being and self-sufficiency. There is no question that literacy will greatly enhance their educational and social development and their chances of gaining access to higher education and employment.

Staff qualities

Staff qualities may be the most crucial feature in any child care or educational program that have deaf and hard of hearing children. In fact, everything hinges on the ability of the staff to meet their needs. It is not simply a matter of adapting the environment or providing technological aids, but how "deaf-friendly" the staff is towards such children. The respondents in the survey strongly emphasized that knowledge and understanding of deafness and its issues, not to mention specific training, are essential to the provision of early intervention and education services to such children and their families.

There are many advantages to having deaf adults in the classroom:

1. They serve as role models not only for the children but also as resources for their hearing colleagues who can learn from them how to relate to deaf children and how to sign properly.
2. They bring with them a rich knowledge of Deaf culture, history, and so on, not to mention experience of growing up deaf in a hearing world.
3. Deaf adults sensitize their hearing colleagues to the needs of deaf children and help them move from a "helper" role to that of collaborators and show them how to regard and respect Deaf persons as individuals rather than as "special cases".
4. Deaf adults can show their hearing colleagues how to manage the behavior of deaf children.
5. Parents of deaf children will be able to visualize what their deaf children will be like when they grow up.
6. Deaf adults are more attuned to the physical environment needs of deaf children such as lighting, lines of sight, "visual noise", and seating arrangements.

Choices for deaf children and their families

I would like to quote an American philosopher, Ralph Barton Perry,s "Ignorance deprives men of freedom because they do not know what alternatives there are. It is impossible to choose to do what one has never 'heard of'". This quote aptly describes the situation in the field of deafness concerning choices.

The issue of choices or lack thereof was raised by a good number of families throughout the survey. It therefore deserves further discussion. It is imperative that choices be made available to the children and their families to help them achieve a measure of personal autonomy or freedom. Unfortunately, the choices are not always made available to them due, in large measure, to the polarity that continues to exist in deaf education.

At the root of the educational polarity is ignorance or the human tendency to build up a wall of isolation around one's favoured school of thought to maintain and increase a sense of power, control, or dominance for the sake of status or prestige. Sadly, the real victims of this longstanding polarity continue to be deaf and hard of hearing children and their families.

The two contentious schools of thought are represented by the medical (usually oral) and cultural (usually sign language) models of deafness. The competition between them has been such that parents are often made to feel as if the choice that presents itself to them is one of "either-or" and hardly or rarely one of "both-and". In laying the blame squarely on the shoulders of the medical model of deafness which tends to deny families access to a complete range of information and solutions, Harlan Lane, Robert Hoffmeister, and Ben Bahan (1995, p.38) note: "Parents have a right to professional advice that provides a balanced view of the possible futures for their Deaf children, including the many possible futures for Deaf people in our society."

How, then, can choices in early intervention and early childhood programs be increased or augmented rather than restricted to one choice or the other? It may help to achieve a paradigm shift from competition to cooperation and to strive to see the big picture that informs us that we are more alike than different. For all of us, whether deaf or hearing, growth is developmental and in need of stimuli for further enriched and enhanced growth. Our needs are universal; among them, the need to love, the need to be accepted as we are, and the need to have value. Members supporting the medical model of deafness might wish to consider the fact that it is the individual who is deaf or hard of hearing who has first-hand knowledge of the condition - a non-fatal one - of deafness or of loss of hearing - which the individual may grow into and perhaps even embrace. In fact it may be character-building for this person. It is the individual's family that has second-hand knowledge of deafness or hearing loss, having lived with the deaf or hard of hearing child from the time of his/her birth. Professionals, unless they are deaf themselves, have a deaf child, or have one or two deaf parents, have only third-hand knowledge of and experience with deafness, which they come by intellectually or vicariously. The role of the professionals is to serve their patients or clients and professionals would do well, therefore, to treat those with first- and second-hand knowledge of deafness or hearing loss as "first among equals" in the planning of their education. It is essential to put people ahead of ideology by apprising them of the range of choices that are available to them at all times over the years.

The big picture also informs us, including proponents of the medical and cultural models of deafness, that perhaps the most insidious aspect of deafness or hearing loss is not the physical condition itself but the ignorance surrounding it, which yields stigma, exclusion, and barriers that we may unwittingly create ourselves. If we wish to tear down the walls of ignorance, a good foothold from which to proceed would be to profess ignorance of the big picture and to make an attempt therefore to perceive it not by walking a mile in the shoes of the other person, which would not be possible due our unique experiential bases in life, but by walking alongside the person wearing the shoes and listening to her/him tell her/ his own story.

The "deaf-friendly" model

To sum up, both parents and deaf persons define "deaf friendly" not so much in terms of physical accessibility and programming but more in terms of personal staff qualities such as patience, understanding and willingness to learn and support, communication access and interaction with other deaf children. The issue here is the best possible environment in which the deaf child can thrive developmentally, and the environment has to be just as completely accessible to deaf children on a level comparable to that of the typical setting for children with normal hearing. In other words, it is a matter of giving deaf children opportunities identical to those available to children with normal hearing. Nevertheless, if there is to be one standard that should be held up to all, it would be the inclusion of Deaf adults in all early intervention and education programs for deaf and hard of hearing children. They are the key to the success of any "Deaf-friendly" approach.

Conclusion

Nearly half of the parents surveyed indicated that they would have done differently if they had to start all over again, and there were two major areas in which they would have done differently: less emphasis on the oral method and more emphasis on sign language and greater advocacy for better education and support for their deaf children.

Many parents complained in the survey about the polarization of the field into the oral and signing camps and the lack of choices available to them. They resent the "either-or" choice they had been forced to take. They also resent being deprived of the freedom of choice to choose whatever communication tools they feel is best for their deaf children and being criticized by professionals, other parents of deaf children, and deaf adults for their choices.

This polarization has harmed, and continues to harm, the lives of thousands of deaf and hard of hearing children and their families. It is our opinion that the time has come to put an end to the age-old oral vs. manual controversy by ensuring that ALL families have access to ALL the tools they need to ensure that their deaf or hard of hearing children develop optimally in ALL areas of development. In order to bring this about, a paradigm shift from the medical model of deafness to a holistic model may have to occur. This is not to say those forms of medical/habilitative treatment of deafness and the science behind them is wrong or offensive. In fact, we believe they can be, and are, beneficial and that a vast majority of their practitioners are sincere in their efforts to help the deaf and the hard of hearing. The problem is that they do not have the knowledge base of the deaf community to work with. It is inconceivable that they could work with deaf children without it; the principle of fully informed decision demands it. We believe that if there is a convergence of views from both models, it will open up exciting new horizons for deaf and hard of hearing children and their families.

In closing, I would like to quote Joanne Cripps (2000, p. xv) who presented an eloquent case for the rights of deaf children in Canada through her book, Quiet Journey: Understanding the Rights of Deaf Children. "Deaf children have the right to be themselves and to experience the natural process of child development." There is no question that this right includes access to natural language and communication through persons who have the natural ability to communicate with them.

Acknowledgment: I would like to acknowledge the significant contribution my colleague, Andrea Sam, made towards this presentation as it is derived from our research report, which we jointly authored.

References

Annual survey of hearing impaired children and youth (1987). Washington, D.C.: Gallaudet University, Center for Assessment and Demographic Studies.

Berger, T. R. (1995). Report of the Special Counsel to the Attorney General concerning claims of sexual abuse of deaf children at Jericho Hill School for the Deaf. Victoria, B.C.: Ministry of Attorney General.

Canadian Association of the Deaf (1994). "Literacy" A position paper. Ottawa: Canadian Association of the Deaf

Carver, R. (1989). Deaf illiteracy: A genuine educational puzzle or an instrument of oppression? A critical review. Ottawa: Canadian Association of the Deaf.

Cripps, J. S. (2000). Quiet journey: Understanding the rights of deaf children. Owen Sound, ON: The Ginger Press.

Cundy, L.H. (1988). The impact the deaf teachers have upon the deaf students: A phenomenological study. Master's thesis. University of Alberta, Edmonton.

Health Canada (1994) Children and Youth with a Hearing Loss: Promoting Mental Health. Health Programs & Services, Health Canada, Ottawa, ON: Minister of Supply & Services.

Lane, H., Hoffmeister, R., & Bahan, B. (1996). A journey into the DEAF-WORLD. San Diego: DawnSign Press.

McCain, M. & Mustard, J. F. (co-chairs) (1999). Reversing the real brain drain. Early Years Study: Final Report. (Advance copy). Toronto: Canadian Institute for Advanced Research.

Meadow, K. & Trybus, R.J. (1979). Behavioral and emotional problems of deaf children: An overview. In L. Bradford & W. Hardy (Eds.), Hearing and hearing impairment (pp. 395 - 403). New York: Grune & Stratton.

Moores, D.F. (1996). Educating the deaf: psychology, principles, and practices. Boston: Houghton Mifflin Company.

Padden, C. (1980). The Deaf community and the culture of Deaf people. In C. Baker & R. Battison (Eds.) Sign Language and the Deaf community: Essays in honor of William C. Stokoe (pp.89-103), Silver Spring, M.D.: National Association of the Deaf.

Rodda & Grove, C. (1987). Language, Cognition and Deafness. Englewood Cliffs, NJ: Lawrence Erlbaum Associates.

STVARANJE PRIJATELJSKOG OZRAČJA ZA GLUHU DJECU

Što je to što omogućava da se razvoj i učenje gluhe djece odvijaju u prijateljskom ozračju? Ovaj rad, temeljen na rezultatima nacionalnog kanadskog istraživanja roditelja gluhe djece, odraslih Gluhih te ranih interventnih i drugih edukacijskih programa, nudi odgovor na to pitanje. Spomenuto istraživanje rezultiralo je kreiranjem posebnog "prijateljskog" modela skrbi za gluhu djecu. Ispitanici svih triju uzoraka slažu se da ključ uspješnog obrazovanja i razvoja gluhe djece leži u okolini "prijateljskoj" gluhoj djeci. Mnogi roditelji ukazuju na duboku polarizaciju i politizaciju na području gluhoće, kojom su prisilno dovedeni u situaciju "ili-ili". Izraženi su i zahtjevi za promjenom načina na koji se odvija rana intervencija te načina na koji se gluhoj djeci i njihovim obiteljima pružaju informacije o gluhoći, ali isto tako i potreba mijenjanja stavova dijela stručnjaka i članova zajednice gluhih prema različitim načinima komunikacije koji su na raspolaganju obiteljima s gluhom djecom. Suštinska stvar su prava gluhe djece na razvoj i obrazovanje u okolini koja zadovoljava i integrira njihove potrebe - socijalne, jezične, emocionalne, kognitivne i obrazovne potrebe.

Key words: gluha djeca, zajednica gluhih, edukacija gluhih, pismenost, školska znanja, komunikacija gluhih

BILINGUAL EDUCATION FOR THE DEAF: EXAMPLES FROM EVERYDAY TEACHING AND LEARNING IN SWEDEN

Lisbeth Henning & Signild Salander
School for the Deaf, Lund, Sweden

Abstract

In 1981 the Swedish parliament recognized Swedish Sign Language as the first language for people born deaf. As a consequence it was also stated that the education of deaf children should be in Sign Language and that Swedish should be taught as a second language. The transition from oral education had already begun via sign-supported speech in the 1970s, but for the full implementation of the new curriculum (from 1984), further training was necessary. Teachers were offered studies in Sing Language at the University of Stockholm, and courses in Swedish as a second language were organized at, for instance, the University of Lund. A production of new instruction material began, and two methodological handbooks were written in order to support the teachers in this new situation. Parents were offered economic support to learn Sign Language. Twenty years after the recognition of Sign Language, one might ask what has happened in the education of deaf children in Sweden since then? Has there been any progress? Have the teachers learnt enough Sign Language? What are the advantages of bilingual education for the children, for the family? What are the problems? This paper will try to answer these and other questions on bilingual education in Sweden.

Key words: *bilingual education, Sign Language, Swedish Sign Language, deaf, deafness*

Special schools organising education for deaf children in Sweden have existed since 1809 but compulsory education for deaf children was not introduced until 1889. For deaf school children as well as for hearing children the Swedish government has always given directions in the form of a national curriculum describing the aims of the education and the methods recommended. However, the aims for special schools for the deaf were not the same as for the corresponding schools for hearing children. For a long time deaf pupils were not expected to be able to reach the same level of competence as their hearing peers. The subjects that were taught were fewer and a lot of energy was put on speech training, on teaching deaf children how to pronounce a few words or sentences correctly and on lip-reading; most of the time with very little success. I have studied some old curricula and handbooks written by teachers for the deaf; the main item in them always seemed to be how to teach the spoken language to deaf children. Sign language was often mentioned as something which could be both useful and even necessary for the deaf among themselves but never as something which could be used as a language of instruction at school. What strikes me among other things when I study these old handbooks of methodology is the strong conviction that language is the equivalent of spoken language only. The written language (and the teaching of it) is all the time regarded as secondary to the spoken form. Swedish deaf education was for more than a hundred years based on oral methods just like the rest of the world and on the belief that sign language was not a real language.

When I started as a teacher for the deaf in 1977, I was not prepared for what I was going to meet. I teach at the secondary school level so my pupils are aged 14 - 17. The pupils that I met in my first years as a teacher made me wonder what was wrong with the education at special schools. I was (and I still am) of the opinion that deaf children are normally equipped when it comes to their cognitive abilities, but here I was confronted with teenagers who were very poor at reading and writing. They were also very ignorant about the world and they did not expect to be understood or to understand other people. In short, they had no self-esteem and they were not aware that they had rights as human beings of getting a good education.

However, the 1970s were a period of changes in special schools for the deaf. They stopped being completely oral schools. Many teachers used sign-supported speech or signed Swedish; a few even started using proper sign language. But the methods for teaching were still on a monolingual (one language) basis, and Swedish was considered as THE language, the one and only that mattered. Most teachers were unwilling to just sign without speaking simultaneously. This resulted in a sort of mixed-languages-situation where neither Sign Language nor Swedish was properly performed. Since the two languages have totally different grammatical systems it is not possible to speak and sign simultaneously without violating the structure of both languages.

The situation at special schools was getting better, though, not only thanks to the opening up for more signing but also because of the fact that parents began using Sign Language in communication with their small children. An opinion was formed, demanding more use of Sign Language in the schools, and in 1981 the Swedish government and parliament stated that Sign Language is the first language of the deaf.

As a consequence of this statement, the government presented a new curriculum for special schools for the deaf and hard of hearing in 1983. This was the first time that we had a curriculum, which was the equivalent to that of the mainstream schools for hearing children. The syllabus was the same for all subjects except for music which was substituted by drama and rhythm, and special syllabuses for languages. The new idea was to introduce a conception of bilingual education for deaf children. All instruction in deaf schools was to be performed in Sign Language, whether it was mathematics, history, physics or something else. Sign Language and Swedish became separate subjects on the timetable. We also got a new syllabus for English and other foreign languages. Swedish was to be taught as a second language, just as was the case with the immigrants that had come to Sweden. Swedish implied primarily the written form of Swedish. Speech training was to be of minor importance and mainly for children with residual hearing. As was stated in the curriculum, it is important to realise that the two languages - Sign Language and Swedish - perform different functions for the pupil. Whereas Sign Language is learnt naturally and spontaneously, Swedish has to be acquired through instruction. Sign Language is the child's primary means of acquiring knowledge and is the language used in direct communication with others. The child's social and emotional development is primarily achieved by way of contacts in Sign Language with parents and others. Swedish is the language that is used by the child's surrounding environment. All books, newspapers and other kinds of information are given in Swedish. The goal for special schools is to prepare the pupils so that they can "read well enough to have a solid foundation on which to acquire knowledge, information and experience for themselves through the medium of newspapers and periodicals, reference works and works of fiction and non-fiction." It is also important to prepare them for an adult life where they can be integrated into society under the conditions set by themselves. We do not believe in integrating deaf children during their school period. The reason for this is that deaf children need to grow up and be educated in an environment where Sign Language is the primary mode of communication. They must be able to see people, both deaf and hearing, communicate in Sign Language on everyday matters, they must be able to eavesdrop, just like hearing children do all the time.

For deaf children the process of learning to read is not comparable to a hearing child's reading development, since the deaf child also has to learn a new language at the same time. An important factor in this process is that the child has a well-functioning first language, Sign Language. By means of Sign Language the child gets knowledge about the world, a knowledge that is an important prerequisite for successful reading. In view of this it is important for special schools to offer individual support for children who are deficient in their sign language. It is also essential to keep the two languages apart from each other, i.e. not to give the impression that there is a one-to-one correspondence between words and signs. A Swedish word may sometimes correspond to a sign, but more often a sign corresponds to a Swedish phrase or even a whole sentence. A child who is taught to read by mapping single words to single signs will soon be lost. The meaning of the whole sentence must be grasped, not the single words only.

The reform in 1983 had been foreseen for a couple of years and was brought about by many co-existing factors, such as the following:

- The oral school had not been successful over the years.
- In the 1970s, research in the linguistic and psychological fields showed that a deaf child, given the opportunity to communicate in Sign Language with parents, teachers and other people in his or her environment, was able to achieve a lot more than had been expected from his or her earlier. Research showed, for example, that deaf children, who acquired Sign Language in a natural way and as early as possible, had an age-adequate language when they began school. Given these opportunities, deaf children were functioning just like any hearing child of the same age, both linguistically and in other respects.
- Deaf organisations, the parents' association and many professionals as well demanded changes and new teaching methods in special schools and the recognition of Sign Language as the first language of deaf children. The fact that deaf adults, parents and professionals working with the deaf were united in their demands had a great impact on the authorities.
- Research on Sign Language showed that it is a full language with its own grammar.
- A new view on handicapped persons was adopted; it's the environment that needs to be changed in order to meet the demands of the individual, not the contrary.

- For a couple of years parents had been taught Sign Language and were able to communicate with their children and, of course, they also wanted the school to have full communication with the pupils

So, how was this new curriculum welcomed by the teachers?

At first, many teachers thought it was a strange idea that Swedish children, born in Sweden and with Swedish-speaking parents, should have Swedish as a second language. Some felt bitter and angry because what they had been doing for many years, all the efforts they had put down in teaching deaf children, was now considered "wrong" (quotation marks). The parents, however, who felt they had been struggling for a very long time, were very positive and now demanded immediate changes and results.

There were, of course, also many teachers who welcomed the reform and who were enthusiastic about the changes that were going to come. Unfortunately, the National Board of Education did not realised the need of further training of the teachers at special schools. Further training was needed both in Sign Language and in teaching Swedish as a second language for the deaf. Initially, the problem was solved locally by the different special schools in varying ways. Short courses were arranged, some teachers started projects in their classes in order to try out new methods especially for teaching Swedish. After some pressure on the authorities, a group was established in 1985. The group was connected to the National Board of Education and consisted of two teachers from each special school, i.e. 15 persons, including one representative from the Board. The aim of this group was to stimulate, initiate and support different educational projects in order to write a handbook for the methods of bilingual education. The group also discussed and suggested new educational materials that were needed and the kinds of further training that were needed for the teachers. There was also some co-operation with the University of Stockholm and the Swedish Deaf Organisation (SDR).

As a result of all these activities projects were started at different schools, a lot of discussions took place and two handbooks were written (one about educational methods and the other about Swedish grammar as seen from the point of view of Sign Language.) At this stage the authorities had realised that they had to supply money for at least a six-month course in Sign Language at the university level for all teachers and also a similar course in Swedish as a second language for the deaf. The government decided to finance a ten-year project (which started in 1989) where two to four teachers from each special school got the opportunity to study Sign Language at the University of Stockholm or of Örebro for six months. The budget covered salaries, all travel expenses, as well as board and lodging.

As for Swedish as a second language it has been up to each school to solve the problem of further training. At our school we chose to contact the Department of Nordic Languages at the University of Lund to develop a course for our specific needs. The National Board of Education helped us finance a three-year educational program, which was finished in June 1994. Eighteen of our own teachers participated and also three teachers from another special school. The course gave us insight into the problems and the possibilities in our teaching of Swedish as a second language. We discussed and penetrated the many questions that we had on how deaf children learn to read and write. I can't say that we have all the answers today, but we have come a long way. We have discovered that many of the problems our pupils meet when learning Swedish resemble the problems that immigrants have when they learn Swedish. We have discussed the consequences of the fact that we only deal with the written form of Swedish. How many times, for example, does a child have to see a word, fingerspell it, write it and sometimes also mouth it before it can be memorised? What sorts of texts do we need to present to the children? The texts must be interesting, in the beginning easy but not oversimplified. We have learnt that the pupils' production of written texts may come very late, and we have learnt to analyse their texts from the point of view of finding what they actually master instead of just finding faults. We also discussed such matters as: attitudes to minority languages, the bilingual situation in the family, early reading with deaf children, deaf children with reading and writing difficulties, etc.

You might ask now: Has the introduction of bilingual education been successful? What are the advantages? What has happened in the years since 1983? To me personally there has never been any doubt that this is the right way to instruct deaf children. An important factor is, of course, everyday communication in a language that the deaf person can always understand. It is also a question of attitudes: if the teachers and other staff members at school are fairly fluent in Sign Language and use it for communication, we send out a message that this is a language that has a value of its own, that it is useful and can be a means for teaching and learning new things.

The use of Sign Language gives all pupils the possibility to understand what is being said; not only the very smart ones that are good at lip-reading and Swedish. By using Sign Language as a means of explaining Swedish and by making comparisons between the two languages, you get a good basis for developing the child's literacy.

Mastering Swedish in its written form is also very important. It gives our pupils a means to take part in society by reading newspapers, watching captured TV programs and films, and by using their text telephones in order to contact both deaf and hearing persons. They can write to friends, relatives and authorities. They can learn new things by studying books, pamphlets and magazines on their own. They can get an advanced education by studying and reading the relevant literature.

We have not totally abandoned the spoken language. When children start school, the first training in reading and learning the letters of the Swedish alphabet is also connected to an articulation program with or without the voice. All children must know about speech and what speech is, and each child will be treated individually and in accordance with his or her needs. If a child has an interest in and the capacity for speech, he or she will get individual speech training. There is also a link between Sign Language and Swedish. Sign language is silent but it does definitely not lack lip movements. Some of the lip movements are genuine sign language but some have a connection with the corresponding Swedish word. In this area it is very helpful if the speech therapist can work together with the Sign Language teacher.

In 1994 a new curriculum (Lpo94) was introduced in Sweden. For special schools it is still based on the bilingual idea and the language of instruction is still Sign Language. The difference from the old one from 1983 was that the national tests given in the final year in the subjects Swedish, English and Mathematics are compulsory also for special schools. Until 1994 it had been up to the schools to decide whether to participate or not. This is one of the reasons why I believe in bilingual education. Ten or fifteen years ago it would not have been possible. But perhaps the main reason for my belief in bilingualism is the fact that my pupils have a self-confidence and a self-respect which make them feel they are on equal footing with the rest of us. They can take responsibility for their own acts and lives, they can make claims on others, they can take care of themselves even when they find themselves in new situations and with new people.

DVOJEZIČNO OBRAZOVANJE GLUHIH: PRIMJERI IZ SVAKODNEVNOG POUČAVANJA U ŠVEDSKOJ

Godine 1981. švedski je Parlament priznao švedski znakovni jezik kao prvi jezik ljudi koji su rođeni gluhi. Također je utvrđeno da se obrazovanje gluhe djece treba odvijati na znakovnom jeziku, a da švedski jezik gluha djeca trebaju učiti kao drugi jezik. Prijelaz s oralnog poučavanja učinjen je već sedamdesetih godina, korištenjem znakovnog švedskoga, ali za potpunu implementaciju novog programa (od 1984.) bila je potrebna daljnja edukacija. Učiteljima su ponuđeni programi učenja švedskog znakovnog jezika na Sveučilištu u Stockholmu, a također i tečajevi švedskog kao drugog jezika (npr. na Sveučilištu u Lundu). Kreiran je didaktički materijal, napisani su priručnici za učitelje. Roditeljima je bila ponuđena financijska pomoć za pohađanje tečajeva znakovnog jezika. Dvadesetak godina nakon priznavanja znakovnog jezika, mogli bismo se zapitati što se dogodilo s obrazovanjem gluhe djece u Švedskoj. Je li postignut ikakav napredak? Jesu li nastavnici naučili dovoljno znakovnog jezika? Koje su prednosti dvojezičnog obrazovanja za djecu, a koje za obitelj? Koji su problemi? Ovaj rad nastoji dati odgovore na ta pitanja.

Ključne riječi: dvojezično obrazovanje, znakovni jezik, švedski znakovni jezik, gluhi

THE INFLUENCE OF BILINGUAL EDUCATION ON DEAF PUPILS' WRITING SKILLS - EXPERIENCES FROM THE BILINGUAL SCHOOL ATTEMPT AT THE HAMBURG SCHOOL FOR THE DEAF

Klaus-B. Günther, *University of Hamburg, Germany*
Ilka Schäfke, *University of Hamburg, Germany*

Abstract

Starting from the school year of 1993/94 the first German attempt was made at the Hamburg School for the Deaf to educate two classes of deaf pupils bilingually. Initially established because of the wishes of parents, the main points of the Hamburg Bilingual Education/School Project have been the following: 1) Bilingual lessons taught by a deaf and a hearing teacher as a team (one person uses one language); 2) Usage of both the German Sign Language (DGS) and German in its spoken form (supported by "signed German" [LBG] and a special sign system representing individual phonemes [PMS]) and written form from the very beginning in the communication between pupils and teachers. The overall aim has been to enable the deaf pupils to develop age-appropriate communication as well as cognition and to experience not only the language but also the culture of both worlds. The traditional oral education neglected the question of written language acquisition by deaf pupils. The bilingual project, on the other hand - considering the important role of writing in society, which has not diminished through the development of the new media in the last decade, and the fact that written words are much less fleeting than spoken ones - tried to support writing in the best possible way. Deriving from this a wider project has been initiated to follow the development of text production (precisely, the production of stories) under the conditions of bilingual education more closely, but also compared to other hearing-impaired (not only deaf) students who have been differently educated. In the absence of adequate instruments of research, we had to develop our own or modify others to analyze different aspects of text development. The texts were collected by the teachers themselves to avoid the typical "testing situation" and to ensure a more natural one. As starting points for the written narratives a comic strip (3th/4th grade) and a short Disney movie (6th/7th grade) have been chosen to ensure maximum motivation and comparability between them. The analysis of the data allows several statements relating to the question of how bilingual education promotes the acquisition of text production skills.

Key words: sign language, manual communication, bilingual education, writing, literacy, deaf, language skills

The Hamburg Bilingual School Attempt

Starting from the school year of 1993/94 the first German attempt was made at the Hamburg School for the Deaf to educate two classes of deaf pupils – one in the first and one in the second grade – bilingually.

Initially established because of the wishes of parents, the main points of the Hamburg Bilingual Education Project have been the following:

- Bilingual lessons taught by a deaf and a hearing teacher as a team (one person uses one language);
- Usage of both the German Sign Language (GSL) and German in its spoken and written form from the very beginning in the communication between pupils and teachers (supported by "signed German" [LBG] and a special sign system representing individual phonemes [PMS]).

The overall aim has been to enable deaf pupils to develop age-appropriate communication and cognition and to experience not only the language but also the culture of both worlds with the deaf teacher as role model. This concept differs from the Swedish bilingual concept insofar as (German) sign language is not the only classroom language but is used in parallel with written/spoken German. Of course, for the pupils, GSL is their main and adequately developed language – the younger they are, the more it is so – but this strong language allows the weaker one to be built up steadily, too. This teaching method can combine both the sign language and the aural-oral promoting possibilities of the present day.

Even though the project itself officially ended in 2000, the bilingual teaching continues. It has been modified to suit the conditions of secondary school.

The teaching of writing skills

The traditional oral education neglected the question of written language acquisition by deaf pupils. The bilingual project, on the other hand – considering the important role of writing in society, which has not diminished but increased through the development of the new media in the last decade and the fact that written words are much less fleeting than spoken ones – tried to support writing in the best possible way.

In order to help their deaf pupils to develop adequate skills in German, the teachers brought them into constant contact with it, starting with written words and sentences on the blackboard while discussing a subject in both languages, and later by reading books and translating them into GSL. The use of sign language and this constant training in translating GSL into German written language and vice versa either in class or at home on their own enabled the pupils to work on texts above their prevailing level of knowledge, since the meaning of unknown words, idioms and phrases could be discussed and clarified.

This close relationship between sign language and written language can also be found in the manner of teaching writing skills. Due to the importance that has been attached to texts in the education of these deaf pupils in the form of fairytales, stories, reports and other text types, writing has not meant producing isolated sentences either but has always been embedded into a context. This means that the semantics have been stressed rather than the morphosyntactics, which, of course, remains a goal as well. Older texts written by the bilingual classes (3rd/4th grade) show clearly, in terms of their structure and expression, the impact of the stronger sign language, whereas the younger ones (6th/7th grade, for examples see below) verify a retreat of those elements and a development towards a more standardized style of writing. To achieve this and to enable the pupils to work independently, the student teacher Cord Harries developed ways to separate the process of revision from the process of correction. Whereas revision means improving the contents of the text, correction means checking it for spelling and other grammatical mistakes. While making a holiday reading book in the 6th grade, the pupils first collected ideas, then each of them wrote a text and corrected it with the help of inflection and conjugation tables hanging in the classroom. The teacher himself only corrected mistakes coming from yet unknown grammatical phenomena, others were marked and a comment was written next to it to enable the pupil to look it up himself/herself. Later the text was presented to the class both in the corrected written form by the use of an overhead projector and in GSL by the author. In the next step the classmates discussed the contents of the story and suggested improvements, which the author could accept, decline or modify during the following revision. This structure could be repeated until the author declared his text finished. Then it was typed and printed.

This procedure is still followed in writing lessons. A brainstorming is made to help those pupils who do not come up with their own writing ideas so easily and the text is written and corrected by the author himself/herself with the help of a list of grammatical phenomena already discussed in class, which some of the pupils have already acquired. Then the content of the text is discussed in a "writing conference" and revised.

It seems that this way of teaching leads the pupils to a functional competence in German written language. Especially the way of treating mistakes as a part of the process allows the pupils to follow their own route in the process of developing text production skills without their motivation being diminished by a constant emphasis on their slowly but steadily decreasing mistakes.

The development of text production skills in written language – Results

The overall development is very encouraging. Comparing the figures for three stories, written in the 3rd/4th, 6th and 7th grade, the numbers show a substantial rise in the texts of most pupils in the number of words used for each story, especially between the 6th and the 7th grade. The structure of the sentences, too, has become more complex and more closely related to the grammar of written German. The frequently found cases of sign language grammar in most of the 3rd/4th grade texts have diminished. Some of the pupils are now so advanced that they do not need the support of the stronger language anymore, while others still depend on it to produce interesting texts and to tie the otherwise isolated sentences together. Other pupils who can not be described as "advanced" either compared to the first group – even though there have been many positive changes in their writing skills towards using standardized German written language – have aban-

---

[1] Categories modified and taken from Boueke et al. (1995): Wie Kinder erzählen. Untersuchungen zur Erzähltheorie und zur Entwicklung narrativer Fähigkeiten. München.

[2] Without Justus, a pupil who entered the younger group in the 6th grade and therefore did not grow up bilingually.

doned using sign language grammar in their texts as well and now prefer short sentences with a grammar they can handle, which follow the structure of German written language.

As stated above, we did not focus on the development of grammar but included text organization and contents as well (see "Text level" in the table below). We put each text in one of five categories[1], Level 0 being the lowest, Level 4 the highest text organization level. A text belonging to Level 0 cannot really be spoken of as "text", since it is no more than an unorganized list or assembly of words, usually without verbs, whereas a text belonging to Level 4 has a more distinct structure, including exposition, complication and solution, enriched by narrative rather than descriptive elements.

Since each pupil starts his/her process of learning at a different point due to circumstances, ability and motivation, the classes are divided into different levels of performance. To describe in more detail the pupils' development of the written language skills under the circumstances mentioned above, we picked as examples a few sentences of the three out of the total of eleven pupils of these classes. Because of the differences in the English and German language – German needs more inflections than English and is less restricted in the order of words in a sentence – a simple translation, if possible, was not enough to clarify the kind of mistakes made by the pupils. We therefore decided to use three lines, the first line for the German original, the second for the corrected German version with the mistakes marked (bold), the third for an *English word-for-word translation*:

Anna represents the top of the class. Even though her parents can hear, her sign language skills are among the highest in the whole group. She is interested in most subjects and is a very active participant in class. Her knowledge in both languages and mathematics is very good. The texts she produces are very advanced both in terms of semantics and morphosyntactics. Whereas in the beginning she used many structures taken from sign language, she has now abandoned them completely and relies only on her knowledge of written German. Examples:

3rd grade:
Zwei Junge kampf eine Junge name Max und eine Junge name Leo
Zwei Jjunge**n** kämpf**en. E**in Junge **heißt** Max und ein Junge **heißt** Leo.
Two boys fight one boy name Max and one boy name Leo
7th grade:
Er liest den Zettel und sieht, daß der Löwe „Lambert" heißt und gehört andere Volk.
Er liest den Zettel und sieht, daß der Löwe „Lambert" heißt und **einem** andere**n** Volk gehört.
He reads the note and sees that the lion is called "Lambert" and belongs to a different people.

The 3rd grade example illustrates that Anna had few problems with the structure of German written sentences even at such an early age. She puts numerals in front of nouns where they belong and adds the linguistically necessary conjunction "and". Nevertheless, some sign language elements can also be found: The expression "name Max/Leo" instead of "heißt Max/Leo" (=is called Max/Leo) corresponds to the typical sign equivalent. It is interesting that she does not use capital letters ("Name") – as in other cases – since that would be the correct noun. Instead, she uses it as the verb needed in this context. Probably due to the fact that sign languages do not inflect verbs in the same way she does not inflect the verb "kämpfen". The other mistakes result from choosing the wrong number or gender, common mistakes for someone learning a second language. In the 7th grade example Anna uses a far more complex sentence structure including the conjunction "daß" (=that). She made only one mistake by putting the verb "gehört" (=belongs) in the second place, which would be correct in the main clause, but the verb needs to be switched to the last place in a subordinate clause. She also omits the indefinite article, which is not always needed in German, and chooses once again a wrong gender. "Das Volk" (= the people) in German is neutral instead of feminine or masculine. Punctuation no longer is a problem.

Vanessa has problems following the present standard of the group. She has been and still is at the bottom of the class achievement level, however, she has a very positive attitude towards learning and does not give up easily. The German Sign Language is very important for her since it enables her to study contents she cannot understand by reading. A constant positive development can be observed. She knows about her limited writing abilities and therefore needs the teachers' encouragement, but the results show that she also profited from the special way writing skills have been taught. Due to her limited reading skills the construction of a text still poses a problem for Vanessa, but in comparison to texts written in the 3rd grade, in which hardly any grammatical features could be found, she now uses and combines both sign language and German written language grammatical elements to express herself. Examples:

4th grade:

Trffen Hallo sagt Doof. Papa ist eine. Mann Doof ist. Junge zwie.

meet(ing?) hello says stupid. Daddy is one. Man stupid is. Boy two.

7th grade:

kommt Vogel. Der Vogel Fiegen landen Unfall zwichen Baum.

(Es) kommt **ein** Vogel. Der Vogel **flieg̶t**, landet **un**d (**hat einen**) Unfall zwischen (**den**) Bäumen.

comes bird. The bird fly land accident between tree.

Due to the extremely restricted knowledge Vanessa seems to have had in the 3rd grade concerning grammar, we had to omit the German interpretation line. Even so, it is equally clear that Vanessa refers to the comic strip that was used as a starting point but her severe linguistic problems make understanding more difficult for the reader. In this and the following example taken from the 7th grade, some incorrectly spelled words can be found. Usually Vanessa omits letters, once she puts them in the wrong place: "zwie" instead of "zwei" (= two). In the 7th grade she appears to have gained knowledge in the grammar of both GSL and German written language. She obviously masters the structure S-V-O of the German written language and even adds a definite article. On the other hand, Vanessa strings a couple of verbs together, which is possible in GSL as long as they all have the same subject. There are hardly any inflections of verb or noun, Vanessa only uses the singular noun form.

Leon is very difficult to describe. He has been thought to be a very slow learner, having problems remembering the spelling of words which continues to be true today. He is not always active in class and shows particular problems in math. On the other hand,

Table 1.

Name[2]	Boxing story 3rd/4th grade			Peanut story 6th grade			Lion story 7th grade		
	Age	Words	Text level	Age	Words	Text level	Age	Words	Text level
Anna	9;6	125	3-4	11;9	110	4	13;0	731	4
Erik	11;7	47	0-1	-	-	-	16;0	-	-
Florian	8;8	83	3	10;11	161	3-4	12;2	457	4
Katharina	10;0	163	4	11;11	127	3-4	14;5	871	4
Lars	9;7	48	1	11;5	66	2-3	14;0	155	2
Leon	9;10	32	1	12;1	84	2-(4)	13;4	269	4
Michael	9;1	32	1	11;4	83	2(-4)	12;7	178	2-3
Thomas	8;8	43	1	10;11	73	2-4	12;2	270	2/3/4
Vanessa	10;6	22	0-1	12;9	26	1	14;0	119	1

over the years we observed his growing ability to organize his work on his own. In the 4th grade his texts used to be very short but did not appear to be significantly influenced by sign language, which continues to be true today. In the 7th grade he writes a much longer text with an astonishingly vivid and far more interesting story than most of his classmates produce, even though his morphosyntactic knowledge is more restricted. He expresses himself by using short, simple sentences with a grammar he can now handle. Examples:

4th grade:

wein Papa der Jungen Bitte Hafle treifen die Mann schreien die Jungen schau

Der Junge weint **bei (seinem)** Papa „Bitte h**i**lf **(mir)**". **D**ie Männer treffen **sich und** schreien **sich an. D**ie Jungen schau**en (zu).**

cry Daddy the boy please help meet the men shout the boys watch

7th grade:

Alle Schaf und Löwe Schlafen plötzlich hören Der Lowe ein Wolf im Berg. Wolf hat viele Hunger Wolf möcht essen auf Schaf.

Alle Schaf**e** und **der** Löwe schlafen**. P**lötzlich hör**t d**er Löwe ein**en** Wolf im Berg. **Der** Wolf hat viel **(großen)** Hunger. **Der** Wolf möchte **das/ein** Schaf essen.

All (of the) sheep and lion are sleeping suddenly hear the lion a wolf in the mountain. Wolf is very hungry wolf wants to eat sheep.

Leon's 4th grade sentences do not appear to be organised in any manner whatsoever. He knows where to put the article and sometimes even puts the verbs in the second place, but in general he does not mark the beginnings or endings of his sentences. Many elements are missing, mostly reflexive pronouns and prepositions. Difficulties with the spelling of words can be observed, which have not diminished in the 7th grade either, and Leon still needs more time to remember the exact letters needed for a word and their position. Still, there has been a fundamental change in Leon's writing skills. He now organizes exactly what he wants to say, which can even be observed in a part of the text as short as this: Leon first describes a peaceful scene with the herd and Lambert the lion sleeping, which is interrupted all of a sudden by the appearance of a wolf. Afterwards Leon makes the situation of the wolf very clear (he is hungry) and states his intentions (he wants to eat a sheep), which threatens the peaceful group. Furthermore, Leon does not have any problems anymore with German sentence structure, he even switches, when necessary, subject and conjunction ("plötzlich hört..."). He mostly inflects the verbs. The only elements he omits now are some articles which are not needed in GSL. As stated before Leon does not need GSL-structure to express himself. In fact, he only uses one element specifically taken from sign language. The signed equivalent of "auf" defines the relation between two elements. To be specific, in this case it is used to make clear that it is the sheep that is to be eaten by the wolf.

The results of the bilingual group compared to other hearing impaired pupils

To gain a deeper insight into the development of writing skills under the conditions of hearing impairment, a wider project has been initiated. As a starting point for the written narratives the same short Disney movie already used in the bilingual group (7th grade) has been chosen. Two hard-of-hearing and three deaf classes have been tested.

Generally, the hard-of-hearing classes use a more detailed vocabulary than their deaf counterparts. Particularly functional words such as prepositions, articles, pronouns, auxiliary verbs or conjunctions are used far more often and more adequately. The deaf pupils mostly leave those words out and are restricted to the use of nouns, verbs and adjectives. The sentence structure in the hard-of-hearing groups resembles more that of the hearing pupils. Nearly all of them reached Level 4. Only the better half of the bilingual group among the deaf pupils is able to compete with them, but even the lesser half can cope with such an assignment. Slightly less functional words than in the texts of the hard-of-hearing pupils can be found, but the words they omit are mostly articles which have a purely grammatical function. Instead, they show an increased use of relational words that help connect the text. This is partly why the bilingual group reaches the highest text level of all groups, except for the best hard-of-hearing group.

References

Günther, K.-B. & Helmecke, S. (1999): *Text writing of Bilingual Educated Deaf Pupils – A Comparison between 3th/4th Graders in the Hamburg School for the Deaf and the Vänerskolan*. In: European Days of Deaf Education (EDDE), 23-26 September 1999, Öre-bro, Sweden.

Günther, K.-B. & Koll. (1999): *Bilingualer Unterricht mit gehörlosen Grundschülern. Zwischenbericht zum Hamburger Bilingualen Schulversuch*. Verlag hörgeschädigte Kinder, Hamburg.

Günther, K.-B. & Koll. (2001): *Bilingualer Unterricht mit gehörlosen Schülern (II). Abschlussbericht zum Hamburger Bilingualen Schulversuch*. Hamburg (unpublished).

Günther, K.-B. (1998): *Problems of Identity Development of Deaf Children, Part two: Report of the Attempt* Bilingual Education *at the Hamburg School for the Deaf*. In: Weisel, A. (Ed. – 1998): Proceedings of the International Congress on Education of the Deaf, Tel Aviv, July 16-20, 1995. Tel Aviv, 457-461.

Klaus-B. Günther a kol. (2000): *Bilingvální vyučování neslyšících žáků základní školy – etapová zpráva o hamburském bilingváním školním experimentu*. Praha: Ministervo školství, mládeže a tělovýchovy.

RAZVOJ PISANOG JEZIKA DVOJEZIČNO EDUCIRANIH GLUHIH UČENIKA - ISKUSTVA IZ DVOJEZIČNE ŠKOLE ZA GLUHE U HAMBURGU

Početkom školske godine 1993./94. učinjen je prvi pokušaj dvojezičnog obrazovanja dvaju razreda gluhih učenika u Njemačkoj. Prvotno započet zbog želje roditelja, glavne točke projekta bile su sljedeće: 1) Gluhi i čujući učitelj zajedno su kao tim (svaki je koristio jedan jezik) poučavali dvojezične nastavne jedinice; 2) Od samog početka komunikacije između učenika i nastavnika koristili su se i njemački znakovni jezik (DGS) i govorni njemački (uz "znakovni njemački" (LBG) i posebni znakovni sustav kojim se predstavlja svaki fonem (PMS)) te pisanje. Opći cilj projekta bio je osposobiti gluhe učenike da razviju komunikaciju i spoznajne sposobnosti koje odgovaraju njihovom uzrastu te da iskuse ne samo jezik već i kulturu dviju zajednica. Tradicionalna oralna edukacija zanemarivala je pitanje usvajanja pisanog jezika gluhih učenika. Dvojezični je projekt, s druge strane - uvažavajući važnu ulogu pisanja u društvu, koja se nije smanjila razvojem novih medija u posljednjem desetljeću, i činjenicu da su pisane riječi mnogo stalnije od govornih - pokušao što kvalitetnije podržati razvoj pisanja. Iz toga proizlazi širi projekt kojega smo započeli da bismo pobliže popratili razvoj stvaranja pisanog teksta (točnije, stvaranja priča) pod uvjetima dvojezične edukacije, ali i u usporedbi s ostalim učenicima oštećena sluha (ne samo gluhima) koji su prošli drugačiji program edukacije. U nedostatku prikladnih instrumenata istraživanja morali smo stvoriti vlastite ili modificirati postojeće da bismo analizirali različite aspekte razvoja teksta. Tekstove su skupljali sami učitelji kako bi se izbjegla tipična "situacija ocjenjivanja" i osigurala prirodnija situacija. Za početak smo kao primjer pisane priče izabrali strip (u trećem i četvrtom razredu) i kratak Disneyjev film (u petom i sedmom razredu) radi postizanja maksimalne motivacije i mogućnosti usporedbe. Na temelju rezultata istraživanja može se ustvrditi kako dvojezična edukacija pospješuje usvajanje vještine produkcije teksta u gluhe djece.

Ključne riječi: *znakovni jezik, manualna komunikacija, dvojezično obrazovanje, pismenost, gluhi, jezična znanja*

KENYAN SIGN LANGUAGE COMPETENCE: A PREREQUISITE FOR TEACHERS IN HANDLING DEAF BILINGUALISM

Peter Oracha Adoyo

*Institute of Special Education,
University of Hamburg, Germany*

"Teaching the deaf is less difficult than is commonly supposed. We merely have to introduce into their minds by way of the eye what has been introduced into our own by the ear. These two avenues are always open, each leading to the same point provided we do not deviate to the left or right, whichever one we choose. Abbe de l`Epee (1776)".

Abstract

The purpose of this paper is to discuss language accessibility for deaf children to enhance bilingualism in the Kenyan classroom. The deaf community has now and again complained of the current practices utilized in educating the deaf, especially in the language of instruction. The paper briefly highlights the changes in the classroom methodologies that have taken place without much success. The paper argues for Kenyan Sign Language competence as a prerequisite for the deaf educator to participate in the deaf bilingual programmes, future advantages of which for the deaf are also outlined. Teachers' attitude toward KSL[1] and the lack of competent teacher trainers are discussed as obstacles to KSL competence. Suggestions on how to tackle these problems are provided and discussed in the section "The way forward".

1. Introduction

Deaf education has been one of the most frequently and controversially discussed area for many centuries and numerous developments and changes in the system have occurred in the past several years in search of a better medium of instruction. Yet the question remains unresolved as to which method of communication should be adopted. The changes moved from pure oralism[2], to total communication[3] and now to sign bilingualism.

As the current preferred approach, bilingual strategy for educating deaf children is now strong in current linguistics and educational theories. Deaf children's need to acquire

---

[1] Kenyan Sign Language
[2] Oralism is a communication method for the deaf which uses only speech
[3] Total communication is an education policy that encouraged teachers to use all means of communication at their disposal, e.g. sign language, English, pantomime, drawing, fingerspelling, etc.

a natural signed language as a basic ground for second language acquisition is being recognized worldwide. As a result, spoken languages, particularly the reading and writing of the surrounding codes are now being taught to deaf students as second languages. These changes have marked an important transition in the history of deaf education.

The language of communication used in school not only affects the child's achievement in language development, but also influences his or her ability to learn other contents the school offers. For education, therefore, overall success will depend on the quality of the instruction. The quality of the instruction the teacher delivers in turn depends on the language used in the classroom. Thus, the two most important variables for deaf students as pointed out by Lane, Hoffmeister & Bahan (1996) are the quality of instruction and the time spent on the task.

However, congenital[4] deafness, which constitutes a larger proportion of deaf children, imposes a severe threat to the development of a verbal language. Consequently, individuals with severe to profound hearing impairment as we know must rely on vision to learn about and interact with the world (Lynas, 1994). Their native modality will be vision and therefore their desired language will be the one that is presented and processed visually and it must be - signed language. Therefore, everyone involved in the care for, development and education of the deaf children has, a primary concern to activate the visual language capacities within the deaf child to enable his/her linguistic development and communication in their full complexity.

2. The Kenyan situation

Despite the serious changes that have taken place in this area, many schools for the deaf in Kenya are still using simultaneous communication in instruction, which, statistically, has failed elsewhere. Children have been expected to receive content transmitted to them in the language that the teachers themselves have not mastered.

Kenya used oralism from 1957 to 1986, when the system changed to total communication, which in essence turned to be Signing Exact English, a communication method that has now dominated classrooms for the deaf in Kenya.

Although Signing Exact English (which most of the Kenyan deaf educators confuse with Kenyan Sign Language) is being used in schools and training institutions, researchers elsewhere (Erting, 1985; Mammor & Pettito, 1979) have revealed that during its use, teachers fail to represent English accurately due to modality difference, i.e. vocal and gestural output. Johnson et al. (1989) argue that the simultaneous communication suffers not only from distortion, but also from omission of obligatory words, which do not fit the rhythmic pattern of English speech, resulting in distorted information, which are incomprehensible to the deaf. This situation has made the deaf to lag behind hearing counterparts in all measures of academic achievements.

A number of studies in Kenya (KSDC[5], 1979; Nkangi & Mbindyo, 1981; Makumi, 1985; Kamunge report, 1988), have documented that deaf education in this country has

---

[4] Deafness that has occurred from birth
[5] Kenya Society for the Deaf Children

Sign Language, Deaf Culture & Bilingual Education

not lived up to its original expectations and that the children finish school semi-illiterate. All investigations have pointed to the medium of instruction as the major obstacle to the academic development and have subsequently called for a change to the approach.

The fact that most children (DCHP)[6], i.e. 95% of them (Conrad, 1979) do not have access to the acquisition of the first language early enough makes them arrive at school with restricted linguistic and social preparation. The impact of this on the structure of schooling is that the school must prepare the children for acquisition of the first natural language for second language acquisition, socialization and development of world knowledge (Cummins & Swain, 1986; Liddel & Johnson, 1990). These tasks, generally undertaken naturally in their infancy at home, must take place in school. This therefore means that the teachers must deal with the issues which this paper calls "first language repair work" while at the same time teaching curriculum in order to make up for the deficit.

3. Sign languages

Sign languages are formal, socially agreed on, rule-governed symbols that are generated in nature (Stokoe, 1960; Klima & Bellugi, 1979; Kyle & Woll, 1985; Wilbur, 1987). Sign languages are separate languages distinct from spoken languages. While in spoken language the physical expression takes the form of articulatory configuration in the vocal tract, which modifies breath to produce relatively discrete units of speech sounds, sign language expressions are based on manual and nonmanual configurations that constitute discrete visual-gestural signs (Okombo & Akach, 1997:133). Though different in the modes of expression, signed and spoken languages are equivalent in their communicative potentials.

Sign languages like spoken languages have internal structure. The phonological level consists of articulatory parameters known as hand configurations, movement, location and orientation of the palm (cheremes). Specific combination of two or more of these parameters (always including hand configuration) may lead to the formation of specific meaningful sign units. Varying any of these parameters leads to the formation of a different sign. For instance, in Kenyan Sign Language, the right active fist landing on the left open palm in space means **"PERMISSION"**, whereas the right "B" handshape with left orientation landing on the same open palm means **"TRUE"**.

One of the most outstanding morphological properties of sign languages is the polysynthetic nature in which two or more ideas are packed in one sign. For example, in KSL, the sign **"to look for a long time"** consist of the root word LOOK-AT plus another morpheme to show the extent of duration (LOOK AT + LONG-TIME).

Like spoken languages, sign languages do not have fixed word order. The following word orders are common: SVO, OVS and topic comment. The changes are normally influenced by several factors, one of which is the grammatical relation of who does what to whom. This syntactic domain is characterized by nonmanual signals that mark the

---

[6] Deaf children of hearing parents
[7] sign languages

modal properties of a sentence. In this way, we are able to separate statements, questions and also identify emotions. For instance, in KSL, the sentence **"Peter went to school"**, a simple declarative sentence, is represented by three manual signs as follows:

(Pst) PETER GO SCHOOL. This sentence has no facial expression because it is a neutral sentence. Since it is in past tense, it is marked by a past marker superscript, pst at the beginning of the sentence.

However, the question **"Did Peter go to school?"** would be represented as follows:

(Pst) PETER GO SCHOOL

The distinction would be marked by the presence of nonmanual signs (NMS) comprising eyebrow raise, head forward, body forward, which would be represented by the NMS written as "q".

The foregoing explanation of KSL sheds some light on its viability as a complete language. Although not much extensive research has been done on it like in other languages, Okombo (1994) has pointed out that it is capable of handling educational demands necessary for the classroom situation.

The advantage of SL[7] in enriching the lives of the deaf cannot be overemphasized. As a language of instruction within bilingual framework in deaf education, SL has created excellent educational and professional opportunities for the deaf in many parts of the world e.g. USA and Sweden, just to mention a few.

4. Education language policy.

The Kenyan education language policy states that the child's first language or the language of the catchment area should be used as the medium of instruction for the first three years of school. This justifies our advocacy for KSL "repair work to facilitate learning. Based on Skuttnab Kangas' (1994) definition of mother tongue using identification, competence, and function criteria, we are convinced that KSL appropriately becomes the mother tongue for the deaf Kenyans. This therefore entails its use as classroom medium of instruction. The question is; how competent are the teachers in KSL, not only for teaching the language but also for using it in the delivery of curriculum?

The question of teaching the language must be addressed because, though deaf children may acquire sign language in the natural setting provided by the school community of the deaf, the degree of competence they require for educational purposes and for complex discourse in their adult life after school cannot be achieved from mere exposure to a language, whether spoken or signed.

A survey by Adoyo (1995) revealed that out of twenty-one (21) teachers in a school for the deaf, only two teachers (9.5%) showed competent knowledge of KSL. This kind of situation is common in almost all schools for the deaf in Kenya. The reasons for this are numerous. Firstly, our teachers` training institutions lack KSL specialists. Secondly, though the teachers interact daily with the native speakers (deaf children) who can provide them with an ideal environment for signing, there is still a negative attitude toward KSL as a medium of instruction. This is paradoxical because research on sign bilingualism elsewhere has shown success.

5. Sign Bilingualism

In their research comparing bilinguals and monolinguals, Hakuta (1986) and Lambert (1977) noted that bilinguals have high cognitive flexibility, are more sensitive to semantic relations among words and are creative in solving problems. One way of approaching bilingualism in the education of deaf Kenyans would be to let KSL share with English the role of the medium of instruction in the teaching at all levels of education (Okombo, 1994). KSL would be the medium of active communication, while English would play the role of written communication, either in writing or via finger-spelling.

The implications for the Kenyan deaf students, who must learn written language, e.g. English, are clear. Bilingual education using KSL as the language of the classroom communication will teach subject matters better and it will impact background knowledge and skills that will facilitate the learning of English. As the deaf children become bilingual, they will be more capable of a variety of cognitive skills, resulting in improved academic achievement, which of course is our ultimate objective.

From the foregoing explanations we can see how useful it is for a deaf child to be bilingual. We must, however, understand that it is the first language that will facilitate this, which is in this case KSL. However, the foregoing evidence shows the teachers' lack of KSL competence. How will they manage a language and deliver curriculum contents through a medium of instruction that they are not competent in? The solution is to re-educate the teachers and reduce the prejudice that leads to oppression.

6. The way forward

The recommendations as set out under this section fall into two categories: teacher training and prejudices.

6.1. Training

One major problem concerning the introduction of KSL as a subject and medium of communication in the education and training of the deaf is the lack of qualified personnel in the training institutions. As Okombo (1994) puts it, "*our training colleges, including Kenya Institute of Education, do not have trainers who are competent in KSL.*" One

---

[8] British Sign Language
[9] German Sign Language

way of tackling this problem, as has been done in well-known centres for deaf studies, e.g. in Bristol, UK (BSL)[8], and in Hamburg, Germany (GSL)[9], is to have deaf Kenyans, as well as sign language instructors, working together with linguists who can handle the theoretical aspects of the programme. The Kenyan policy makers will have to ignore the academic certificate requirements for the deaf at this initial stage if they truly want the programme to set off. The ongoing programme at Maseno University where a native deaf and a bilingual instructor are working in collaboration is a move in the right direction.

New changes and developments in society, research and schools, as well as in the area of deafness now demand innovative approaches in teacher preparation. For instance, research in schools with young deaf children points to the need for learning in an environment in which communication is consistently accessible and clear. Evident, too, is the awareness that a strong foundation in the first language is important, together with potentially positive effects of a bilingual strategy to education, suggesting a need for new methods of instruction and a high competence of sign language for the teachers of the deaf.

The teachers' level of understanding and skill in communication and language, regardless of particular modes of communication, should be the focus of teacher preparation. There is need to understand the way linguistic behaviour is affected by the children's communication mode. The critical issue of whether to use a natural sign language or the signed form of a spoken language as the appropriate linguistic base for the deaf must be viewed by the teacher trainers.

Most of the students who go into teacher education are hearing students who may or may not have had contact with sign language. There is a need to provide an intensive immersion course in KSL so that they can concentrate on developing language competence with which to deliver curriculum contents. Emphasis should also be laid on the teachers' ability to understand the signing of young children, as this is often different to adult signing. It is also important to recruit deaf members as teaching assistants. It should be ensured that culturally deaf individuals have a central role in these programmes.

It has been observed that student teachers of the deaf in Kenya are not gaining the appropriate knowledge needed for work within a bilingual framework. They do not have ample opportunity to learn or effectively apply Kenyan Sign Language, to study the linguistics of the language or to become knowledgeable in Deaf culture. In addition, the curriculum does not offer training in the areas of bilingualism. The training has failed to emphasize the critical relationship between language, cognition, culture and the process of total human development and learning. There is a vital need to incorporate these areas in the teacher's curriculum.

Many a time, deaf and hearing people at workplace find themselves involved in very difficult and challenging situations that end up in conflicts. Difficult self-examination and working to understand what it means to cooperate for a common goal in a culturally diverse environment should be a part of the teacher training.

The continued search for literacy for deaf children will require teachers of the deaf to acquire new techniques, including code-switching, the ability to move from sign language to the signed or written form of spoken language, depending on the instructional needs of that particular moment. Education officers, inspectors, as well as teachers, need to become knowledgeable about new research findings and teaching techniques. There is a need for teacher trainees who are well-prepared in content areas as well as in pedagogy. Apart from high communication skills, teachers of the deaf must possess the essential content background and expertise to teach subject matters such as science, mathematics or geography.

In Kenya, all schools for the deaf are residential institutions forming a "deaf community." This becomes an ideal environment for KSL acquisition. The teachers should take advantage of this to improve their KSL skills while at the same time attending rigorous school-based in-service training.

Misplacement of skills when teachers are posted from training institutions is another key issue which needs urgent redress. It is quite common to find trained teachers of the deaf posted to schools for the physically/mentally handicapped against their will. This is unprofessional and unfair, not only for the teacher but also for the deaf child who cannot be taught elsewhere due to the lack of professionally qualified personnel. It deprives deaf children of talented teachers whose skills are merely wasted elsewhere. Teachers must work in their relevant areas of specialization if we truly want to produce desirable results.

6.2. Prejudices

Many uncritical Kenyan minds including teachers still believe that African languages are inferior to the languages of the West. A recent conversation with a Kenyan deaf adult shocked me when he proudly said that he was using American Sign Language because Kenyan Sign Language is for the young deaf children and those with low education. This is very unfortunate as it has resulted into tension and struggle within the Kenyan deaf community. The tension is often a result of a lack of information, awareness and exposure. As Gallimore (1993) observes, it can also be a result of oppression itself, as sometimes members of an oppressed minority begin to work against each other. Freire (1990) calls this "horizontal violence". Some key deaf Kenyans have differed on which sign language dictionaries should be used in schools. This situation will continue to delay research and development of KSL. There is a great need for unity in order to overcome this "horizontal violence" which has been used by the observers as an excuse for postponing desirable changes within the educational establishment.

Many teachers still doubt the status of Kenyan Sign Language as a real language due to the assumption that language must be spoken. This attitude is difficult to defeat. It is connected with the ideology of colonial education in Africa, which recognized those who speak English as elites that belong to a class of their own. This mentality has made teachers prefer Signing Exact English (a bimodal artificial communication which uses signs mapped on the English word order) to Kenyan Sign Language. Consequently, KSL has become a victim of neocolonialism. This violation of linguistic human rights must be resisted at all costs as it deprives deaf children (who keep languages alive) of the use and development of Kenyan Sign Language.

One of the main attitudinal problems for teachers is the feeling that KSL as a language is not viable as a medium of instruction and that it has no capacity to serve as a medium for communicating complex ideas the school curriculum offers. As Okombo (1994) puts it, *"Such attitudes totally ignore the unlimited creative ability of human languages as any language can make the necessary adjustments to accommodate new ideas as long as its users really want to use it in communicating those ideas."*

6.3. Conclusion

In general, we have seen that deaf Kenyans need to be educated through the medium of their own language, KSL, not only to master the curriculum contents but also to become bilingual and capable of participating in complex discourse in both KSL and written English as these will later be important in their career and social life. This is only possible with the guidance of a teacher with KSL competence.

7. References

**Abee de L`Epee, C.M. (1776)**: Institutiondes sourdes et muets, par la voie des signes methodigues. Paris: Nyon Revised. L`Epee (1784) English translation (excerpts), American Annals of the Deaf (13), 1861, 8-29.

Adoyo, P.O. (1995): An investigation of Kenyan Sign Language Development. Unpublished PGDE Dissertation, University of Bristol, U.K.

Cummins, J. & Swain, M. (1986): Bilingualism in Education. New York: Longman.

Deuchar, M. (1984): British Sign Language. London: Routledge and Kegan Paul.

Erting, C.J. (1978): Sociocultural dimensions of deaf education. Belief systems and communication interactions: In Sign Language studies, pp. 111-126.

Freire, P. (1990): Pedagogy of the oppressed. New York Continuum.

Gallimore, L. (1993): How to utilise American Sign Language as the language of instruction in the classroom. In Gallaudet Research Institute working paper 89-3. Gallaudet University, Washington, D.C.

Hakuta, K. (1986): Mirror of Language: The Debate on Bilingualism. New York: Basic Books.

Johnson, R.E. & Liddel, S. (1990): The value of ASL in the education of the deaf. In Garretson (ed.). Communication issues among deaf people: A deaf American monograph, pp. 59-63. Silver Spring, MD: National Association of the Deaf.

Johnson, R.; Liddel, S.; Erting, C. (1989): Unlocking the curriculum. Principles for achieving access in deaf education. Washington, D.C. Gallaudet University Research Institute, USA.

Kamunge-Report (1988): Education and Manpower training for the next decade and beyond. Nairobi, Government Printer.

KSDC (1979): Final report on deaf education, Nairobi, Kenya.

Klima, E. & Bellugi, U. (1979): The Signs of Language. Cambridge, Mass, London Havard University.

Lambert, W. (1977): Culture and Language as factors in education. In F. Eckman (ed.) Current themes in linguistics: Bilingualism, experimental linguistics, and language typologies. Washington, D.C.: Hemisphere Publishing.

Lane, H.; Hoffmeister, R.; Bahan B. (1996): A journey into the Deaf world. Dawn Sign Press. San Diego, California.

Larson, D.N. & Smalley, W.A. (1972): Becoming Bilingual: A guide to language learning. Practical Anthology. New Canaan, U.S.A.

Lynas, W. (1994). Communication options in Deaf Education. Compton Terrace England: Whur Publisher.

Makumi, E.C.N. (1995): A study of special education programme in Kenya with special emphasis on education of hearing - impaired and causes of their semi-illiteracy. Unpublished Thesis. Kenyatta University.

Mammor, S. & Pettito, L. (1979): Simultaneous communication in the classroom. How well is English grammar represented? Sign Language studies (1979): SLS 99-136, Linstock Press, Inc.

Nkangi & Mbindyo (1981): Head teachers' views on poor performance of deaf children. In Yego E. (1986): The status of sign language of the deaf and measures for improvement in Kenya. In Finnish Association of the Deaf (ed.). East African Sign Language seminar. Debre Zeit, Ethiopia. August 20-26, 1990. Helsinki: FAD, 31-38.

Okombo, O. (1994): "Kenyan Sign Language. Some attitudinal and cognitive issues in the evolution of a language community". In Ahlgren & Hyltenstam I.K. (eds.). Bilingualism in Deaf education. Hamburg: Signum, 37-54.

Okombo, O. & Akach, P.O.A. (1997): Language convergence and Wave phenomena in the growth of a national sign language in Kenya. In De Gruyter (1997) (eds.): Linguistic issues in Sub-Saharan Africa. International Journal of the Sociology of Language,125, pp. 131-144.

Sass-Lehrer, M., & Martin, S., D. (1992): "New directions for deaf education: A proposal for action in teacher preparation". In Martin, S. & Mobley, R. (1992) (eds.): Proceedings of the first International Symposium on Teacher Education in Deafness: Gallaudet University.

Skutnabb-Kangas; T. (1994): Linguistic human rights. A Prerequisite for bilingualism. In Ahlgren, I. & Hyltenstan (eds.): Bilingualism in deaf education, Hamburg: Signum, pp. 139-159.

Stokoe, W. C. (1960): Sign language structure: An outline of the visual communication system of the American deaf . Studies in linguistics. Buffalo, NY: University of Buffalo.

Wilbur, B. P. (1987): American Sign Language Linguistic and applied dimensions. Boston: College-Hill Publication.

KOMPETENCIJA UČITELJA U KENIJSKOM ZNAKOVNOM JEZIKU: PREDUVJET ZA DVOJEZIČNO OBRAZOVANJE GLUHE DJECE

Cilj ovog rada je rasprava o dostupnosti jezika gluhoj djeci u svrhu poticanja dvojezičnosti u kenijskim učionicama. Zajednica gluhih opetovano se žali na trenutnu praksu koja se koristi u obrazovanju gluhih, osobito vezano uz jezik na kojem se poučava. Rad ukratko opisuje promjene u metodologijama koje se nisu pokazale osobito uspješnima. Kompetentnost u kenijskom znakovnom jeziku preduvjet je koji učitelj gluhih mora zadovoljiti da bi sudjelovao u bilingvalnim programima za gluhe. U ovom radu prikazane su i buduće prednosti tih programa. Raspravlja se o stavovima učitelja prema kenijskom znakovnom jeziku i nedostatku jezične edukacije za učitelje, što predstavlja prepreku postizanju kompetentnosti u kenijskom znakovnom jeziku. Navedene su sugestije kako riješiti te probleme.

Ključne riječi: *znakovni jezik, gluhi, školovanje gluhih, dvojezično obrazovanje*

TOWARDS BILINGUAL EDUCATION IN THE RESIDENTAL SCHOOL FOR DEAF AND HARD OF HEARING IN LJUBLJANA: LANGUAGE AND SELF-CONFIDENCE

Nicole Kuplenik

Residential School for Deaf and Hard of Hearing Children, Ljubljana, Slovenia

Abstract

In the field of deaf education, most effort is put forth into language learning. From the linguistic and sociological point of view, in teaching both spoken language and sign language we encounter a number of stumbling blocks. Students at ZGN Ljubljana (Residential School for Deaf and Hard of Hearing) fall short of satisfactory linguistic competence in either language. Our aim is to guide them to a certain level of linguistic competence in one or both languages. The question is why the level of academic achievement in our students can't compare with the level of regular schools' students in spite of employing the principle of total communication in education. Obviously, in the field of language learning, this is not enough. Therefore, some questions have to be asked to change our perspective: 1) Is learning of the national spoken language reasonable at all if by the end of school it can't be used to communicate successfully? How are we to improve our students' insufficient language structure (in both spoken and sign language) that is inadequate in spite of applying various teaching methods and a lot of hard work? In my opinion, systematic effort is only put forth in building the structure of spoken language while systematic teaching of sign language is put aside, since our students from hearing families learn sign language mostly from their peers. And yet at the end of school their sign language structure seems to progress to a much greater extent than that of spoken Slovene. The latter functions as the second language. I believe our task should be to concentrate systematically on building the students' metalinguistic knowledge of sign language, which would also result in the improved structure of the second language - national spoken language. Thereby, the level of reading and writing skills would get significantly better. 2) Learning, language and self-esteem are intertwined characteristics of personality; by systematically improving them, personal identity is developed and thereupon group identity (Deaf Power) is built. The three intertwined characteristics influence each other: self-esteem gives motivation to learn, successful learning builds self-esteem, high self-esteem manifests in language by encouraging language learning and improving language structure, a well-developed language structure assists in expressing one's personality which improves self-esteem … The three characteristics have come a full circle. The paper deals with the experiences and projects of ZGN Ljubljana (School for the Deaf and Hard of Hearing) that lead to a better language competence in spoken as well as in sign language and the long-term effects this work will have on the self-esteem of our students and thus on the deaf population.

Key words: deaf, bilingual education, identity, deaf identity

Introduction

The greatest emphasis in deaf education is put on language acquisition. Linguistic competence of deaf students in spoken language is rather insufficient in most cases. Nevertheless, their sign language - Slovene Sign Language (SSL) - structure is often inadequate, too, since it is usually learned from peers after the period critical for learning the first language. Their low linguistic competence has severe negative influences, not only on language lessons or school work. It affects various areas of one's performance. Language is a tool of one's social life which defines us as human beings.

Deaf students in Ljubljana School for the Deaf and Hard of Hearing (ZGNL School) have low linguistic competence in both spoken and sign language. The objective of the School is to provide them with skills for a successful communication in their future environment. In spite of the consistent use of the total communication (TC) principle the level of academic achievement of our students is hardly comparable to the one of hearing students in regular school. Therefore some questions spring up regarding the acquisition of language.

1. Dilemmas in teaching language(s) at ZGNL School

A lot of time and effort is invested in teaching spoken language: lessons in Slovene language and literature, lessons in (spoken language) communicational skills, individual training in aural and oral skills. All this work is highly systematic and student-oriented – the national spoken language is taught through second language methods, communicational skills provide them with reading, writing and discourse communicational skills, individual training gives students a chance to do extra work with their poorer skills (understanding and producing written texts, lip-reading, creativity in different communicational situations ...).

The total approach has been used consistently is for the last fifteen years. This approach has been vital since our student population is highly heterogeneous, especially in the secondary school.

At first, this principle has been viewed as a teaching method, although time has proved some weak points of this view: using TC as a teaching method can negatively affect language acquisition. In communication, TC gives the student a "potpourri" of linguistic and non-linguistic elements from which no linguistic system can be derived. Since it is used only as a means of getting a message across, it contains elements of two or more languages and many non-linguistic elements, all of them used in a non-systematic way. If the language structure (two, in our case) isn't strong enough, TC can bring more harm than good to the user. This is especially true for deaf children from hearing families who haven't acquired the first language.

1.2 Dilemmas regarding academic achievements

If the level of academic achievement is measured by the linguistic competence in spoken language, we can say that the use of TC as a teaching method hasn't really brought any progress, though its benefits are easily perceived: our students seem to be more versed in general matters and their self-image seems to be improving. The general level of the national language competence remains more or less the same. Therefore the deaf remain a marginal group since their access to information is highly limited, which makes them dependent on the hearing population.

The great dilemma in the education of the deaf is whether teaching the national language makes any sense at all. During his or her schooling (altogether 12 to 14 years) our average deaf student doesn't learn Slovene well enough to communicate successfully with hearing people. What methods should we use to improve the poor language system of our students? Their language structure (in both spoken language and sign language) remains incomplete in spite of all the systematic work and various teaching methods used.

In my opinion this is caused by the fact that systematic educational work is only invested in the acquisition of the spoken language. Its language structure is taught over a long period of time and never sufficiently grasped, while sign language is learned from peers in non-school situations and mastered quite well in a rather short period of time. From the point of view of an average deaf student, Slovene always remains in a position of the second language, even if the deaf student doesn't master SSL.

Therefore, our task is to put more effort in teaching SSL in a school environment in order to achieve a higher level of linguistic perception of SSL. It would also undoubtedly affect the linguistic competence in Slovene, especially in writing.

2. Language and self-image

Language not only provides us with categories for conceptualizing the external reality, but also corresponds to what we want to express (the internal reality) and the relationship between both. What we express through language is tightly connected to our views, opinions, emotions, values – our self-image. It is also a means of bonding with the community we belong to and identify with. That's why every community identifies so much with its language. If one is incapable of establishing any social bonds, one can't identify with the community in question and thereby also the need of establishing those bonds declines. And since deaf children experience many failures in communication at an early age, they have little motivation to learn the spoken language.

To some extent the structure of our mother tongue[2] "selects" for us what is necessary and less necessary for us to notice. On occasion, different languages focus the attention differently.

In a way, we are more or less slaves of our mother tongue in our thinking and our way of comprehending the world[3]. When we start to learn other languages we begin to realise how relative and arbitrary the way in which our own language describes the world is. Every language we learn anew broadens the horizons, opens new possibilities and teaches us new values. Therefore, bilingualism is an advantage, especially if the two languages differ in the communication code they use (auditive and visual).

---

[2] In the case of the deaf this term is inappropriate since they originate in various environments – using sign language or spoken language.
[3] Skutnab-Kangas, 1981: 5.

The deaf in a hearing society experience great social pressure since their poor competence in spoken language puts them at a disadvantage. On the other hand, segregated education enables them to identify with the deaf community through SL[4], all the more since hearing people use it as little as possible.

Regarding social identification through language, there are severe problems for deaf students in regular schools who mostly don't have any contact with SL or the deaf community. Integration in regular schools is becoming more common, because they provide a higher level of academic achievement and more options in education, however, these deaf students are often isolated and don't feel like an equal part of the hearing society. They mostly don't identify with the deaf community either. Quite some systematic work has been done to keep those students in touch with the society they might become equal members of. If those deaf students would eventually turn away from the deaf community it would in the long term mean lowering of the general level of education in this population, which also affects the possible wider use of SSL.

3. Trends in ZGNL School

The hearing teachers in ZGNL School use SSL more or less fluently, however, it is their second language (L2) and they therefore can't represent a language model for the deaf students. Since in the educational process it is important to convey messages accurately, bilingual forms of school work have been introduced.

In ZGNL School in Ljubljana the TC principle is used with its benefit to individual-oriented communication. Teachers employ elements of SL as a means of communication. In classroom situations, they communicate directly with students, but interpreters are used as well, giving the learning process a bilingual dimension. TC gives the deaf student an access to integral information equal to the one given to a hearing student. A drawback of TC is that it isn't an appropriate means of constructing and complementing the structure of either language – it might even have a negative influence on the already learned language structure[5].

3.1 Bilingual classes in primary school

It has already become clear that the principle of TC can't assure success in language acquisition (which also affects all academic fields directly or indirectly in terms of linguistic competence). Therefore, our work in ZGNL School has introduced teaching methods supporting two language systems separately. Since the school year 1995/96, some lessons in the primary school have been taught by two teachers. Several positive effects of this project have been reported by teachers: children taught in both languages have shown more interest in school work and tend to grasp more general information, the level of forgetting has rapidly decreased, motivation for reading has appeared at an early age, the children easily comprehend and produce written texts.

---

[4] Sign language.
[5] Košir, 1998.

3.2 Using interpreters in classroom

In the secondary school, the use of interpreters has started to become more co-mmonplace. At first, they were only used in activities outside the school (excursions, exhibitions etc.) After the evening school was established, interpreters were also used in a classroom environment, which turned out to be a great success. Today, using interpreters in classroom is becoming a part of our daily teaching practice. Thus, teachers' and students' work is easier and more fluent, language perception is ensured, the deaf students can strongly identify with SL and the hearing teacher acknowledges the students' basic right to communicate in their first language. The interpreter in classroom surmounts the obstacles in communication and conveys a complete information. This form of work also enables both language systems to be conveyed as a whole: the structures remain separate and therefore evident, which brings a return in national language lessons.

3. Comparative work in spoken language lessons

At first, I have used SL only as a means of communication in Slovene lessons. About a year ago, I have started to draw the students' attention to differences between the languages. The motivation for school work has evidently risen, and my students have started to point out some differences themselves. There is more comprehension of grammatical categories. It has also enabled me to become more aware of my own mother tongue and it has become easier to explain elements of grammar to my students. The next step was to compare grammatical categories in both languages.

This must have been quite hard for my students since they haven't thought of their own language as something that can be researched or even compared to some other language. In our discussions, I have also established that they don't even see SL as a language. To them, it is just "a means of communication". They only use the term "language" when they refer to spoken languages. They had also had no experience in taking a scientific view of their language; they have been doing it with Slovene since primary school, but seeing SL in this light was something completely new to them.

We started to use comparative work in language lessons last September and immediately achieved results: the students have become aware that spoken language is "just a language" and not a means of repressing the deaf by hearing people; that SL is a language equal to any other; they have comprehended that learning a language is needed in order to master it – this goes for both languages; they have become aware that through Slovene lessons they can also learn something about their own language. It has become easier for them to grasp some grammatical categories of Slovene and understand their use. They put more effort in comprehending written texts – they are not ashamed to ask what they don't understand, questions also referring to general information in texts.

This is only one of the initial steps towards bilingualism. The goal of Slovene lessons remains the learning of the spoken language and its literature. Comparative methods facilitate the work, but in order to see SL as an equal part of our community and as an unquestionable right of the deaf, it is necessary to introduce it as a school subject. In ZGNL School a project has started to develop a curriculum for its introduction into primary school. Government institutions responsible for education have expressed their moral support for it.

3.4 What to expect

It would be rather unrealistic to expect the most of the deaf population to master spoken language. However, bilingual work in deaf education will most likely cause an increase in language competence in both languages and long-term effects in the fields directly or indirectly affected by linguistic skills, as it has been proved by many schools for the deaf all over the world. From the linguistic point of view, abundant and integral linguistic information at an early age is necessary to master a language. But bilingual teaching methods will bring more than that: this way, a lot of other information is conveyed: the respect for basic human rights, tolerance and the necessity of acquiring various social skills in order to live as a part of the community.

The main goal of ZGNL School is to teach communicational skills so the deaf students would be able to integrate in their home environment. This can be achieved not only through the sufficient use of spoken language, but also through general social skills and through a positive self-image. For the deaf, this mostly means identification with the deaf community, and since more and more deaf students attend regular schools with the expert help of ZGNL School, I believe it is the duty of our school to provide links to the deaf community.

4. Conclusion

Learning, language and self-image are tightly interconnected elements of one's personality and by systematically upgrading them all personal identity is built. The three elements influence each other: self-confidence affects learning motivation, successful learning improves self-confidence, which is expressed through communication with others; successful communication gives rise to the need to learn the language, a well-acquired language structure enables one to appropriately express oneself, which again improves self-confidence.

By improving the perception of SL, the perception of the majority language is improved as well, since the users are enabled to compare the structure known to the structure learned. Bilingual methods bring information on both languages and both cultures not only to the native users (the deaf) but also to the members of the majority. An indirect effect of introducing bilingualism (and bicultural elements) into school is a greater acceptance of the deaf by the hearing society, starting from the hearing teachers in school.

5 Bibliography

Martin, D.S. (ed.) (1989): Cognition, Education and Deafness. Directions for Research and Instruction. Gallaudet University Press, Washington DC.

Chomsky, N. (1989): Znanje jezika. Mladinska knjiga, Ljubljana.

Inclusion. Best Practices for Students who are Deaf or Hard of Hearing. http://www.sesa.org./agency/docs/incldhh.html

Košir, S. (1998): Utemeljevanje totalne komunikacije. Defectologica Slovenica, 1/VI, 64–71.

Ljubešič, M. & Stančič, V. (1994): Jezik, govor, spoznaja. Hrvatska sveučilišna naklada, Zagreb.

Skutnab-Kangas, T. (1981). Bilingualism or not. The Education of Minorities. In: Multilingual Matters 7.

Svartholm, K. (1995): Deaf policies in Sweden. http://www.zak.co.il/deaf-info/old/sweden.html

Toporišič, J. (1992): Enciklopedija slovenskega jezika. Cankarjeva založba, Ljubljana.

Vogler, C. (1995): Deaf Children in Swedish Kindergartens. http://www.zak.co.il/deaf-info/old/kindergarten.html

PREMA DVOJEZIČNOM OBRAZOVANJU U ZAVODU ZA GLUHE I NAGLUHE U LJUBLJANI: JEZIK I SAMOPOŠTOVANJE

U školovanju gluhih osoba, najviše se truda ulaže u učenje jezika. No, u poučavanju govornog jezika i znakovnog jezika nailazimo na poteškoće i s lingvističkog i sa sociolingvističkog stajališta. Učenici u Zavodu za gluhe i nagluhe (ZGN) u Ljubljani zaostaju u jezičnoj kompetenciji u oba jezika. Naš je cilj dovesti ih do određene razine jezične kompetencije u jednom ili u oba jezika. Postavlja se pitanje zašto razina akademskog uspjeha naših učenika nije usporediva s uspjehom učenika koji pohađaju redovne škole, bez obzira na to što se u edukaciji koristi totalna komunikacija. Očito je da to nije dovoljno kad je u pitanju učenje jezika. Stoga, kako bismo promijenili perspektivu, moramo postaviti određena pitanja: 1) Ima li učenje nacionalnog govornog jezika uopće smisla ako se nakon školovanja ne može koristiti za uspješno komuniciranje? Kako možemo poboljšati nezadovoljavajuću jezičnu strukturu (govornog i znakovnog jezika) koja je neprikladna unatoč različitim metodama poučavanja i mnogo napornog rada? Mislim da se trud sustavno ulaže u izgradnju strukture govornog jezika, dok se sustavno podučavanje znakovnog jezika ostavlja po strani, budući da naši učenici iz čujućih obitelji uglavnom uče znakovni jezik od svojih vršnjaka. Međutim, ipak se na kraju školovanja čini da je jezična struktura znakovnog jezika napredovala mnogo više od govornog slovenskog. Slovenski govorni jezik funkcionira kao drugi jezik. Vjerujem da bi naš zadatak bio koncentrirati se na izgradnju sustavnog metajezičnog znanja o znakovnom jeziku, što bi također poboljšalo strukturu drugog jezika - nacionalnog govornog jezika. Time bi se razina vještine u čitanju i pisanju znatno poboljšala. 2) Učenje, jezik i samopoštovanje ispreletene su karakteristike osobnosti; sustavno ih poboljšavajući, razvija se osobni identitet, a time gradi i grupni identitet (Deaf Power). Ove tri isprepletene karakteristike utječu jedna na drugu: samopoštovanje motivira na učenje, uspješno učenje jača samopoštovanje, visoko samopoštovanje očituje se u poticanju učenja jezika i poboljšavanju jezične strukture, razvijena jezična struktura pomaže pri izražavanju vlastite osobnosti, što poboljšava samopoštovanje.... Te tri karakteristike čine zatvoreni krug. U radu su prikazana iskustva u ZGN u Ljubljani i projekti kojima je cilj poboljšanje jezične kompetencije, kako u govornom tako i u znakovnom jeziku, te dugoročni utjecaji na samopoštovanje naših učenika, a time i na zajednicu gluhih.

Ključne riječi: *gluhi, bilingvalna edukacija, identitet*

THE WORLD OF FAIRY TALES: SOFTWARE FOR DEVELOPING FUNCTIONAL AND EMOTIONAL LITERACY SKILLS IN DEAF CHILDREN

Vesna Ivasović, Lidija Andrijević, Tereza Szavai
«Slava Raškaj» Centre, Zagreb
Tvrtko Maras
Zagreb

Abstract

Since in Croatia no educational software for the deaf is available, we decided to use our practical and theoretical knowledge in order to develop a programme which will help deaf children to develop functional and emotional literacy. The programme is based on contemporary concepts of psychology and psycholinguistics of bilingualism and language competence, as well as on the insights about the importance of emotional literacy and its effect on psycho-social adjustment of children. The software has been designed for children of the older pre-school age and for the pupils in grades 1-4 of the primary school. The aims of the programme are the following: 1) the acquisition of the vocabulary of Croatian sign language and Croatian spoken language; 2) the understanding of the contents communicated in Croatian sign language, written and spoken language; 3) the development of metalinguistic awareness - since fairy tales are told in both sign and written language, the child develops a sense of both languages through the comparison of the two languages; 4) the acquisition of the vocabulary of emotions; 5) the recognition of emotional states; 6) the development of self-evaluation skills; 7) the understanding of the cause-and-effect relationship, the development of logical thinking and moral reasoning. This programme consists of the learning phase and the phase in which the acquired skills are checked. The software is made in such a way that it is possible to add new contents and expand it in a simple way. It has turned out that the combination of the work on the computer and the application of the fairy tales has a positive effect on the motivation in learning. Although a good teacher is irreplaceable, the computer has many good educational qualities: it is patient, remembers the pupil's success in a permanent and objective manner, it is not frustrated by the pupil's slow progress, it can easily store many educational materials, it can give the most appropriate assignments according to the pupil's achievement.

Key words: deaf children, deafness, sign language, literacy, emotional intelligence

Introduction

The natural language of prelingually deaf children which they acquire spontaneously and with ease is sign language. As early as in the 1960s linguists proved that sign language is a real language, linguistically complex and sophisticated, fully adapted to visual and spatial modality (Stokoe, 1960; Klima & Bellugi, 1979). It is processed in the left hemisphere, approximately in the area where spoken language is processed (Poizner, Klima & Bellugi, 1987).

There is a widely spread prejudice that sign language is universal. Quite to the contrary, each country has its own national sign language. There are numerous dialects, too. Research has shown that sign language acquisition phases in deaf babies are identical to spoken language acquisition phases in hearing babies, the only difference is the modality of language acquisition (Pettito & Marentette, 1991).

Today the deaf are considered a linguistic minority and in many countries sign language has been officially recognized, e.g. in France since 1830, in Sweden since 1981, in the Czech Republic since 1998, in Thailand since 1999, and since recently in Slovenia. UN, UNICEF, UNESCO and the European Parliament promote, among other things, the preservation and development of sign languages of individual member/ signatory countries, they encourage its use in the education of deaf children, in their families and communities, as well as the development of interpreters' services.

Functional literacy and bilingualism

Many deaf children fail to achieve the level of functional literacy (reading and writing skills) of hearing children. However, this does not mean that they are not able to master written language well, but only reveals wrong and inefficient practices used in teaching the language of the hearing environment to deaf children. Recent research has made it possible to understand the reasons for traditional problems in the education of deaf children.

In spite of the fact that more than a half of world population uses two or more languages in everyday life, prejudices about bilingualism are still widely spread. The unrealistic definition of a bilingual as a person about equally competent in both languages was rejected a long time ago. Bilinguals are persons who use two or more languages (or dialects) in everyday life. This includes persons who speak one language and write another, persons who speak two languages with different degrees of fluency (and cannot read or write them) and it is persons who are about equally competent in both languages (which is rare). Bilinguals acquire and use languages to various purposes, in various life situations and with various people. The needs and the usage of the two languages are completely different, and it is for this reason that bilinguals rarely achieve fluency in both languages (Grosjean, 1998). Deaf persons who regularly communicate in sign language and in the language of their wider community (e.g. in writing) are bilingual. Deaf bilinguals and hearing bilinguals have many traits in common, but they also have some specific qualities.

There is a strong theoretical support to bilingual education of deaf children. Research has shown that the linguistic development is slowed down and more difficult if information is incomprehensible, inaccessible in any manner or significantly below the level of a person's competence or experience. This does not apply only to deaf children but also to hearing children belonging to minority groups. It is not difficult to imagine how it affects their education.

More than three decades of research in the field of bilingualism suggest that the competence in the first language represents a basis for the acquisition of the second language.

This is also confirmed by results obtained on deaf respondents. The first language and the second language are complementary and not mutually exclusive; it has been demonstrated that the first language competence is a consistent and strong predictor of the acquisition/learning of the second language (Grosjean, 1998). The first and the second languages do not occupy separated brain areas - once the competence in one language is developed, it serves as a basis for the acquisition of other languages.

In relation to deaf children of hearing parents, deaf children of deaf parents show superiority in cognitive, emotional, social (Kolod, 1994; Desselle, 1994) and linguistic development, as well as in school achievement. It has also been demonstrated that in hearing children the learning of sign language at an early age leads to better results in tests of non-verbal intelligence, visual perception and discrimination, spatial memory and the understanding of spoken language vocabulary. Various attempts have been made to explain the fact that deaf children of deaf parents achieve significantly better results on non-verbal intelligence tests even than their hearing peers. The explanation that this is a consequence of additive bilingualism seems the most logical. Additive bilingualism will develop where the first language of the child has neither been neglected nor suppressed. The first language must enjoy about the same social prestige as the language of the wider social community. The concept of additive bilingualism involves two languages on the same footing that enrich a person's cultural identity (Stančić & Ljubešić, 1994). On the other hand, if the first language of a child is held in low esteem by society and is being suppressed from usage, the subtractive bilingualism will develop - the second language is developing at the expense of the native language, which is being suppressed and undervalued. The fact that bilinguals achieve better results on various tests of cognitive abilities may be attributed to their higher mental flexibility and easier formation of concepts, higher ability of manipulating two symbolic systems and detailed analysis of semantic features (Hamers, 1998).

The practice has confirmed that the so-called bilingual-bicultural education provides the best results in developing literacy and generally in acquiring school knowledge by deaf children, but also by hearing children belonging to minority groups. In the majority of developed countries this approach to the education of deaf children is used. In some it is even compulsory, e.g. in Sweden since 1981, as well as in Denmark, Portugal, Venezuela, etc.

The basis for a bilingual education is the acquisition of sign language in a natural manner, in other words as early as possible in childhood, in an interaction with deaf adults - during the same development period as in hearing children. Written language is learned as the second language and academic knowledge is transferred in sign language. It has been demonstrated that bilingual education leads to an increase in self-esteem and the development of bicultural identity due to the acceptance of and a positive attitude toward the minority language, which again leads to better school achievement (Baker, 1997).

The fact that the results of recent research in Sweden do not suggest that deaf children of hearing parents lag behind deaf children of deaf parents in cognitive, emotional, social and linguistic development and in school achievement confirms the efficiency of bilingual approach to deaf education (Mashie, 1995).

Vocabulary

Among pre-school and primary-school children there are significant individual differences both in the number of words they understand (passive vocabulary) and in the number of words they use (active vocabulary), which has far-reaching consequences for their general social and educational achievements. In studying children' vocabulary we make a distinction between its quantitative growth and the development in terms of meanings that requires particular attention.

With children the individual conceptual meaning of word prevails, as a result of the selection of meanings from the vocabulary offered by speech community. This process takes place in a social context and complex situations through common experiences in the interaction between the child and the parent.

Research suggests that a parent who has the same hearing status as his or her child (e.g. both are deaf) will be more successful in attracting and maintaining the child's attention, which will encourage the development of the child's self-awareness and other aspects of the child's social and emotional development at an early age, which all together represents a pre-requisite for a normal acquisition of vocabulary.

Oral speech

The child's ability to develop oral speech depends on many factors. However, there are two principal pre-requisites: biologic potential and an intrinsic motivation or interest. Factors related to potential and motivation may be divided into several specific areas in deaf and hard of hearing children: residual hearing, usefulness of the hearing aid, language competence, support by the family, intelligence, the child's and the family's attitudes, the attitude of the person chosen by the parents as their counsellor and the possibility to choose the manner of rehabilitation and education. Each of these factors has a complex role in the development of speech skills.

Whether a deaf or hard of hearing child will develop comprehensible oral speech mostly depends on the degree of accessibility of spoken language. Children who have less residual hearing, have, in other words, a very limited access to the auditory part of speech and cannot use their hearing to control their own speech, are faced with an extremely difficult task. Although there are exceptions, children with a smaller auditory access to oral speech are less likely to develop functional speech skills. Motivation is often affected by the degree of auditory information accessibility since accessibility makes oral speech more meaningful. However, although the level of motivation, which may to a great extent affect the development of speech skills, may be encouraged, it cannot be increased by force.

The critical factor of the development of speech is the development of linguistic competence. A deaf or hard of hearing child with a good basis in sign language will learn to speak more easily. Research has shown that deaf children of deaf parents are significantly better in spoken language than deaf children of hearing parents. A deaf or hard of hearing child who already understands the world around him or her and can fully transfer his or her own thoughts, is more capable of learning and ready to learn the skills required for the development of oral language skills. Recent research has shown that there is a link between competence in sign language and literacy in spoken language. The knowledge of written language is very important for the development of competence in spoken language. When a deaf or hard of hearing child starts to read, he or she may create a link between the printed word and the spoken word, particularly when the hearing rehabilitation worker practices listening and speech exercises with stories and sentences that are meaningful for the child (the child understands them) as early as in the phase when the language structure is still being modelled. This visual support facilitates the learning of sound combinations in the new vocabulary.

Written language also offers a deaf child full access to language structure, providing a clearer model of the spoken language syntax than the one obtained from speech signals. The knowledge of the structure of spoken language is particularly important in lip reading since it helps filling up the gaps by the anticipation or guessing of what cannot be read from the speakers' lips. Therefore, early acquired literacy which is developed by reading written stories translated into sign language also facilitates the development of speech.

Lipreading

Lipreading may be defined as the distinguishing and understanding of words by observation of the speaker's lips, facial expressions, gestures, postures, characteristics of the situation, linguistic factors and auditory information available to the lip-reader. In other words, all the mentioned factors facilitate lipreading. Although lipreading is very difficult, tiring and frustrating, deaf persons do it every day - some better, some worse. Even the best lipreaders obtain only partial information since many sounds cannot be seen on the lips. A successful lipreader compensates this deficiency of sensory data by making the best of his or her previous knowledge of the language structure and of the linguistic and situational context. This is a very demanding activity and even the most competent lipreaders must fill up the gaps by guessing. For persons with residual hearing lipreading is significantly easier.

Some researches suggest that there is a correlation between lipreading and competence in sign language. Since lipreading does not reflect only visual-perceptive aspects of speech perception but also the knowledge of the language, it is assumed that there is a correlation between lipreading and other measures of linguistic competence, too.

Lipreading may have a significant share in developing independence and increasing self-confidence in situations in which communication is in spoken language. Lipreading is an important part of communication therapy. Deaf children are encouraged to anticipate what will be said in a certain speech situation. This process of anticipation (situational and linguistic) has a positive effect on the child's ability to function in various situations in hearing environment.

Many authors believe that lipreading may be improved by exercise. This means that it is not necessary to teach the child how to lipread but this process takes place in a structured, pleasant atmosphere in which deaf children can acquire lip-reading skills. Consequently, the analytical approach (effort to visually distinguish isolated sounds) is not recommended, but an empirical, synthetic approach aimed at developing receptive speech language abilities through meaningful activities. Exercising takes place on the synthetic or pragmatic level, sounds are presented within words and phrases as in a real conversation. Synthetic activities are functional by nature, "surrounding" the key words and phases by context. This is more similar to real life situations and is therefore more motivating and meaningful than analytical tasks.

Video presentation on computer enable repetition that is indispensable in acquiring lipreading skills because the same phrases may be repeated without variations as many times as needed. Lipreading should be carried out from the context because it is impossible to lipread all the individual words; if a child is trying to do this, frustration he or she experiences will interfere with lipreading.

Although lipreading is a difficult task, we have included it in our programme because the great majority of deaf persons relies on that skill in their everyday communication with the hearing. It has been demonstrated that the development of literacy particularly contributes to the improvement of lipreading skills. Specifically, due to the fact that a large number of sounds cannot be seen on the lips, deaf persons should rely on phonetic, lexical or grammatical redundancy. Knowledge of the language is an inseparable part of guessing, which is indispensable in reconstructing the parts that are missing.

Emotional literacy

The role of language competence in acquiring academic skills is fundamental. However, language competence is related to mental health as well; it is indispensable for the development of self-control, self-esteem, identification and understanding of the environment. Consequently, language has an important role in school achievement, too, as well as in general psychosocial adjustment (Bebko & McKinnon, 1998). We have therefore included the development of emotional literacy in our programme.

Emotional literacy is a wide term, but its basic meaning is the ability to identify and name one's own emotions (Steiner, 1997). Emotional literacy consists of two main components. The first is the ability to precisely describe one's emotions in three-word sentences: I feel happy, scared, motivated, excited, proud.... The other refers to the vocabulary of emotions, i.e. how many words of emotions are ready/available when needed. Emotional literacy is the basis for other abilities, such as the following:
- ability to understand others;
- ability to express one's emotions appropriately;
- self-motivation ability;
- ability to regulate emotions;
- ability to solve problems and assess risks;
- ability to solve conflicts;
- ability to empathize.

Research has shown that children who are emotionally literate
- have a higher self-confidence;
- have better school achievements;
- have a greater self-esteem;
- have less behavioural problems;
- are more optimistic;
- deal with their own emotions more easily.

Although "emotional illiteracy" primarily affects us on the individual and family levels, it is significant in education, too. Schools educate children and help them achieve a good quality of life. This may be accomplished by understanding and solving problems, acquiring knowledge of the world, developing practical skills necessary for a productive life and learning how to live in peace with oneself and the environment. Teachers who are emotionally literate, i.e. understand their own emotions and the emotional of others, will be more successful in teaching these skills to children.

How do children learn about emotions? The most frequent manner in which children learn is observation and modelling. They literally observe other people's behaviour in emotional situations and model themselves on them or imitate them, most frequently their parents, brothers and sisters, peers and teachers. Most families do not pay attention to that. If a child's emotions are not recognized, the child may grow up thinking that emotions do not matter and should be ignored, both one's own and those of other people.

Research has shown that deaf children of hearing parents, in comparison to their hearing peers and deaf peers whose parents are deaf, are less mature emotionally and more inclined to aggressive behaviour, outbursts of anger, impulsiveness, external locus of control and low self-esteem. Deaf children with hearing parents are deprived of the so-called vicarious learning - unintentional learning by observation. Deaf children of hearing parents are deprived of a great amount of information that is available to hearing children. The main hindrance to the social adjustment of deaf children is the lack of efficient communication between the child and the parents. Since they, on account of this, get fewer explanations of the causes and consequences of social and emotional behaviour of others, they experience more difficulties in self-regulation and their ability to learn from social interactions is reduced (Greenberg & Kusche, 1993). Their reduced understanding of other people's reactions to their behaviour results in their having a less correct picture of themselves and a low self-esteem.

It is considered that in hearing children impulsive and aggressive behaviour is a consequence of their lack of understanding of social situation and the lack of self-control, i.e. interruption in the acquisition of internal speech, which results in a poor self-regulation of behaviour (Kendall, 1991).

Since a deaf child is exposed to scanty communication, an interruption in verbal self-control may result (Greenberg & Kusche, 1993). Impulsiveness of deaf children of deaf parents is smaller in comparison to deaf children of hearing parents because the latter share the communication system. It has been demonstrated that deaf children are less accurate in recognizing emotional states than hearing children and have a poorer vocabulary of emotions. Understanding one's own and other people's emotions is indispensable for mature social and emotional reactions. It is not the deafness itself that leads to emotional and social problems, but secondary consequences of hearing impairments. The most important secondary effects of deafness are the lack of appropriate cognitive, linguistic and social experiences, inappropriate manner of rearing (overprotective or rejective) and difficulties in communication between the child and the mother.

A pre-requisite of efficient self-control and problem solving is the ability to recognize emotions. The acquisition of the vocabulary of emotions and subtle conative meanings greatly facilitates verbal mediation of affective states, which is a pre-requisite for self-control, cognitive understanding of emotional situations and problem solving. Therefore, it is important to teach children how to recognize and distinguish emotional states and expand their vocabulary of emotions, which is usually very poor in deaf children. The target is to achieve better understanding of links between emotions, behaviours and cognitive processes. This facilitates identification and understanding of motives and behaviours of other persons. Children learn how to recognize emotions of other persons, acquire the techniques of assessing their own emotional states, drill attributes that link causes and effects. They develop the ability to understand how a person's behaviour affects the behaviour of other persons and how it influences their own behaviour.

Children should be suggested that emotions have their specific names and that the more names of emotions they know, the better they will be able to understand emotions and talk about them to other people. Calling an emotion the right name increases personal power and calling it a wrong name reduces it (Kaufman & Raphael, 1990). It is important that children realize that emotions themselves are neither good nor bad, neither right nor wrong, but that some are pleasant and some are not. Children learn that emotions are signals that carry important information. If people learn to pay attention to what the emotions are telling them, they can use this information for making a decision on what to do next.

It is critical that a child learn to observe his or her internal states, recognize an emotion he or she feels and assess its intensity. For younger and linguistically less competent children a scale is used which contains pictorial descriptions of certain emotional states and degrees of their intensity. The so-called "barometer of happiness" is used, on which respondents need to assess how they feel on a scale rating from 1 to 10 degrees. The sentence "I feel ..." with the name of emotion is used as well. Self-assessment where the name of an emotion felt by the child has to be filled in enables the child to share his or her emotions with a minimum of difficulties and to understand that emotions are changing. In a similar manner children are encouraged to use these drawings in an empathizing identification with characters from fairy tales and in this way to learn how to recognize the changes in emotional states in written materials as well. This technique is efficient with children who have various emotional problems, e.g. children who are shy, withdrawn or very aggressive and prone to outbursts of anger.

From pre-school age to adolescence people experience similar emotions, but situations provoking them change in terms of quality and complexity. As children grow, they become more capable of applying cognitive skills to more abstract issues related to emotional experiences. They, for example, begin to realize that emotions are not only a result of momentary situations but may also occur as a reaction to memories from the past, that it is possible to experience several emotions at the same time, that the existence of conflicting emotions may lead to ambivalence, that emotions may be consciously hidden from others, that they may be changed under the influence of internal and external sources, that a disharmony between behaviours, situations and internal states may arise, etc.

Why fairy tales?

Everything in a fairy tale seems familiar and clear to children. First, the language of fairy tales is clear and functional, without ornaments, the beginning is quite simple and introduces the reader directly into the story, and is followed by rhythmic strings of sentences, which are for the most part independent or linked into a sequence by conjunctions and disjunctives.

Although the fairy tale world is magic and unreal, the fantasy is well-organized and harmonious, subject to strict laws of composition, and episodes in the fairy tale make a coherent whole and are repeated rhythmically with gradation and an increase in tension.

The basic structure of the fairy tale is familiar to children; it is entirely built of action, events, adventure, and never describes a tranquil state. In a fairy tale comic, tragic and dramatic parts alternate, which enables the child to actively identify with the heroes' actions. Children often and with temperament take sides with the weak, humiliated and hurt, get angry with the evil and mean characters and despise the stupid and hypocritical ones. The story of the fairy tale is simple and clear: in the end the evil fails and the good always wins, which corresponds to the child's notion of life as something magic and cheerful. In this manner children learn to despise violence, insincerity, malevolence and breaking of promises, empathizing and feeling sorry for a hero who is in trouble and enjoying the rightful victory of the honest, brave, good hero with a strong character; and thus learn to evaluate good and bad human characteristics.

One should not forget the fact that fairy tales present the power of imagination as the magical ability that encourages and recognizes creation and creativity as the greatest values.

1. OBJECTIVES

The objectives of the programme are the following:
1. Acquisition of the vocabulary of Croatian sign language and Croatian spoken language;
2. Understanding of contents told by Croatian sign language, written language and oral speech;
3. Development of metalinguistic knowledge - since the fairy tale is told in both sign language and spoken language, the awareness of both languages is developed because a comparison between them is possible; children begin to realize that these are two different languages and discover the differences and similari-

ties between them; they, in other words, acquire metalinguistic knowledge - the ability to think about and discuss their own linguistic processes;

4. Encouraging the development of listening and speech skills;
5. Exercising lip-reading skills:
6. Acquisition of the vocabulary of emotions;
7. Recognition of emotional states;
   The objective is to make the children recognize emotions on drawings and photographs and to realize that all of us experience emotions. They learn non-verbal signs that help us understand which emotion a person is experiencing. The child should indicate a possible reason for that person's emotion, what could have provoked it. For each emotion the child determines whether it is pleasant or unpleasant. Pleasant emotions are marked with yellow and unpleasant with blue.
8. Acquisition of self-assessment skills;
9. Understanding of cause-and-effect relationships;
10. Development of logical thinking and moral reasoning.

2. USERS

The programme has been designed primarily for deaf and hard of hearing children, but with simple modifications, i.e. the disabling of certain modalities, it is applicable to other user groups as well. Users are, consequently, the following:

1. Deaf and hard of hearing children;
2. Hearing children who are learning sign language as the second language;
3. Hearing children of the upper pre-school age and primary school classes 1-4;
4. Children with language difficulties;
5. Children with motor impairments;
6. Children with the attention-deficit and/or hyperactivity disorder;
7. Older children with delayed cognitive development (up to and including mild mental retardation).

3. STAGES OF THE PROGRAMME

The first part of the programme covers learning and includes the following stages:
1. A presentation of the fairy tale in pictures with the aim of understanding cause-and-effect relationships, i.e. overall understanding of the fairy tale's story;
2. For children fluent in sign language: the fairy tale is told in sign language; a person may pay attention to the manner in which a message is conveyed (grammatical rules) only if he or she understands the message;
3. Key words for a certain picture; with the key word written, drawing, sign or speech are displayed in sequence;
4. With each picture, sentences are displayed in sequence - in sign language, wri-

tten and spoken language:

5. Emotions are presented through a video recording of facial expressions and through drawings; with each facial expression, the sign for the emotion, word or speech are displayed in sequence; acquisition of the names of emotions in various language modalities.

The second part of the programme covers the testing of the acquired skills and includes the following:

1. Putting the pictures in order in accordance with the story;
2. a) Searching for the written word (displayed in sign language, spoken) in an individual picture;
   b) the same, but all pictures are displayed on the screen;
3. Associating sentences to pictures - displayed in sign language, written or spoken language;
4. Exercising the writing of key words according to the criteria of task levels;
5. Writing a sentence to each picture:
   a) fill in the missing word;
   b) words are mixed;
   c) writing sentences;
6. Questions - displayed in sign language, written, spoken language;
   Several answers are offered. The aim is to link the situation in the fairy tale to the child's own experiences, development of logical thinking, moral reasoning, understanding of social situations, understanding of humorous questions and questions encouraging creative thinking;
7. Recognizing whether an emotion presented in a video recording or drawing is pleasant or unpleasant by associating a blue or a yellow marking;
8. Presentation of an emotion in a video recording or drawing - searching for appropriate word or sign, i.e. recognition of spoken word;
9. How a character from the fairy tale feels in a certain situation (in an individual picture) - the target is to recognize an emotional state;
10. Recognition of the intensity of a character's emotional state (boiling pot);
11. Recognition of a certain emotional state in a situation where all pictures are displayed on the screen;
12. Recognition whether the behaviour presented in a drawing is good or bad and the assessment of what the character in the drawing feels in that situation; beside the pictures from the fairy tale, other situations from everyday life are presented;
13. Assessment of the child's own current emotional state and its intensity on one of the rating scales.

This software is designed in such manner that new contents may be added to it and it can be expanded in a simple way. Consequently, we are planning to make up stories in which the heroes will be deaf children. This has turned out to be extremely motivating for learning (Mashie, 1995). Such picture-books made up of drawings and video recordings have a positive effect on the development of self-esteem and linguistic skills: reading about deaf children and their lives in a positive context, learning grammatical rules of one's own language and learning the written and spoken language of the wider social community from the perspective of the second language in comparison to one's own language.

4. References

Baker, C. (1997): Deaf Children: Educating for Bilingualism. *Deafness and Education (JBA-TOD)*, 21/3, 3-9.

Bebko, J. M. & McKinnon, E. E. (1998): Assessing Pragmatic Language Skills in Deaf Children: The Language Proficiency Profile. In: Marschark, M. & Clark, D. (Ur.), *Psychological Perspectives on Deafness, Vol. 2.,* (243-264). London: Lawrence Erlbaum Association.

Deselle, D.D. (1994): Self-esteem, Family Climate, and Communication Patterns in Relation to Deafness. *American Annals of the Deaf, 139*, 322-28.

Greenberg, M.T. & Kusche, C.A. (1993): Promoting Social and Emotional Development in Deaf Children. Seattle: University of Washington Press.

Grosjean, F. (1998): Living with two languages and two cultures. In: Parasnis I. (Ed.): Cultural and Language Diversity and the Deaf Experience. New York: Cambridge University Press.

Hamers, J.F. (1998): Cognitive and language development of bilingual children. U: Parasnis I. (Ed.): Cultural and Language Diversity and the Deaf Experience. New York: Cambridge University Press.

Kaufman, G. & Raphael, L. (1990): Stick Up for Yourself. Every Kids Guide to Personal Power and Positive Self-Esteem. Minneapolis: Free Spirit Publishing.

Klima, E. & Bellugi, U. (1979): The Signs of Language. Cambridge, MA: Harvard University Press.

Kendall. P. C. (1991): Child and Adolescent Therapy. Cognitive-Behavioral Procedures. New York: The Guilford Press.

Kolod, S. (1994): Lack of a Common Language: Deaf Adolescents and Hearing Parents. *Contemporary psychoanalysis, 30(3),* 634-650.

Mashie, S.N. (1995): Educating Deaf Children Bilingually. With Insights and Applications from Sweden and Denmark. Washington DC: Gallaudet University.

Pettito, L. A. & Marentette, P.F. (1991): Babbling in the manual mode: Evidence for the ontology of language. *Science*, 251, 1493-1496.

Poizner, H., Klima, E. & Bellugi, U. (1987): What the Hands Reveal about the Brain. Cambridge, MA: Massachusetts Institute of Technology Press.

Stančić, V. & Ljubešić, M. (1994): Jezik, govor, spoznaja. Zagreb: Hrvatska sveučilišna naklada.

Steiner, C. (1997): Achieving Emotional Literacy: A personal program to increase your emotional intelligence. New York: Avon Books.

Stokoe, W. (1960): Sign Language Structure. Burtonsville MD: Linstok Press.

Sažetak

Nepostojanje sličnih softwarea na našem tržištu ponukalo nas je da naša praktična i teorijska saznanja iskoristimo u svrhu izrade programa koji će pomoći gluhoj djeci, ali i drugim skupinama korisnika, da razviju funkcionalnu (čitanje i pisanje) i emocionalnu pismenost. Razvijajući program oslanjali smo se na teorijske postavke psihologije i psiholingvistike bilingvizma i razvoja jezične kompetencije, na rezultate najnovijih istraživanja provedenih na gluhim ispitanicima te na spoznaje o važnosti emocionalne pismenosti i njenom utjecaju na psihosocijalnu prilagodbu djece. Software je namijenjen djeci starije predškolske dobi te učenicima nižih razreda osnovne škole. Ciljevi programa su sljedeći: 1) usvajanje rječnika hrvatskog znakovnog i hrvatskog govornog jezika; 2) razumijevanje sadržaja ispričanog hrvatskim znakovnim jezikom, pisanih jezikom i oralnim govorom; 3) razvoj metajezičnih znanja - budući da je bajka ispričana i na znakovnom i na pisanom jeziku, razvija se svijest o oba jezika, jer su moguće usporedbe između njih. Djeca počinju shvaćati da se radi o dva različita jezika i otkrivaju razlike i sličnosti. Dakle, stječu metajezična znanja - sposobnost razmišljanja i raspravljanja o vlastitim jezičnim procesima; 4) usvajanje rječnika emocija; 5) prepoznavanje emocionalnih stanja; 6) usvajanje vještine samoprocjene; 7) shvaćanje uzročno-posljedičnih odnosa, razvoj logičkog mišljenja i moralnog rezoniranja. Program se sastoji od faze učenja i faze provjere usvojenog. Software je tako koncipiran da je moguće jednostavno dodavati nove sadržaje i stalno ga proširivati. Pokazalo se da kombinacija rada na računalu i primjene bajki djeluje izrazito motivirajuće na učenje. Iako je dobar učitelj, naravno, nezamjenjiv, ipak, kompjutor kao nastavno pomagalo ima brojne pozitivne osobine: strpljiv je, učenikov uspjeh pamti trajno i objektivno, ne frustrira ga spor napredak učenika, lako pohranjuje mnoštvo edukacijskih materijala, a, ako je dobro programiran, može prema postignuću učenika zadavati najprimjerenije zadatke.

Ključne riječi: gluha djeca, gluhoća, znakovni jezik, pismenost, emocionalna inteligencija

SIGN LANGUAGE AND DEAF EDUCATION IN CROATIA

Sandra Bradarić-Jončić
Department of Hearing Impairments, Faculty of Education and Rehabilitation Sciences
University of Zagreb, Croatia
Sanja Tarczay
Croatian Association of Deaf-Blind Persons «Dodir»,
Zagreb, Croatia

Abstract

This paper considers the current situation in Croatia concerning the status of Croatian Sign Language and its place in the education of deaf children and youth. Deaf children in Croatia today attend special, as well as regular schools and preschools. Early intervention programmes encompass oral programmes exclusively. The overall communication programmes in preschools and schools include either oral approach or a combination of the oral approach and the use of signed Croatian. The value and potential of Croatian Sign Language (HZJ) for a healthy and successful development of deaf children has not been recognized yet, neither among professionals working with deaf children nor among the members of the deaf community themselves. The prerequisites for implementing bilingual programmes in the educational system are elaborated.

Key words: *deaf, bilingual education, sign language, sign language interpreters*

Social status of sign language

The situation concerning the status of sign language in Croatia is only partly satisfactory; a certain awareness of the significance of manual forms of communication for the life of the deaf does exist, but it almost exclusively refers to the use of signed Croatian.

The Croatian Sign Language (HZJ) has not been recognized as a language at all. Many even do not know that it exists, and what potential it has for the development of communication skills and the education of deaf children, as well as for an improved access to information and efficient communication of the deaf in general.

In Croatia HZJ is used only by prelingually deaf in their mutual communication. Signed Croatian (simultaneous communication - speech accompanied by signs from the Croatian Sign Language) is absolutely dominant and the *only system* that has its place in the education of deaf children, the media and courses. Signed Croatian is present in several schools for deaf children with the unofficial total approach to education, in the media (in three Croatian Television programmes: news for the deaf and hard of hearing, a programme on health and a programme on sports for youth) and in the few sign language courses.

Croatian Sign Language is, however, not present in any of the mentioned aspects of deaf's social life. Currently, elements of HZJ are being gradually introduced into a two-year course conducted by the Croatian Association of Deaf-Blind Persons "Dodir", as well as in teaching students in the HZJ course at the Faculty of Education and Rehabilitation Sciences in Zagreb.

In Croatia the status of manual forms of communication has not been officially/legally regulated (not even signed Croatian, of which there is some kind of awareness, let alone HZJ), and neither has the issue of funding interpreters' services. This has its implications for the functioning and availability of interpreters' services for the deaf, which in turn effects the unsystematicality in the training of interpreters. All this together has far-reaching effects on the availability of information to the deaf and, even more importantly, to the accessibility of education for the deaf and their school qualifications being below their real potentials.

Finally, this has an effect on the social power of the deaf community, which lacks critical mass of prelingually deaf intellectuals who would generate and disseminate new ideas, directly articulate the views and aspirations of their community and be the agents of progress in their social community, as the intellectuals in all other communities use to be. The deaf community in Croatia should be empowered, particularly in this educational aspect.

There is also a lack of modern, efficient HZJ courses. Efficient courses and/or programmes of learning HZJ as a foreign/second language are a prerequisite for many other changes in the system of the education of deaf children and youth, from modified university education programmes for the teachers of deaf children to modified education programmes for the deaf children and youth themselves using HZJ, especially early intervention programmes for the hearing parents and their small deaf children.

Efficient language courses and/or training programmes are an important prerequisite for the education of sign language interpreters as well, among others of educational interpreters, who play an important role in new models of educational integration of deaf children. In Croatia there are no systematic and verified interpreter training programmes, neither for signed Croatian, nor for HZJ.

Since 1998 the Association "Dodir" has conducted various programmes and workshops in Zagreb with a view to effecting changes in the accessibility of sign language to the deaf and the deaf-blind. The Association has started a pilot two-year sign language course involving four levels. An effort was made that the courses are held by native deaf speakers. So far three generations of attendants have finished the course. In the original form the courses were in signed Croatian but contained many elements of HZJ used in deaf families. In order to achieve the quality of the courses needed for their verification, an additional education of deaf persons was gradually introduced in parallel with the two-year courses. Several workshops were organized, mostly held by foreign deaf or deaf-blind trainers, where the deaf learned the basics of the linguistics of sign language and how to plan teaching units and topics and got an insight into approaches and methods. Two deaf trainers were sent to a one-year training programme to Gallaudet University, USA. In order to significantly improve the quality of courses and create critical mass of deaf teachers, a project of two-year university education of the deaf supported by interpreters was started in cooperation with the Teacher Training College. It is the first time in the Republic of Croatia that all lectures are continuously interpreted for deaf persons into sign language. Not only a positive influence on the self-esteem of the deaf and the development of their awareness of their own language and value was observed, but also a progress in the Croatian spoken language.

The development of HZJ curricula is significantly impeded by the absence of the HZJ grammar description. The problem is also posed by the relative insufficiency of the HZJ vocabulary, which lacks technical terms needed for the acquisition of school contents by deaf children in their first language and in general, so that many technical terms have to be articulated in the phonological form of the spoken language (by finger-spelling), which slows down the communication and makes it less efficient.

For this reason, in parallel with the continuation of the work on the HZJ grammar description, efforts should be made to develop this language, especially a vocabulary of technical/scientific terms of HZJ, those related to educational work in particular, in order to ensure, at the end of years-long efforts, the linguistic prerequisites for organizing bilingual education of deaf children and youth. In HZJ, many technical/scientific terms have not even been borrowed from other sign languages but are, as already discussed, articulated by fingerspelled words of the Croatian spoken language.

Education of deaf children in Croatia

The first school for deaf children was established in 1885 in Zagreb. Today centres for the education and rehabilitation of deaf children exist in regional centres of Croatia, two in Zagreb and one each in Split, Rijeka, Varaždin and Osijek. Within these centres pre-school, primary school and secondary school education programmes are conducted, including predominantly an oral and (unofficially) total approach in education.

Some of these schools are residental, and other are daily schools. Besides, for many years now deaf pupils have been integrated into regular primary and secondary schools. There are more than 200 children and adults with cohlear implants in Croatia today.

Maternity hospitals are equipped with newborn hearing screening instruments, which significantly reduces the age of hearing impairment identification.

For small hearing impaired children there are early intervention programmes, however, only in the framework of the oral educational approach, i.e. aimed at the development of listening skills and speech and the acquisition of spoken language. They are designed for families with children under 3 years of age. After the programme deaf children (as soon as possible) join a special kindergarten for deaf children. However, as discussed above, HZJ has no place in the system of the education of deaf children in general, and pre-school educational programmes are not an exception. There are no programmes of early bilingual development that would systematically assist the hearing parents in learning HZJ and early sign language communication with their child.

In kindergartens, primary and secondary schools fostering the total approach, simultaneous oral and sign communication is present.

The right of the deaf to interpreters' services is not regulated. Deaf children and youth integrated in regular primary and secondary schools in their schoolwork must rely solely on their oral-aural communication skills since there are no educational interpreters available.

The first continuous educational interpreting started in 2000 with the enrolment of a deaf (deaf-blind) student in the Faculty of Education and Rehabilitation Sciences, University of Zagreb. In recent years the trend has continued with the enrolment of several deaf students in the Teacher Training College (N=3) and in the School of Management of the School of Economics in Zagreb (N=1). Also, one deaf and one deaf-blind student are enrolled in a graduate study program at the Faculty of Education and Rehabilitation sciences, University of Zagreb.

At the moment in Croatia only one deaf teacher is employed. If we wish to prepare the ground for bilingual education of deaf children, a certain number of deaf pre-school and school teachers need to be trained.

Conclusion

Implementing new alternatives to the continuum of deaf education in Croatia demands complex activities of the scientific, deaf and professional communities:

1) Description of HZJ grammar and the development of vocabulary, especially of technical/scientific terms;

2) Development of HZJ courses based on modern principles of second/foreign language learning/teaching - for the existing and future teachers, the existing and future interpreters, particularly educational interpreters, for hearing parents of deaf children;

3) Organization of an efficient interpreters' service which would, among other, enable a larger number of deaf young persons to achieve university level education; also legal regulation of its work and funding;

4) Curricula development for the bilingual education of deaf children
   - including the programmes for facilitating the acquisition of the first- and the second language;
   - acquisition of academic knowledge in the first and the second language;
   -learning about the values, customs and cultural endeavours of the deaf and hearing communities;

5) Curricula development for professional preparation of teachers for the deaf that would qualify them for the realization of the above mentioned programmes, with such an instruction in sign language that would qualitatively and quantitatively differ from the existing ones; deaf pre-school and school teachers for deaf children ought to be trained as well.

References:

Ahlgren, I. & K. Hyltenstam (eds.) (1994): Bilingualism in Deaf Education. Hamburg. Signum Verlag.

Kyle, J.G. & B. Woll (1985): Sign language: The study of deaf people and their language. Cambridge University Press.

Lane, H.; Hoffmeister, R. & B.Bahan (1996): A journey into the Deaf-World. Down Sign Press, San Diego, (CA).

Neal Mahshie, Sh. (1995): Educating deaf children bilingually. Pre-College Programmes, Gallaudet University, Washington, D.C.

Pickersgill, M. (1990): Bilingualism and the education of deaf children: Part 1 – theories, models and factors. Deafness and Development, 1, 1, 10-15.

Pickersgill, M. (1991): Bilingualism and the education of deaf children: Part 2 – Implications and theoretical considerations. Deafness and Development, 1, 2, 1-3

Pickersgill, M. (1997): Towards a bilingual education for deaf children. Deafness and Education, 21, 3, 10-20.

UNESCO (1994): The Salamanca Statement and framework for action on special needs education. Paris, UNESCO.

United Nations (1994): The Standard Rules on the Equalization of Opportunities for Persons with Disabilities". New York, United Nations.

Valli, C. & C. Lucas (1992): Linguistics of American Sign Language. Gallaudet University Press. Washington, D.C.

ZNAKOVNI JEZIK I EDUKACIJA GLUHIH U HRVATSKOJ

U radu se razmatra status hrvatskog znakovnog jezika (HZJ) i njegovo mjesto u edukaciji gluhe djece i mladeži. Znakovni jezik nema svoje mjesto u edukaciji gluhih. Sustav manualne komunikacije koji se neslužbeno koristi u obrazovnim ustanovama je simultana oralno-znakovna komunikacija, dok vrijednost i potencijal HZJ-a za razvoj gluhe djece još uvijek ne prepoznaju ni stručnjaci, a niti sami pripadnici zajednice gluhih. Razmatraju se pretpostavke uvođenja dvojezičnog obrazovanja u postojeći sustav edukacije gluhe djece u Hrvatskoj.

Ključne riječi: *gluhi, bilingvalna edukacija, dvojezično obrazovanje, znakovni jezik, tumači*

REAL ACCESS TO INFORMATION: INTERPRETING FOR DEAF RESIDENTS WITH MINIMAL LANGUAGE SKILLS

Noel T. Traynor

The University of Central Lancashire, Preston, United Kingdom

Abstract

In a 2-year joint project with Deafway, a Residential Care Unit for Deaf people, the focus is on Communication Disadvantage for those residents who have mental health difficulties and/or minimal language skills. The research aims to examine the roles of various professionals involved in resident's review meetings. Of prime interest is if, and how, the interpreter processes the information and transmits it at a level appropriate to the resident's needs. Review meetings are video-filmed and analysed, with the agreement of all parties involved. The interpreters acknowledged that this would provide an opportunity to evaluate their own skill in adapting language to meet resident's needs. Following the meetings, both the Chairperson and interpreter/s are interviewed to determine how successful they feel the communication has been.

During phase one of the Project (April - August 2000), we observed a number of factors which were inhibiting the active participation of residents. After discussion, we have drawn up a new set of rules for the conduct of Case Review meetings, and aim to set out training guidelines for working with residents in this situation. During their training, interpreters should benefit from the Project's examination of the linguistic process of adapting from high-level spoken English to a minimal signing level, whilst still conveying full information. We will be able to offer examples of this processing in action, through which they can gain practical experience. We believe this is the first time this has been done in Britain. Phase 2 of the Project will examine communication and participation success in the light of our recommendations. It is hoped the Project will affect residents, and that it will influence mental health care and interpreter training.

Key words: sign language, minimal language skills, mental health, sign language interpreting, interpreter training

Introduction

This paper will discuss the research project currently being undertaken jointly by the University of Central Lancashire and the charitable organisation, Deafway. Both institutions are based in Preston, Lancashire, England. The University of Central Lancashire has an established "Deaf Studies" team, and a proven record in both the teaching of and research into issues concerning deafness, deaf people, and British Sign Language. Deafway has, for many years, been a source of support for deaf people and the Deaf Community in the north west of England, offering educational, community and social services to deaf people of all ages. Situated on the outskirts of Preston, it also provides residential care to around 35 deaf people with mental health difficulties. The residents at this home are people with varying needs and characteristics: some have mental ill-ness; some have other mental health or behavioural difficulties; others have learning di-sabilities. All are deaf. In this joint project, the two partner organisations are investi-gating access to information for deaf people in the residential care environment. Of par-ticular concern is access for people with *"minimal language skills"*. This term origina-ted in The United States of America; in Britain, as yet, we do not have an alternative, so we use this one, but it is a term that may, in the course of time and with further research, change. At this point, however, and for the purposes of this paper, we will use the estab-lished terminology.

Background to the Project

During 1999, The University of Central Lancashire approached Deafway with a pro-posal to set up a joint research project. Following an agreement, the University and Deafway then jointly approached the National Lotteries Charities Board, a large natio-nal body providing funding for research into social issues, to apply for funding in order to carry out the project. Main focus of our project was the *communication disadvan-tage*. An essential component of the Deafway residents' care programme is the six-monthly *Case Review Meetings*, in which individual residents meet formally with the professionals involved in their care: day to day "care" workers (both Deaf and non-deaf) employed by Deafway, external professionals such as social workers, and clinical team members; also involved are members of the residents' families. Most relevant to this paper is the involvement of Sign Language Interpreters, whose vital role is to enable communication between the deaf residents and the hearing persons involved in the case reviews. Communication is paramount, for the case reviews mark important stages in the residents' lives in care.

There are two landmark statements that are particularly relevant to the situation of these deaf residents. UN Standards Rule No. 5 recommends that all states and countries throughout the world should ensure that all citizens are equal and have *access to any process that they are involved in*, within any part of society. This emphasis on 'access to any process' does seem highly pertinent given the situation of the deaf residents in their case review meetings, where decisions are taken about their future, which may pro-foundly affect their lives. Another relevant international statement comes from the European Parliament. Croatia is not yet a part of the European Community, but one does anticipate that it will achieve its aspiration to become so in the future. In 1988, a European Parliament Resolution recommended that sign languages throughout the member countries and states be recognised as having equal status to spoken languages, and stated: *"sign language interpreters are one of the means by which the deaf gain access to information needed for everyday life"*. This very significant recommendation was re-affirmed in 1998.

A further source of reference is the European Society for Mental Health and Deafness, who, in 1999, *"used the acronym INCLUDE to emphasise that Intervention with No Communication Leads to the Undermining of the Rights of Deaf Europeans"*.

This is exactly the issue that the project is considering, and is, indeed, an issue we all should consider further. If a person does not have communication, she/he does not have access, and without access a person cannot participate.

The research

The research team from the University comprises two Deaf British Sign Language (BSL) users and two non-deaf persons; both of the hearing researchers have good BSL, and one is, in fact, a Registered Qualified Sign Language Interpreter. The first phase of the two-year project involved data collection by means of video-recording some of the case review meetings, described above, in their original, unchanged format; that is, case review meetings as they had been conducted for some years, with an established routine and procedure. It was felt that, although the Deaf residents were in attendance at these reviews, there was an element of doubt as to whether or not they were, actually, able to participate in and fully understand the meetings. One could easily be deceived by the head nods from the residents, that appeared to happen at appropriate times to indicate approval; it could be the case that, in reality, the residents may not truly be involved.

The team then scrutinised the skills and qualifications of the sign language interpreters employed to interpret for the case reviews. The process we used included interviewing the interpreters after each case review recording was completed. We asked for interpreters' views and examined their responses. Our aim was to find out if the interpreters felt that they were understood by the client during meetings, and if they felt that communication had been achieved or not. Access was the main focus.

The case review meetings take place at six-monthly intervals; over the two-year period of the project, we would have the opportunity to observe, record, analyse and draw conclusions from three of the residents' meetings. The project was divided into "Phases" of six months each: Phase 1 and Phase 2(a) involved collection of data from the status quo; during Phase 2(b) training of interpreters and Deafway staff was begun, and draft recommendations made for changes to the meetings. Before Phase 3 could proceed, more training of interpreters had to be done, and a process of *language modification* was undertaken by the Deaf researchers. This latter looked at the sign language used by the interpreters in the meetings, which was often "over the heads" of the residents, and suggested ways of modifying their language to meet the communication needs of the residents. At the end of Phase 3, and the completion of the Project, it is anticipated that final recommendations will be available in published form, which will be of use not only to Deafway but also to other establishments dealing with the residential care of Deaf people with minimal language skills (MLS).

The 'subjects'

Several of Deafway's residents were chosen to be involved, and, with their informed consent, chose to be involved, in the project. Some are mentally ill, identified as having schizophrenia; other have disabilities within the range covered by the term autism; one has behavioural problems; thus the residents selected represent a wide range of mental health difficulties. One is affected by physical symptoms of cerebral palsy, which restricts movement and has an effect upon her communication. There is also variation in the level of language skills among these residents, and significant differences in the methods of communication they use. Some of the residents do have a high level of language skills, using BSL, albeit very idiosyncratic in its use. Other residents use very simple sign, which may be BSL-based or their own home-signs and gestures; one of the autistic persons appears to understand simplified BSL but never, himself, signs or speaks to any significant degree.

The main issues for research

The questions had to be asked: *during the case review meetings, is information provided in such a way that the residents can understand, do they respond appropriately, and can the interpreters understand their responses?*
We considered three main issues:
- the quality of interpretation;
- the quality of facilitation by the team leaders and key workers involved in the case review;
- the environmental factors of the room being used for the case review meetings.

Usually, the case review meeting would include: the sign language interpreter; the Team Leader (responsible for supervision and organisation of the care staff); the resident's Key Worker (this is the term used at Deafway - in other situations it may be Individual Rehabilitation Officer or similar); the resident's social worker; a member of the resident's family; someone from the Clinical Team - perhaps a psychologist or a doctor; and, of course, the resident him/herself.

Research methodology

Before the research began, the two Deaf researchers met the residents individually, and had the opportunity, informally, to look at the level of language used by each person. In order to evaluate the success of communication during the meetings, we had, firstly, to assess the residents' communication abilities; we also needed to request their permission to allow us to video-record the meetings. It would have been unacceptable to arrive at a case review meeting with video camera equipment without having previously informed the resident of the reason for it. For this reason, the two Deaf researchers met the residents individually, in their own room or flat, to discuss and explain the research and the Project. It was essential to have the Deaf researchers do this, as they were more easily able to adapt their own language to meet the communication needs of the residents, and in turn understand the residents' sometimes obscure signing. At the same time, Deaf residents would feel more comfortable with Deaf people, who understood not only their language but also their culture and, in this way, had perhaps a deeper empathy and the ability to communicate directly and on the residents' own terms.

Though the non-deaf researchers have high levels of BSL, they are, essentially, of "the others", and it could be said that Deaf people are more at ease with their "own kind".

In this way, "informed consent" was gained. This initial meeting was also an opportunity to gain an understanding of the varying levels of sign language used among the residents, to enable the project to proceed successfully. It was by no means an easy process, as communication with the residents can be very difficult; the primary objective was, however, that *they* understood.

The non-deaf researchers met with the interpreters, the family members and the social workers, to request permission to video-record the meetings. While some people were taken aback by the request, we did gain the approval of all participants to record the meetings. The two Deaf researchers then analysed the video recordings. Many hours were spent in discussion, and we were able to create recommendations for changes to be made to improve the success of the review meetings. The Deaf researchers, together with the non-deaf researcher who is also a qualified interpreter, considered the translation of any contributions made by the resident. They also scrutinised the language used by the interpreters upon whom the Deaf residents would be relying for information. This done, some recommendations for possible changes were drafted.

Interim results and recommendations

Phase 1 of the project involved ten residents. Ten case review meetings were video recorded, and from analysis of these the research team compiled the following draft recommendations regarding areas or issues for change:

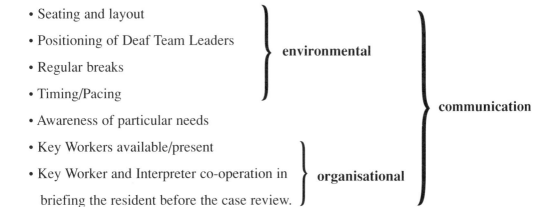

• Seating and layout

• Positioning of Deaf Team Leaders

• Regular breaks   } environmental

• Timing/Pacing

• Awareness of particular needs   } communication

• Key Workers available/present

• Key Worker and Interpreter co-operation in   } organisational

briefing the resident before the case review.

It was suggested that Interpreters might also benefit from:
- Meeting Team Leader before Case Review –
  - to clarify and establish working practice
  - to gain information about the resident and the situation
- Meeting key workers before the briefing with the resident, to gain vital information and enable preparation
- Meeting and preparing with any co-worker interpreters involved in the case review

Environmental changes

The seating arrangements at the case review meetings were considered, and it was found that, more often than not, the meetings were held in a very small room with unsuitable tables. This seemed to be having a detrimental psychological effect upon the residents: in a room that was restricted and confined, there was less contribution on the part of the resident. It was observed that in a more spacious and airy room, the resident was more inclined to contribute. If the people present were too close in proximity to each other, there was less opportunity for the resident to contribute. The researchers also observed the importance of having Team Leaders seated in an appropriate place. Where a resident is seated immediately next to the Team Leader, they may feel less able to contribute, as they are tempted to look at the person next to them and not at the interpreter opposite.

Review meetings often continued for lengthy periods of time with no break, and that was causing difficulties. For the resident the meeting is an unusual and strange environment, in total contrast to their usual routine of quiet activity and relative calm. In the meeting they are surrounded by authority figures from the non-deaf world, communicating in speech which the resident has to follow through an interpreter. Their concentration span is limited, perhaps by their learning difficulty or mental health condition, and affected by their residential care environment; in most cases they were overwhelmed, confused by the bombardment of information, and easily fatigued. A tendency by the professionals perhaps to rush through the meeting, to enable them to deal with it quickly, was not helpful to the resident. With all this input of information, where was the opportunity for the resident to respond, consider, or rest?

The resident relies on the interpreter for access to information; the interpreter therefore requires adequate skills to ensure understanding. This means adapting the language register and providing more visual information to make it more meaningful to the resident. This process requires a great deal of time, and it was concluded that the meetings need to be paced more slowly to allow the interpreter time to adjust their interpretation to the needs of the resident. It was also suggested that meeting conversations be categorised. For example, if medication was being discussed, it would be necessary to inform the resident of the topic at the start. Once the topic had been discussed, it would be necessary to clarify to the resident that the meeting was moving on to a new topic. The guidelines recommend that the meetings should therefore have clear subject markers and adequate breaks.

Organisational changes

From observations of the residents in their homes, researchers were able to consider their own, natural environment. They observed everyday activities and conversations between residents. What was noted here was the marked difference between the pace of life in the natural environment and the one-hour "crash" case review meeting. Once one understands the naturally slow pace at which the residents live and receive information, it is possible to appreciate that attendance at a sudden one-hour meeting may make it difficult to absorb the mass of information presented to them. For this reason, the key worker (or rehabilitation officer) has the responsibility of monitoring the improvement of the resident over the six-month period between reviews. This person is involved with the resident daily, and is the person who knows the resident best. Every case review meeting must, therefore, involve the key worker. Often the meeting will be arranged and, because of illness, shift patters and so on, the key worker may not be available. This may mean a substitute key worker is in attendance, and s/he will briefly read aloud the meeting papers. In this case, the worker is not fully aware of the situation for the resident and they will read at a fast pace. This will mean that the interpreter does not have the time to adjust their interpretation, and the resident may not be able to follow the meeting. If a key worker who is familiar with the resident is present at the meeting, they will be able to pace the meeting appropriately; in turn, this will allow the interpreter the time to interpret successfully to the resident.

Further recommendations regarded the interpreters. It was felt that the interpreter would benefit from a pre-meeting with the client. This would allow them the opportunity to establish communication with the client, and would also allow time to read the communication profile pertaining to the client. The interpreter should also be able to meet the key worker prior to the meeting, to clarify any terminology from the meeting report. The interpreter may want further information about specific medication, for example. In order to present the information visually, the interpreter may need to ascertain the colour of each tablet, etc., as this will be how the resident refers to the item. Reference to colour of tablets will be useful during the meeting, and the interpreter will be able to present the information visually to the resident. Preparation before the review is, therefore, vital, and will enable the interpreter to work with more confidence.

Training and Language modification

Case review meetings vary and it may be, for example, that the resident is placed at the residential home under the Mental Health Act. Placements of this nature involve certain stipulations, and the residents will need to be informed as to the reason for their placement. In this case, it is important that the interpreter is adequately trained, as should be the team leader and key worker. The training for interpreters working in this situation should include language-modification training. An example of this can be seen in the production of the sign statement YOU CARRY-ON STAY HERE made by one interpreter. The resident is obviously not going to be dispersed into the Deaf Community and left to cope independently, and therefore the sign CARRY-ON may not be appropriate. One would suggest: MEETING FINISH - <u>YOU</u> NOT FINISH HERE LIVE – NO, YOU

NOT FINISH HERE LIVE, YOU STAY-HERE MUST, SIX MONTHS MORE, OR MAYBE MORE. Fluent high-level BSL, as learned on standard Interpreter training courses, may not be understood; it is necessary to find a more appropriate form of signing to match the residents' level of understanding.

This also applied to discussion of the issue of "personal hygiene". Telling a resident s/he has "poor personal hygiene" means little. If the resident is not aware of the meaning of this term, the interpretation would need to include a visual representation of the concept. The interpretation may therefore be NOT BOTHER, YOU, SHAVE YOURSELF: CLOTHES SMELL, YOU B.O. SMELL — HAVE SHOWER, SHAVE YOURSELF, CLEAN TEETH, SPRAY DEODORANT, WILL LOOK GOOD, FEEL BETTER, SMELL GOOD! A more specific visual representation of the concept will be easier for the resident to understand, and ensure understanding and access to the information.

Interim Conclusions

In conclusion, two main aspects must be borne in mind:

- Firstly, the Deaf resident is the most important factor in the whole environment, and they must have access to what is happening around them. If they have access to the review meetings, their life skills, their independence and their daily living skills will improve.
- Secondly, one must consider the interpreters. Care providers need to ascertain the skills of the interpreter employed in the meetings. The interpreter must be able to make a critical self-evaluation and be able to modify the language they are using to ensure that the resident is able to understand. These are two vital elements. If the interpreter feels that they are not able to relay the information to the resident, then those responsible should seek to provide a Deaf Relay Interpreter who will have the skills to modify their language and enable the resident to access the information.

It is anticipated that the results of this project will be of interest to all organisations providing residential care for deaf persons with the aforementioned minimal language skills, for whom communication disadvantage is a barrier to participation in decision-making about their own lives. It is hoped that the recommendations suggested by the project will have a positive impact upon the lives of deaf people in residential care. It is further hope that the results of this project will be noted by others providing care for deaf persons with mental health difficulties and/or learning difficulties, and that the effects will be wide and far-reaching.

STVARNI PRISTUP INFORMACIJAMA: TUMAČENJE GLUHIM OSOBAMA S MINIMALNIM JEZIČNIM ZNANJIMA

Dvogodišnji projekt u suradnji s institucijom za gluhe "Deafway" bio je usmjeren na komunikacijske teškoće onih korisnika koji su imali problema s mentalnim zdravljem i/ili s minimalnim jezičnim znanjima. Postavlja se pitanje obrađuje li i prenosi li tumač informaciju na razini primjerenoj komunikacijskim potrebama korisnika i na koji način to čini? Sastanci korisnika snimljeni su i analizirani uz prethodni njihov pristanak. Tumači su to prihvatili kao priliku za evaluaciju vlastitih vještina i za prilagodbu jezika potrebama korisnika. Nakon sastanaka održavali su se razgovori predsjedavajućega i tumača kako bi se utvrdio njihov stav o uspješnosti komunikacije. Tijekom prve faze projekta promatrali smo čimbenike koji su otežavali aktivno sudjelovanje korisnika. Nakon diskusije utvrdili smo nova pravila tumačenja, koja će biti uključena i u edukaciju tumača. Tumači trebaju biti osposobljeni kako prenijeti informaciju s visoke razine služenja govornim engleskim jezikom na nisku razinu služenja znakovnim jezikom, a da ta informacija pritom bude potpuna. To će nam omogućiti da u edukaciji tumačima pružimo praktična iskustva vezana uz obrađivanje informacija prilikom prevođenja u takvim situacijama. To je vjerojatno prvi takav pokušaj u Velikoj Britaniji. Druga faza projekta ispitat će uspješnost komunikacije i participacije korisnika po uvažavanju naših preporuka. Nadamo se da će ovaj projekt omogućiti korisnicima veći utjecaj na organizaciju vlastitog življenja u instituciji te da će utjecati na brigu o mentalnom zdravlju i osposobljavanje tumača.

Ključne riječi: *znakovni jezik, minimalna jezična znanja, mentalno zdravlje, prevođenje sa znakovnog jezika, edukacija tumača*

QUALITY OF LIFE OF THE DEAF IN AUSTRIA

J. Fellinger[1], D. Holzinger[1], R. Schoberberger[2], G. Lenz[3]

Abstract

The description of the social situation of the deaf in Austria (325 interviews) demonstrates the existence of a special group of people within the general population. Observations regarding the health-related aspects of quality of life made in the course of preventive medical checkups were compared with a hearing control group of a general practitioner's patients (n=273), who had undergone a preventive medical checkup as well. Although there were significant differences in age, marital status and the percentage of retired persons they do not explain the significant differences in the field of health-related quality of life. The slightly higher average age of the hearing control group would let us expect a worse status of health and higher risk factors, however, the contrary was found. There is a significantly higher number of illnesses and a higher degree of risk factors in the deaf group. The higher degree of somatophysical complaints and nervous tension (30% higher rate among the deaf as compared to the hearing control group) in particular let us assume a higher degree of distress among the deaf population.

Key words: deafness, quality of life, mental health

Introduction

The quality of life of different groups of handicapped people is of increasing interest. Although the situation of the deaf and the use of sign language is being discussed in the public, there is still few data available concerning their quality of life. This is partly due to the fact that the usual instruments such as written questionnaires or spoken interviews cannot be applied.

Deafness

The medical view of deafness focuses on the severity of hearing loss. With profound deafness, hearing loss is higher than 95dB. This figure refers to the loss in the better ear on pure tone audiometry, average across 250, 500, 1000, 2000 and 4000 Hz.

The cultural view refers to the deaf community an individual may identify with. This partly separate cultural group is characterized primarily by its common sign language, its common experience (e.g. attendance of schools for the deaf) and specific formal social structures (e.g. deaf clubs).

---

[1] Out-patient Clinic for the Deaf and Hard of Hearing, Hospital of St. John of God, Linz, Austria
[2] Institute of Social Medicine, University of Vienna, Austria
[3] Department of Psychiatry, Allgemeines Krankenhaus, Vienna, Austria

According to international studies the prevalence rate of prelingual profound deafness in the general population is about 1 per thousand (Ries, 1985, Schein, 1987, van Cleve, 1987).

Quality of life

To describe the situation of the deaf and severely hearing-impaired to a satisfactory degree we have to refer to their conditions of life and compare them with the data relevant to the hearing population.

The number of quality of life studies considering only «hard criteria of success», i.e. pathophysiological parameters, is steadily decreasing. On the other hand, psychic and social well-being, the intellectual and physical performance, as well as the ability to «function» in everyday life, are studied increasingly (Bullinger, 1994). So far, there is no generally accepted definition and theoretical basis of the concept of quality of life, which causes problems in the area of data collection (Weinman et al., 1995). For practical reasons the different variables of quality of life need to be taken into consideration (Fallowfield, 1990). Quality of life refers to the following domains:

- social variables such as personal and sexual relationships, participating in social and leisure time activities;
- work domain, e.g. the possibility to do a paid work you like and to manage the necessary work in the private household;
- psychological aspects such as depression, anxiety and adaptation to illness;
- physical conditions such as pain, mobility, sleep, appetite and sexuality.

Method

Studies that use psychometric scales for the assessment of quality of life very often consist of a comparison of different ways of treatment of chronically ill patients. The study at hand concerns the quality of life of deaf patients and a comparison with a hearing control group. The data of the control group relate mainly to the psychological and physical domains, whereas for the deaf sample their special social and work situation was analyzed, too.

Deaf sample

The «Out-patient Clinic for the Deaf at the Hospital of St. John of God in Linz» offers multi-disciplinary services such as medical and psychiatric care, social help and promotion of communication abilities. Since 1991 more than 1.200 deaf patients have been treated. About 700 of them come from the region of the Upper Austria, i.e. about 60% of all the deaf in this area. The out-patient clinic is very well known among the deaf. We therefore proceed from the assumption that our patient population is quite representative for the adult deaf in general. This assumption is reconfirmed by the high degree of agreement of our sociomedical findings with international results. It is only

Table 1. A comparison of the deaf and hearing sample by number, age, sex, marital status, employment and retirement

	DEAF	HEARING	p
TOTAL	310	273	
AGE	43.3	48.2	0.003
WOMEN/MEN	53.2% / 46.8%	52.2% / 45.8%	N/A
SINGLE	27.8%	8.8%	0.0000
MARRIED	61.4%	83.5%	0.0000
DIVORCED	8.5%	1.1%	0.00009
WORKING	63.7%	61.2%	N/A
RETIRED	20.6%	30.4%	0.000

the multiple handicapped deaf living in institutions or with their families and the very old deaf that are somewhat underrepresented.

From 1993 to 1994 a random choice of 353 of our patients was interviewed in detail (usually in sign language) about social and medical matters and given a preventive medical check-up. 85% are prelingually deaf and 12.7% lost hearing after the age of three.

Hearing control group

The data of a control group of 273 hearing persons who had been to a general practitioner for a preventive medical check-up were analyzed. There is a significant difference between the hearing and the deaf samples regarding age, marital status and percentage of those living in retirement (Table 1). The gender distribution is about equal to that in the general population. We found it quite difficult to find a hearing control group; on one hand, there is a lack of willingness to undergo preventive medical checkups among the general population. On the other hand, only very few general practitioners do the whole program including exact anamnesis.

Results

Social domain

72.5% of the deaf were separated from their families at about 6 years of age due to the attendance of residential schools for the deaf, 27.2% at an even earlier age as a consequence of going to kindergarten.

About 60% of the deaf live in a steady partnership, 22% live on their own, 16% live with their parents or their relatives, about 2% are in institutions. Of those married, 85% have a deaf spouse. This figure demonstrates an interesting phenomenon of how deaf culture comes into being; even though 90% of the deaf have hearing parents, 85% marry deaf partners. Deaf children most often move from their parents, culture and enter the deaf community.

Table 2. *A comparison of the average monthly net income of employed deaf and hearing people (Bauer, 1995)*

	DEAF	HEARING
ATS	10,722.20	13,723.737

47.1% of the deaf have children, usually one or two. 90% of the children are hearing. This figure exactly matches the international situation (Schein, 1979).

More than 70% of the deaf sample are members of a deaf club and almost 50% perceive themselves as very active members. However, even non-members take part in the activities of clubs. Only 15% never attended a deaf club. 65% have exclusively deaf friends. This figure points to the high degree of separation from the hearing world and difficulty to maintain relaxed and enjoyable social relationships with hearing people.

Communication competence is another essential factor contributing to the social domain of quality of life. Linguistic abilities in German were assessed in two separate studies. On average, hearing subjects were able to understand only 32% of the words of spontaneous utterance of the deaf (Holzinger and Fellinger, 1997). According to Markides (1976), language in which a hearer recognizes less than 40% of the words is unintelligible. Another study revealed severe deficits in the knowledge of vocabulary. From the most basic German vocabulary of 500 words, a random choice of twenty deaf subjects understood an average of 93% (Fellinger and Holzinger, 1997).

Work domain

Although two thirds (64%) of the deaf achieved basic vocational qualifications, only 23.3% spend their working lives doing qualified jobs. The awareness that one actually could achieve more under equal conditions certainly influences the individual's perception of this quality of life. The average income of employed deaf people is dramatically below the Austrian average. (Table 2)

Psychological domain

With 45% of the deaf at least one psychiatric disorder was diagnosed (according to the ICD-10 F-categories) by clinical psychiatric examination without the use of standardized epidemiologic study instruments. There is at least one additional disorder in 17% of the cases. From these data we can assume a higher psychiatric morbidity of the deaf as compared to the hearing population. Regarding the distribution of psychiatric diagnoses, we found a high percentage of «neurotic, stress-related and somatoform» disorders, whereas the other disorders show a prevalence rate similar to that of the general population. (Table 3)

The F4 category can be further divided into neurotic disorders (3.5%), adjustment disorders (9.3%) and somatoform disorders (19.3%).

A further important psychological aspect of quality of life we investigated was nervousness, i.e. nervous tension over an extended period of time, which we had observed

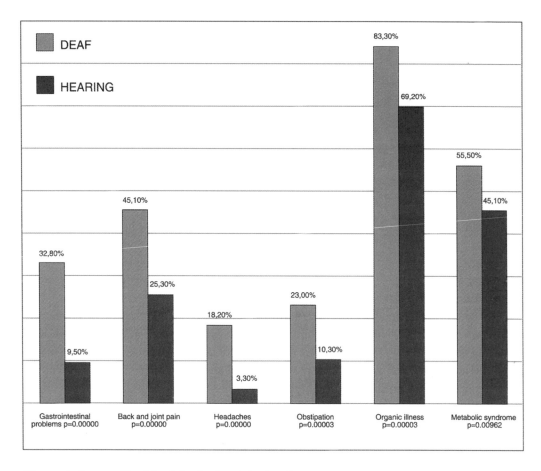

Figure 1. *Status of health of the deaf and the hearing*

to be relatively high in clinical practice. 80% of the deaf women and 64% of the deaf men regarded themselves as nervous. In the hearing control group we found an almost 30% lower rate of reported nervousness; 53.4% of the women and 35.2% of the men (p=0.000).

The results of a survey among the general Austrian population done by the Institute of Social Medicine of the University of Vienna in 1991 were similar (Rieder and Kunze, 1992).

49% of the female and 39% of the male respondents described themselves as nervous. This survey was based on a sample of 1,000 questionnaires randomly selected from more than 100,000 submitted by newspaper readers from all over Austria.

Physical domain

Of the nervous deaf patients 86.2% have somatopsychic complaints. For the non-nervous ones this figure is only 29.3% (p=0.000). A significant influence of nervousness on problems in the stomach area and digestion, problems in the breast region, back and joint pains, insomnia, obstipation and the lack of appetite could be demonstrated.

Despite the younger age of the deaf sample (43.3 years) as compared to the hearing control group (48.2 years), a number of indicators of a worse state of health were found. (Fig. 1) At this point of research it is particularly the metabolic risk factors that objectively show the difference between the deaf (55.5%) and the hearing groups (41.1%). If one of the following parameters was beyond the standard, the subject was included in the risk group; blood glucose level 130 mg/dl (or pathological glucose tolerance), _GT 28 U/I, uric acid 6 mg/dl, cholesterol 200 mg/dl, triglyceride 180 mg/dl.

Discussion

It is the high degree of nervous tension among the deaf that might explain the higher number of health-related complaints. The higher degree of nervousness among the deaf (30% higher as compared to the hearing control group) in particular could be reconfirmed by an even larger study of 705 deaf patients as compared to the general population of Austria (n=100,000).

The lower socioeconomic status of the deaf (as expressed by the difference in income) would let us expect the contrary, i.e. less complaints. Our findings are confirmed by an American study (Zazove et al., 1993), that found a lower subjective status and a higher utilization of physician by the deaf and hard-of-hearing as compared to the general population. Furthermore, the higher number of neurotic, somatoform and stress-related disorders reflect this observation. What are the possible reasons for all that?

It is quite trivial to state that *communication problems* are the primary causes for the worse quality of life of the deaf. However, the relationship can be a very indirect one. The high degree of *isolation* within the hearing world as perceived by our deaf sample (65% report to have exclusively deaf friends) most often starts at a very early age within their own family. Furthermore, the negative effect of *institutional care* (residential kindergarten and school) on the socioemotional development of children has been documented (e.g. Rutter, 1985).

Other findings pertain more to the present situation of deaf adults. As expressed by the social data we presented in the beginning, most of the profoundly and prelingually deaf regard themselves as a part of the sociocultural group of their own. Escobar (1987) has shown, that the expression of emotions and emotional disorders is culture-dependent.

We also need to be aware of the *acculturative stress* most of the deaf steadily perceive in their contact with the hearing society and *the strenuous and often frustrating and humiliating communication* experiences.

Conclusion

The goal of deaf education has mostly been to assimilate them to the hearing society by focusing on teaching them to speak. As a result, many of the psychoemotional and information/knowledge needs of the deaf children and adults have not been considered to a sufficient extent. The deaf have to be given a real choice, to what extent, when and how to participate in the hearing and/or the deaf society. Accepting a specific culture means accepting its language. The use of sign language in early intervention, school and vocational training has to be considered. By legally accepting the sign language of the deaf we could let them know our appreciation of their way of communicating and, finally, of themselves.

References

Bauer, M. (1995): Einkommen unselbständig Beschäftigter nach Wirtschafts- und Berufsklassen-Ergebnisse des Mikrosenzus 1993, in: Statistische Nachrichten 3/1995.

Bullinger, M. (1994): Lebensqualität. In Pöppel E, Bullinger M, Härtler U (eds.) Medizinische Psychologie und Soziologie, p. 369. Chapman & Hall, London.

Escobar, J. I. (1990): Cross-cultural aspects of the somatization trait. Hospital and Community Psychiatry 38:174-180.

Fallowfield, L. (1990): The Quality of Life. The Missing Measurement in Health Care. Souvenir Press, London.

Fellinger, J., Holzinger, D. (1997): Komunikativ-sprachliche Kompetenz gehörloser Erwachsener in Österreich. Teil II: Wortschatz. Published in: Rehabilitation 250.

Holzinger, D., Fellinger, J. (1997): Komunikativ-sprachliche Kompetenz gehörloser Erwachsener in Österreich. Teil I: Zur Verständlichkeit gesprochener Sprache. Published in: Rehabilitation 250.

Linden, M. (1996): Psychische Erkrankungen und ihre Behandlung in Allgemeinartzpraxen in Deutschland, in: Nervenartz 67: 205-215.

Markides, A. (1976): Comparative linguistic proficiencies of deaf children taught by two different methods of instruction – manual vs. oral. The teacher of the Deaf: 307-347.

Rieder, A., Kunze, M. (1992): Epidemiologie der Befindlichkeitsstörungen in Österreich, Psychosoziale Aspekte von Prävention und Therapie. Symposium Psychosoziale Medizin, Vienna, May 1992. Volume of Abstracts.

Rutter, M. (1985): Family and school influences on behavioral development. Journal of Child Psychology and Psychiatry 26: 349-368.

Schein, J., D. (1979): Society and culture of hearing impaired people. In Bradford LJ & Hardy WG (eds.). Hearing and Hearing Impairment. Grune & Stratton, New York.

Weinman, J., Wright, S., Johnston, M. (1995): Measures in Health Psychology: A User's Portofolio – Health Status and Health-Related Quality of Life. Nfer-Nelson, Windsor.

Zazove, P., Niemann, L., Daniel, W., Gorenflo, D., Carmack C., Coyne, J., Antonucci, T. (1993): The Health Status and Health Care. Utilization of the Deaf and Hard-of-Hearing Persons. Arch. Fam. Med, Vol 2., July 1993.

KVALITETA ŽIVOTA I GLUHOĆA

Opis socijalne situacije gluhih u Austriji (N=325) ukazuje na postojanje posebne skupine osoba unutar opće populacije. Zapažanja u pogledu zdravstvenih aspekata kvalitete življenja gluhih ispitanih prilikom preventivne medicinske provjere uspoređena su s podacima kontrolne grupe čujućih ispitanika liječnika opće prakse (N=273), koji su također bili uključeni u preventivno medicinsko ispitivanje. Iako su postojale značajne razlike u dobi, bračnom i umirovljeničkom statusu, one ne objašnjavaju utvrđene razlike u zdravstvenom aspektu kvalitete življenja. Zbog nešto više kronološke dobi kontrolne skupine čujućih očekivali bismo lošiji zdravstveni status i više faktora rizika, međutim, utvrđeno je suprotno. Postoji značajno veći broj oboljenja i viša razina faktora rizika u uzorku gluhih. Posebno veći broj pritužaba na somatopsihičke tegobe i živčanu napetost (30% više gluhih nego čujućih žali se na te tegobe) ukazuje na moguću veću izloženost stresu gluhih osoba.

Ključne riječi: *gluhoća, mentalno zdravlje, kvaliteta života.*